D0847959

THE WAR CRIMINAL'S SON

THE WAR CRIMINAL'S SON

The Civil War Saga of William A. Winder

JANE SINGER

Potomac Books

AN IMPRINT OF THE UNIVERSITY OF NEBRASKA PRESS

Library of Congress Cataloging-in-Publication Data
Names: Singer, Jane, 1947– author.
Title: The war criminal's son : the civil war saga of William
A. Winder / Jane Singer.
Description: Lincoln: Potomac Books, an imprint of
the University of Nebraska Press, [2019] | Includes
bibliographical references and index.
Identifiers: LCCN 2018051031
ISBN 9781612349114 (cloth: alk. paper)
ISBN 9781640121843 (epub)
ISBN 9781640121850 (mobi)
ISBN 9781640121867 (pdf)
Subjects: LCSH: Winder, William A. (William Andrew),
1823–1903. | Winder, John H. (John Henry), 1800–1865. |
United States—History—Civil War, 1861–1865—Biography.
| United States. Army—Biography. | Confederate States
of America. Army—Biography. | United States. Army.
Artillery Regiment, 3rd (1861–1865) | Military Prison at
Alcatraz Island, California. | United States. Army—Prisons.
| Confederate States of America. Army—Prisons. | United
States—History—Civil War, 1861–1865—Prisoners and
prisons. | Fathers and sons—United States.
Classification: LCC E467.1.W764 S56 2019 |
DDC 973.7092 [B]—dc23 LC record available at
https://lccn.loc.gov/2018051031

Set in Questa by E. Cuddy.

Know, my name is lost; by treason's tooth bare-gnawn and canker-bit: Yet am I noble as the adversary I come to cope.

WILLIAM SHAKESPEARE, *King Lear*, Act 5, scene 3

Contents

Illustrations

Acknowledgments

To all the fine scholars, diligent archivists, and generous colleagues who contributed time, energy, advice, and encouragement throughout my study of the life and times of William Andrew Winder, a debt of gratitude is owed.

I began my research in California, the beautiful sunlit state I proudly call home and where many of William A.'s years of service, toil, struggle, and reinvention came into bold relief. For the countless hours I spent at the San Diego History Center with archivist Jane Kenealy, for her wisdom and willingness to allow me to nest among microfilms and view hitherto unseen records that illuminated the unexplored life of my subject, my great thanks. Also, at the San Diego History Center Christine Travers and Carol Meyers furnished valuable images of Old Town San Diego as well as an early lithograph of William A.; your help and attention were invaluable. As well, my repeated requests for materials were always promptly and patiently furnished by diligent and able researchers Ellen Sweet, Linda Canada, Karen Beery (the San Diego Coast District interpretation and education manager), and Ellen Green (volunteer and education service coordinator at the Whaley House Museum). Guire John Cleary, Garner Palenske, Tony Falcon, David J. McLaughlin, Dr. Robert J. Chandler, Kenneth Meza, Sister Barbara Jackson, and Betsey Culp gladly and generously helped expedite my requests for images and information.

At Alcatraz, my good friend and frequent correspondent John A. Martini, the eminent San Francisco historian, former park ranger, city guide, and author, led me deep underground to view the remains of the Citadel, the fortress that stood atop the island where during the Civil War Capt. William A. Winder, serving as post commander, and the men of the Third U.S. Artillery defended the Bay of San Francisco as ongoing threats from Confederate privateers and foreign invaders abounded. Thank you, John, for your time and your abounding knowledge. Lorna Kirwan, the collections manager at the Bancroft Library of UC Berkeley, graciously provided a hitherto unpublished image of William A. Winder at Alcatraz. Rebecca Crowther, the photo archivist at the Center for Sacramento History, furnished me with a rare photograph of Alcatraz and the Citadel. Charles Johnson at the Museum of Ventura County sent me an invaluable cache of personal letters from William A.'s wife, Abby Goodwin Winder.

And figuratively following the route of William A. as he sailed out of California into uncertain waters, I found along the way Robbi Siegel at Art Resource in New York City, Mary Frances Ronan at the National Archives in Washington, and Patrick Kerwin at the Library of Congress Manuscript Division, also in Washington. All were at the ready and most generous with their time.

A very special thanks to Robert Scott Davis, professor of genealogy, geography, and history and director of the Family and Regional History program at Wallace State Community College in Hanceville, Alabama. Bob has been both constant friend and educator as I gingerly ventured into the dark and tragic history of Andersonville Prison.

As I followed William A. to his final, grueling post at South Dakota's Rosebud Reservation, I thank Joyce Burner at the National Archives in Kansas City, Missouri, Prof. Jon Taylor at the University of Central Missouri, Russell Eagle Bear, who is the tribal historic preservation officer of the Rosebud Sioux Tribe in South Dakota, Matthew T. Reitzel at the South Dakota State Historical Society, and Martha Grenzeback at the Omaha Public Library. These fine men and women made my journey to an unfamiliar, faraway place where proud Sioux warriors once freely roamed a true illumination.

And at Portsmouth, New Hampshire, I thank and praise Elizabeth Farish, chief curator at the Strawbery Banke Museum, who always generously gave me her time and allowed me to use in this work some marvelous images of William A.'s wife Abby Winder and her father, Ichabod Goodwin, who was a former New Hampshire governor.

Author John Stewart, my dear friend, was and will remain an important part of my tumbles into the endless rabbit holes of hidden history. I cannot image a time when our work together has not and will not be a thrilling adventure.

To Ann Harezlak, words cannot describe how I value you. And to Tom Swanson Joeth Zucco, Tish Fobben, Rosemary Sekora, Jackson Adams, Abby Stryker, Andrea Shahan, and Natalie O'Neal at the University of Nebraska Press (Potomac Books), your patience and support have been a gift. To Maureen Bemko, your thoughtful and important copyedits have taught and guided me.

To Christy Sears, for your time with my artifacts and ever-good cheer, my thanks.

Finally, to my brilliant husband, Charles Eckstein, and my inspiring and cherished daughter, Jessica Masser, my love to you both, always.

Prologue

During the bone-biting cold of an early January morning he headed quickly up Pennsylvania Avenue on his way to the White House, all the while passing shivering groups of ragged slaves, fur-bedecked gents and their ladies dodging hawkers, and whores hectoring and soliciting the Union soldiers guarding Washington City. In the distance across the Potomac River the glowing watch fires of Confederate soldiers mustering and massing in Virginia were visible to many who peered through spyglasses or perched atop hillsides and even to President Lincoln himself from his vantage point on the second floor of the White House.

As he reached the white-columned south portico that led to the public entrance of the president's office, a guard blocked his way. But upon seeing the soldier in Union blue—with no weapon drawn and no threat apparent—and as he identified himself as Third Artillery captain William Andrew Winder, seeking an audience with Pres. Abraham Lincoln—the guard let him pass. It was easy then, as almost anyone could drop in on Abraham Lincoln to plead for the life of a deserter-son doomed to execution, to listen to a long, folksy story, or to swear loyalty to the man and the war that had divided the capital, where spies from both sides skulked and fears of an invasion by Confederate troops beset city residents.

Finally inside the Executive Office, Capt. William A. Winder, the son of a Confederate general whose last name was well known to Union authorities, told the president that he had recently been transferred to the front with Company M from Fortress Alcatraz, a craggy, fog-bound San Francisco army post and prison where secessionist sympathizers were held. Captain Winder's purpose for this urgent visit was clear. He'd come to swear his allegiance to the Union, to the president himself. He asked that, as his company was already in Washington City awaiting postings to the front, he might be permitted to stay with them and, for the love of God, not be sent back to Alcatraz.

Although Lincoln was seemingly receptive to the captain's plea, could William A. Winder, or any Winder, be trusted? His two civilian uncles had been jailed for treason in Washington City and New York. He was the first-born son of a Confederate general and had a half brother and two cousins already serving in Richmond. Perhaps worse, President Lincoln and his war secretary, Edwin Stanton, had heard rumors of treasonous statements made by the captain to a Pinkerton spy posing as a Confederate courier just after he'd arrived in Washington City. Perhaps the rumors were true.

Introduction

Begin then with my acquisition of a nineteenth-century oil portrait of a man: a stern visage, pale blue eyes, and a haunted, inward gaze. Judging from his black frock coat, its narrow lapels, the formal white shirt, and the style of his long, silver-threaded, patriarchal beard, the portrait was likely done in the mid-1880s. Scrawled on the back in ink was the name *Captain William Andrew Winder, U.S. Army*. The last name was familiar, but he was not. Was this somber, troubled-looking man related to the infamous Winder clan allegedly responsible for the war crimes at Georgia's Andersonville Prison, a place of horror and death long synonymous with brutality in an already brutal war? According to the portrait's inscription, he was at one time in the U.S. Army, but an important question was if he had served the Union or the Confederacy during the Civil War.

Hover in the past, and sometimes there is that rare occurrence when the discovery of an obscure figure—at first a pinpoint of light on a darkened stage—slowly takes shape, with face and form, and, rarer still, resonates with themes of the dissonant past with all its dips, stutters, and cataclysms. Allegations of treason, the definition of patriotism and loyalty, the dividing of a nation, and the aftermath of war, including war crimes trials, and the sins of a father and a father's father are the themes of this work.

This is the saga of William Andrew Winder, a man who appeared in far-flung, improbable places, only to reappear again and again—a cipher, yet a composite of many people fleeing a past or a place. The memory of the world around him—the history he witnessed— was a rare opportunity for a modern scholar to pry the hidden alloys of the past from its rusted hinges. William A. Winder was a player on a uniquely American stage, a metaphor for the recovery and reinvention of a fractured nation and its people during and after the Civil War.

Often mute, always peripatetic, William A. Winder was at times accused of being a traitor, a failure, or, worse, a coward. In the end one bears witness to a life often lived in palpable agony and frustration, a man with an honor-bound conscience and an uncommon ability to forge new beginnings.

Herein lies a story of collective shame and redemption, of prisoners and prison camps, American Indian abuses, nineteenth-century medicine, of railroads, healing, and renewal in the remote outpost of San Diego; of gold and copper mines; of disloyalty and disunion; of the "go-Westers," the hucksters, politicians, pioneers, humbugs, traitors, and generals who blazed through William A. Winder's long life until it sputtered to a close near the gouged earth of a place called Rosebud.

1

Bedeviled Winter of War

T o the beggars, prostitutes, hucksters, and saloonkeepers along the wharf the steamship's arrival at the bustling Port of New York meant fresh business. Ordinary trade. With sails furled, the ship and its huge side-wheel paddles churned through the water, billows of coal dust from a single smokestack obscuring the passengers thronging the upper deck. But as the ship nears and the smoke clears, the sight of masses of soldiers decked out in Union blue is far from ordinary. Seven months into the war, when homegrown boys and newly arrived immigrants are already fighting and dying for the Union, aren't these Yankees late to the fight? Was the ship a floating Trojan horse full of invading rebels? Or perhaps a survivor of the "worst storm in years that struck the Atlantic Seaboard" just two weeks before, when "floodwaters swamped Newark, Manhattan and Newport[,] Rhode Island"?[1]

Not likely. It was clear this was no battered vessel; it was fitted out, sleek, and steady on the water. But to those who regularly scanned the shipping news columns published in the daily press, the impending arrival of the iron side-wheel steamship *Champion*, a star of Cornelius Vanderbilt's Atlantic and Pacific line, was no mystery.

And for the soldiers aboard, the truth was prosaic. The *New York Evening Post* trumpeted the "Arrival of Regulars from California bringing fifteen thousand stands of arms—Springfield rifles with a large amount of ammunition," eight companies of the Third U.S. Artillery, and three of the Sixth Infantry regiments fresh from "occupying barracks at the Presidio and at Benecia [*sic*]."[2]

Many of those troops, the *New York Herald* announced, were "among the guardians of California soil."[3] Along with troops the

1

Champion brought nearly $800,000 in gold specie. And glowering in the ship's iron hold were three fractious prisoners of state. The journey from California to New York had been a grueling slog of twenty-four days. Leaving from San Francisco, the companies of the Third Artillery and Sixth Infantry Regiments had boarded the *Orizaba*, a trusty workhorse of a steamer that plied the Pacific from San Francisco to Panama City. Then came a five-hour journey on the six-year-old Panama Railroad, traveling forty-seven miles from Panama City on the Pacific Coast across the isthmus to Aspinwall. It was a very good road and a beautiful but slow trip in cars with cane seats and wooden blinds instead of windows. Depending on conditions, however, some travelers might notice only that the way was full of violent curves, pestiferous marsh, and tangled forest before reaching Aspinwall, where finally the passengers boarded the *Champion*.

Although the vessel was only three years old, it was "the first iron steamship ever built in the United States."[4] At 1,850 tons, 250 feet long, and built to carry more than seven hundred passengers, the *Champion* was reputed to be little more than a seagoing cesspool, with "tainted meat, dirty tablecloths and sheets, a lack of bathrooms or spittoons," in addition to filthy upper cabins, the stench of offal wafting from steerage, and ill-mannered service.[5] Finally, after twenty-four days at sea, the steamer crossed the bar of Sandy Hook, a series of shoals running roughly south from Long Island to the northern tip of New Jersey and separating New York Harbor from the deep waters of the Atlantic. The *Champion* chugged into the harbor, the hum and thrum of its engines growing louder as it passed the sloops, packets, and other steamers hovering or berthing.

Among the five hundred officers and privates recorded on the *Champion*'s manifest by Shipmaster David Wilson is newly minted Capt. William Andrew Winder of the Third U.S. Artillery, the commander of Company M.[6]

Born on December 3, 1823, in Baltimore, William A. in 1861 is thirty-eight and a seasoned soldier honed and hardened by army service throughout the country. When the Civil War began he was a first lieutenant stationed at Alcatraz, a rocky, fog-shrouded outpost-turned–federal fort a mile and a half from shore in the Bay of San Francisco, where news of the bombardment of Fort Sumter arrived twelve days after the historic onslaught. With mostly army deserters and miscreants jailed at Alcatraz, Captain Winder's transfer to the front was a prized and welcome assignment. Although more than ready to fight the rebels, he will be forced to wage a very different kind of war. His loyalty and his very honor will be tried and tested. So if he is at first a blurred image, frozen and faceless in the frames of an old stereoscope viewer—a soldier among many soldiers amassed on the ship's deck—he will come into bold relief, for this is his story.

Now, as the long-awaited sight of Manhattan comes into view, Captain Winder must summon his men. No matter their rank or station, they are a brotherhood forever bonded by a disaster at sea that had decimated their ranks. Many members of the Third Artillery "comprise the survivors of the regiment," the *New York Evening Post* reported, "nearly all the remainder of which were lost" when the steamer *San Francisco* pitched headlong into a hurricane in the mid-Atlantic on her maiden voyage in December 1853.[7]

Aboard that doomed vessel, performing heroically as the crippled ship drifted for fourteen days, was young 2nd Lt. William A. Winder. As he frantically bailed water from the hold while huge waves swallowed the upper deck and washed two hundred comrades away, he tended to those stricken with cholera, as time and again three would-be rescue ships tried but could not breach the turgid waters. Finally, when help did arrive, the ship had become a "floating coffin."[8] William A. Winder's heroic efforts earned him and other shipmates—including his cousin, 1st Lt. Charles Sidney Winder—official commendations for bravery from their native state of Maryland. The wreck shattered William A. with the tragedy of many lives lost, passengers and soldiers alike, and, as he later recounted, it resurrected his own personal trauma of having nearly drowned as a small child. "I have met several times with serious accidents on water," he recalled. "I have never gotten over my nervousness." He nevertheless faced those furious gales and always found land. Now, eight years after the loss of the *San Francisco*, on this calm, crisp November morning as the *Cham-*

pion glides along the glassine waters of the New York Harbor and noses into the dock, perhaps he does not yet see the darkening skies, the coming of a very different kind of storm that will forever change his life.[9]

But for now, as the *Champion* is finally docked in the harbor, to enliven the weariest of voyagers there is music as the regimental drummers strike up the brass bands. Feet tapping, a patriotic song or two, amid nods and good-byes to the soldiers who will wait aboard the ship to see everyone safely ashore, witness the civilian passengers as they leave the ship. There are wealthy, high-hatted gents and silk-clad ladies and their servants from the cabin class. From steerage come the laborers, immigrants, and laundry workers. And emerging from the hold under guard are three belligerent California *prominenti* detained by Gen. Edwin Vose "Bullhead" Sumner, who had replaced Gen. Albert Sidney Johnston as commander of the Department of the Pacific when the latter had resigned to serve the Confederacy. Determined to save California from being another divided state, Sumner demanded that "the troops hold their [Union] positions" and concentrate on rooting out disloyal citizens.[10] Just relieved of his command of the Department of the Pacific by his own brother-in-law, Gen. George Wright, Sumner was eager to join Gen. George McClellan's Army of the Potomac. Not the least of his missions that day was to deliver his prisoners to Union authorities. They were "former California senator William Gwin, attorney and state senator Joseph Lancaster Brent[,] and San Francisco government attorney Calhoun Benham."[11] These well-known California Copperheads (or Peace Democrats sympathetic to the Confederate cause) were "men whose secession leanings were so strong that they felt they had to leave for the Confederacy."[12]

On December 2, 1861, these men were "granted a parole by an official at Fort Hamilton in New York Harbor" after pledging not to act against the Union in any way.[13] "Whereas Gwin remained a private citizen throughout the war, Brent and Benham both became Confederate officers, Brent rising to the rank of brigadier general."[14] Although Gwin, Brent, and Benham would "be placed on Governor's Island, to await the order of Government," had they been able to flee their captors and melt into Manhattan, a divided borough that once "boldly flirted with leaving the Union," they would have found sympathy, if not the means to escape to the Confederacy.[15]

Afoot and prospering in the staunchly Democratic city are cotton brokers fattened by longtime trade with the South, as well as Copperheads led by Democratic mayor Fernando Wood, who favored the secession of Manhattan early in the war. The mayor's stance underscored a belief that "slavery wasn't so much a moral as an economic necessity." In his view the city "made its reputation—and the lion's share of its revenues—by supplying goods and services to the slave South," and it stubbornly continued to hold itself apart from the rest of the Union. In part because Mayor Wood's brother Benjamin owned the *New York Daily News*, the widely read anti-Lincoln mouthpiece that the mayor had gifted to his sibling, the newspaper ginned up like-minded readers.[16]

And of course there was William Magear "Boss" Tweed's Tammany Hall political machine. Democratic in theory but not practice, Boss Tweed's machine ruled the city. In spite of other voices, such as Horace Greeley's *New York Tribune*, which urged Union troops to take Richmond and end the war, bribery, corruption, and intimidation held sway above all else. But for Capt. William A. Winder, hearing the joyful cries of mothers, brothers, fathers, and children rushing to embrace loved ones as the regiments muster and prepare to march up Broadway, there would not be a single blood relation to welcome him home. Most of them had "gone over to the dragons," as New York City diarist and fervent Union loyalist George Templeton Strong wrote, damning those who'd turned tail, turned traitor, and swarmed south.[17]

Driven by Lincoln's election on November 6, 1860, further irritating already inflamed sensibilities, ignoring the president's pleas to "rely on the better angels of our nature," and further enraged by his promise to contain the spread of slavery, uncountable numbers began massing in Richmond to swear loyalty to the newly formed Confederacy. Among them was the Winder clan.[18]

First to go was Capt. William A. Winder's cousin, Capt. Charles Sidney Winder, who had left the Third Artillery on April 1, eleven days before war was declared. On April 21 William A.'s father, Maj.

5

John H. Winder, a hard-handed martinet with more than thirty-eight years of service in the U.S. Army, resigned his commission and went to the Confederate capital at Richmond. John H. Winder's second son, William Sidney Winder—known as "Sidney" or "Sid"—and another cousin, Richard Bayley Winder, joined John there. John H. Winder's third son, John Cox Winder, an engineer before the war, was first a Confederate captain, then a major "placed in command of Company A, Second Engineers," at North Carolina's Fort Fisher.[19]

Noting John H. Winder's arrival in Richmond, the War Department clerk and diarist John Beauchamp Jones took an immediate dislike to the "stout gray-haired old man from Maryland applying to be a general, . . . the son of the General Winder whose command in the last war with England unfortunately permitted the City of Washington to fall in the hands of the enemy."[20]

It was true that Gen. William Henry Winder's failure to hold the lines at the Battle of Bladensburg, Maryland, during the War of 1812 and his inability to prevent his troops from throwing down their weapons and running from enemy rocket fire allowed the British an undefended and unobstructed path across the Potomac into Washington. They sacked and burned buildings until they reached the White House, setting it afire. The "Bladensburg Races," as the American rout was derisively termed, nearly caused the demise of an infant nation, and the defeat made Gen. William Henry Winder an object of scorn and suspicion and led to his being court-martialed. Although cleared, his army career was over and his reputation in tatters. His biographer notes that even his closest friends felt it necessary to refer to Winder as 'that most unfortunate general' of the war of 1812."[21] This was a humiliation for all the Winders, including the disgraced general's namesake son William H. and his brother Charles H., but especially John H., who like his father was a soldier and who wanted desperately to restore honor to the family name by serving a cause the Confederate president deemed "just and holy."[22]

Born in Maryland on February 21, 1800, at Rewston plantation in Nanticoke (present-day Wicomico County, originally part of Somerset and Worcester Counties), John H. Winder was from a storied, patrician Maryland family boasting of judges, generals, lawyers, and a governor. He was a West Pointer, veteran Indian fighter with notable service in the Mexican War, a failed plantation master, and ultimately a peripatetic Third Artillery officer unable to rise above the rank of major in the U.S. Army. At sixty-one, too old to fight and too fired up not to, he was promoted to the much-coveted position of brigadier general in Richmond on June 21. Rumor had it that his old friend Confederate president Jefferson Davis had succumbed to his constant petitions, finally awarding Winder his first assignment as inspector general of the camps, a position that made him "responsible for overseeing the fitting out of soldiers for field duty . . . handling discharges, returned deserters and medical care for sick and wounded soldiers."[23] Six months later Winder "was given command of the Department of Henrico." On March 1, 1862, he received his next post, as "commander of the Federal prisoners in Richmond . . . and Danville," and it gave him sweeping powers.[24]

John H. Winder, the man who would come to be known as the "formidable dictator of the Capital," would see his career reborn in Richmond.[25]

John H. Winder's reign of terror began when, with a growing reputation for brutality to Union prisoners as well as his own people, he hunted down and incarcerated those suspected of disloyalty to the Confederacy—anyone deemed a threat to the government. Part of the crackdown on Richmond citizenry was first made possible by an earlier product of the Confederate Congress: "An act respecting Alien Enemies." Pres. Jefferson Davis had proclaimed, "I do hereby warn and require every male citizen of the United States" over the age of fourteen and "now within the Confederate States" that if they should "adhere to the Government of the United States" and "not declare themselves a citizen of the Confederate States, they must depart from the Confederate States within forty days or will be treated as *alien enemies*." Worse, if any alien left the Confederacy and returned to the United States (i.e., Union territory), they "shall be regarded and treated as an alien enemy" and, if made prisoner, would be turned over "to the nearest military authority, to be dealt with as a spy or [a] prisoner of war."[26]

7

With this dictate many innocents, suspected spies, and underground Unionists were later rounded up and jailed by Winder's much-feared "force of civilian detectives," composed of petty larceny detectives from Baltimore, Philadelphia, and New York. Known as "plug-uglies," they were given free rein and "interfered intolerably with citizens going about their lawful business."[27]

With illegal arrests and the eventual suspension of habeas corpus when martial law was enacted, the fears of Winder's police state becoming a harsh reality, and the price of food and dry goods skyrocketing, Winder's biographer writes, "Richmond was a rather grim place . . . and Winder was blamed for much of the despair."[28]

William A., the last of the Winders left in the Union Army over this long winter of 1861–62, must have known that in spite of the "dragons" that summoned most of his family, surely there was comfort in knowing that his wife, Abby, and eleven-year-old son, Willie, might soon join him in Washington. Would the reunion be bittersweet or bitter? He was a Winder, after all. His beautiful, musical, and extremely competent wife—they'd married on December 24, 1850, in Portsmouth, New Hampshire—was well aware of his family's disloyalty. Perhaps she feared that her husband might be torn and tested by their defection and that their son might be ridiculed or worse by the stolid and solid residents of her home state—most if not all had voted for Abraham Lincoln. Abby's father was former New Hampshire governor Ichabod Goodwin, a Unitarian, abolitionist, and passionate Lincoln man. As soon as war was declared and Lincoln had sent out the call for "seventy-five thousand volunteer militiamen to fight for the Union for a period of just ninety days . . . [Goodwin] set up recruiting offices throughout the state." Volunteers—more than two thousand men streamed in—eventually made up the First and Second Regiments of New Hampshire. "Fighting Governor Goodwin," who at first funded the regiments with personal and borrowed funds, thrilled to the sight of Union flags everywhere he looked.[29]

With William A.'s blood kin rooted deep in the Confederacy, his father-in-law positioned as the sworn enemy of those kin, and William A. himself now squarely at the seat of war in Washington, he surely looked back to the days of dread before the war began, when it seemed he might remain at the front. Possibly with his consent, Ichabod Goodwin and his daughter had decided to pursue a position for William A. as a paymaster with the Union Army. It was a plum job. Only a few were awarded the post, which required appointment by the president. At a salary of eighty dollars a month and the rank of major, paymasters traveled with the troops to the front, where they set up in mobile tent offices to disburse pay to the soldiers. Although armed, they would not be fighting with the troops unless dire conditions required their support; surprise attacks, friendly fire, or unforeseen emergencies could require a paymaster to raise his weapon. Surely the Goodwin clan would have discussed William A.'s plight with him in person or by mail. Would he too bolt south or would he turn his back on the Winders to remain with the Union? What would he choose to be—a paymaster or an artillery officer in the bloody chaos sure to come? On April 11, one day before the firing on Fort Sumter, the *New Hampshire Sentinel* reported, "Percival Pope of this state has been appointed a second Lieutenant and Captain Winder, a Paymaster in the army."[30] This article made it seem that William A.'s position was a fait accompli. It was not.

Two months later, on June 24, 1861, Ichabod Goodwin wrote to President Lincoln from Portsmouth, New Hampshire: "My daughter . . . wife of Lieut. W. A. Winder [Goodwin was not yet aware of his son-in-law's promotion to captain] . . . goes to Washington in behalf of her husband, asking that he may be appointed a Paymaster. . . . Mr. Winder has seen much service, had been stationed for . . . years in California. He is a native of Maryland and has passed most of his life in the states that are True as himself to the Union. This is the only favor I have asked for one of my immediate family, or connection, and hope it may be granted." Soon came an answer to Ichabod Goodwin's request that President Lincoln appoint his son-in-law paymaster—a one-page quarto endorsement signed "A. Lincoln" and penned vertically on the integral leaf of the June 24 letter signed by Ichabod Goodwin and addressed to Lincoln. The president replied, "I have written some letters or notes in behalf of persons as Paymasters in the Army. . . . I am entirely willing for Capt. William A. Winder of Maryland, [to] be appointed a Paymaster in the Army."[31]

Although Lincoln appeared willing to make the appointment, Abby, not waiting for an official answer, went straight to Washington to lobby for the post. For two weeks she went about the city vouching for her husband's loyalty and urging someone, anyone in authority to grant him a paymaster's job. If in fact the appointment came while William A. was in California, communication with the West Coast was spotty at best. Letters and newspapers took three to four weeks by ship and, depending on weather and road conditions, three to four months overland. And then, in a seeming miracle of wire and engineering, of splicing and connecting, on October 25, 1861, a long-awaited telegraph line finally connected New York and San Francisco. Imagine the thrill as the first message crackled through the wires, then raced from telegraph offices on opposite sides of the country to both cities' mayors. San Francisco mayor H. F. Teschemacher rejoiced: "San Francisco to New York sends greetings and congratulates her on the completion of the enterprise which connects the Pacific with the Atlantic. May the prosperity of both cities be increased, and the projectors of this important work meet with honor and reward."[32]

There was little honor and certainly no reward for Captain Winder, however, in spite of his intrepid wife and devoted father-in-law's efforts, for treason roosted on the home front.

William A.'s civilian uncle, attorney Charles H. Winder, a fifty-two-year-old "citizen of Washington of notoriously disloyal character," was arrested on September 9 by the Union Army provost marshal, Gen. Andrew Porter, for having "a quantity of disloyal correspondence from him to his brother William H. Winder of Philadelphia."[33]

The same day Charles Winder was arrested he was "examined and questioned" at the provost marshal's office by E. J. Allen, the wartime alias of Detective Allan Pinkerton, head of Gen. George McClellan's secret service. Although E. J. Allen's true identity was not revealed to Charles H. Winder at the time of his interrogation, his critical part in the evolving drama of William A.'s time in Washington City will be fully illuminated in the following chapter.

Notable are some excerpts from the transcript of the questions Allen asked Charles H. Winder. Notable are the answers he gave. For example, Allen asked, "Do you know, Mr. Winder, on what charge you are brought here?" Winder answered in all innocence, "I have not the remotest idea." Perhaps he guessed it was because of a "violent discussion about the war" he had had with an unnamed Englishman when he loudly declared, "I am all for the South from the crown of my head to the soles of my feet." He denied he'd done "anything against the North," and although he admitted he would "like to serve my people in the south," and if he did he would do it "openly and aboveboard," he added—and one can imagine a raised voice, a verbal shot at the Yankee interrogator—"I would fight you to the death if I had the power." After more questioning he admitted, "I am acquainted with a large number of officers in the Southern Army. General John H. Winder is my brother." And with this came the following: "I have not corresponded with any of them since the war commenced."[34]

In fact Charles H. Winder *had* written to his brother John H. Winder on August 20, 1861, five months after the war began. In that letter he reported that one Dr. Edward Taylor desires "to be absolved from his parole," as he had been captured in Richmond. In addition Charles H. tells his brother that William A.'s wife "Abby left here a few days ago," after trying to get her husband a paymaster's job: "Wm. still in California his object was to get a paymaster's appointment." This letter would have been deemed treasonous—any letter written from the North to the South, particularly to a Confederate officer, was forbidden, and Charles H. Winder could have been charged with far more than defiant secessionist proclivities.[35]

In addition to E. J. Allen's interrogation of Charles H. Winder on September 9, excerpts of letters Charles H. wrote to his brother William H. before and just after the war began were seized. Describing his unyielding devotion to the Confederate cause and bemoaning the "military garrison" that was Washington, on April 17 Charles H. wrote, "I know we are better organized, that in the coming contest we are more than a match for them. . . . When I say 'we' I mean the Confederate States." There were many letters and many sentiments like this in his correspondence to his brother, as well as to men of growing prominence in Richmond.[36]

One of several depositions made against Charles H. Winder the day after his arrest on September 10 was that of his neighbor George Theodore McGlue: "I have had conversations with C. H. Winder frequently, and from the language used I have regarded him as a violent secessionist and enemy of the Union. He said he was in favor of Jeff Davis and that he'd be damned if Lincoln would ever be inaugurated in the city."[37] On the same day one W. H. Parker swore that Charles H. Winder was "receiving dispatches from Richmond stating that Jefferson Davis was not dead but that he was present at the opening of Congress by the Rebels." When Charles H. Winder offered to show Parker the dispatch, "I declined seeing it," Parker stated.[38]

Surprisingly Charles H. Winder was released on a conditional parole on October 15, carefully watched, and warned, as noted in a letter of November 30 from Secretary of State William H. Seward to the provost marshal, Gen. Andrew Porter: "General: Mr. Charles H. Winder's parole which expires on December 1 may be extended for sixty days further, but it is indispensably necessary that he should abstain from political conversation. He has already been reported to me as publicly expressing treasonable sentiments within the past month. It will not be in my power [sic] this exemption from confinement if he does not himself cooperate in the regulations prescribed. Very respectfully, your obedient servant, William H. Seward."[39]

Charles H. Winder cooperated. His brother did not. William H. Winder, an extremely wealthy Maryland-born Philadelphia attorney and correspondent for the New York Daily News—a well-known anti-Lincoln publication—was arrested in Philadelphia on September 11. At fifty-three, the bold, successful William H. Winder never hid his southern sentiments and dared government authorities to arrest him. A warrant was issued: "War Department, Washington, September 11, 1861. William Millward, U.S. Marshal, Philadelphia: You are directed to arrest William H. Winder and transfer him to the charge of Col. Martin Burke at Fort Lafayette. Simon Cameron, Secretary of War."[40]

On the same day, U.S. Attorney George A. Coffey wrote to Secretary of War Simon Cameron: "William H. Winder, of this city, has been arrested for treasonable correspondence with rebel officers in obedience to a dispatch sent on from Provost-Marshal General Porter. We find scores of letters in Winder's possession to and from many traitors—Breckinridge, Burnett, Vallandigham, Halleck, of the *Journal of Commerce*, etc.," noting that "he has destroyed or concealed the letters from his brother, Charles Winder, of Washington." Even more damning was an accusation that "Charles Winder and William H. Winder knew of the intention and plan of taking Washington last April. Please order the marshal of this district at once to take William H. Winder to Fort Lafayette. He is a constant conspirator and should not be at large."[41]

By September 13 the constant conspirator was an inmate at Fort Lafayette, a military prison "built on a small rock Island lying in the narrows between the lower end of Staten Island and [L]ong Island." William H. Winder was housed behind twenty-five- to thirty-foot walls, "with outdoor exercise limited." It was a place where the "foul water" (when water was available at all) was contaminated by dirt and bacteria. The notoriously bad food—"fat pork and beans, a cup of thin soup and undrinkable coffee . . . bread on alternate days"—must have been a great shock to the gentleman lawyer.[42]

Defiant from the moment he arrived, locked into a dark and damp cell, William H. Winder wrote copious correspondence protesting his incarceration and the seizure of his papers, said to contain treasonous correspondence. Although he had expressed sympathy with the rebellion publicly and on paper, he claimed he had never regularly corresponded with his brother the Confederate general, John H. Winder, after the war began. (This may or may not have been true since all his correspondence was seized by the authorities, deemed treasonous, and lost or suppressed during and after his incarceration.)

Yet on the morning of November 16, while his uncle William H. sat fuming and unrepentant in prison, Union captain William A., in spite of the sure knowledge he had of the recent arrests of his uncles and with angry government authorities wary and watching, marched in orderly lockstep with a portion of the Third Artillery and Sixth Infantry. As crowds cheered, they paraded up Broadway to the accompaniment of a "full and splendid band." Hurrah the soldiers, hurrah! But who were they, exactly? The *New York Herald* gave a shaky and befuddled glad-hand to the event: "Nobody knew what regiment it was, where it came from, or whither it was going," but the *Herald*'s readers were assured that the men were "a double compliment to our national pride and to the drill and discipline of our gallant volunteers."[43] In a bit of a fog as well, the *New York Commercial Advertiser* reporter stated, "It is not known to what duty they will be assigned." However, the journalist noted that they "were all well-drilled men," as some had "stripes on their arms denot[ing] having served twenty years."[44]

It was "a rare and most brilliant sight," the *New York Evening Post* gushed.[45]

After the glittering parade the troops were to remove to their temporary barracks in City Hall Park until called to the front. The Union-loyal *New York Times* expected a "better use for them occurring nearer home."[46] What better use might lie in store for William Andrew Winder, as he leaves the barracks and boards a steamer traveling down the coast, around Hampton Roads, into the Chesapeake Bay, and up the Potomac River to Washington City? On this November morning, with California and sea disasters a world away, he leaves a place where being a Winder is tinged with peril. He is adrift with no compass and no guide.

2

The Double Agent and the Captain

Washington City, the once-sleepy southern town that Capt. William A. Winder had known, was now seething, pestiferous, and paranoid. With his uncle, Charles H. Winder, recently paroled and under close observation, William A. now navigates a much-changed landscape. Throughout the city are hospitals teeming with mutilated, weakened, and diseased troops. The lists of the sick and wounded, nameless and simply numbered according to the hospitals that care for them, were a tally of men who came stumbling or borne by litter from many regiments: New York, Michigan, Pennsylvania, Wisconsin, and New Jersey, to name a few.[1]

For those hungry for distractions and guffaws, Canterbury Hall advertised "Frank Bower, The Chief Impersonator of the Happy Darky," and King's National Circus announced "Ella Zoyara, the sensationalist," who promised breathtaking acts.[2]

Spreading comfort and doses of venereal disease to fresh recruits far from home were the prostitutes swarming Union camps. Hidden among sedate mansions and throughout the infamous Swampoodle District were brothels doing booming business. Should infection occur from these romps, fear not—an ad in the *Evening Star* consoles, "Dr. Johnston will cure all diseases of imprudence" and warns those waking to sexual arousal of the "terrible disorders arising from solitary habits of youth."[3]

And with many city streets so muddy, so fetid and marshy that typhoid fever is borne through canals polluted by rotting army mules, offal, defective plumbing, and filthy drinking water, the disease is rampant. Worse, heavy rains have so flooded the Potomac River that it "washed downstream the uniformed corpses of

Federal soldiers who had died weeks earlier, in the Battle of Ball's Bluff, thirty-four miles above Washington."[4]

Rebel and Yankee spies prowl across the Potomac as a Confederate invasion is looming. All loyal Union eyes turn to the strutting, magnetic, and notably bigoted Gen. George Brinton McClellan, chief of all Union forces. President Lincoln had appointed him to that top post on November 1. It is worth a look at a few passages from McClellan's copious, intimate, gossipy, and often shocking letters to his wife and confidant, Mary Ellen. He complained that he found the "Army just about as much disorganized as was the Army of the Potomac [when he was overall commander] . . . no system, no order—perfect chaos." He assures her (and himself) that "I can and will reduce it to order. I will soon have it working smoothly," but he almost immediately contracted typhoid fever, thus halting the prospect of the winter offenses so longed for by Lincoln.[5]

"The original gorilla," McClellan called the president of the United States in one of the numerous letters in which he viciously denigrated the commander in chief. "What a specimen to be at the head of our affairs now!"[6]

In a letter to his friend Samuel M. Barlow about Lincoln's views on what he termed the "nigger question" and about his own belief that the war should not be about the abolition of slavery, McClellan wrote, "I am fighting to preserve the integrity of the Union— and no other issue. . . . Help me to dodge the nigger—we want nothing to do with him."[7]

In spite of McClellan's personal stances—at times he appeared to be a closeted foe of the Union—roundups of Confederate sympathizers, the seditious enemy within, increased daily.

More than determined to root out such traitors was the detective Allan Pinkerton, aka E. J. Allen, a wily Scot and devout abolitionist with views antithetical to McClellan's. He had lately been summoned to be the head of the new secret service department. Pinkerton's reputation as a Chicago detective and former head of the secret service for McClellan's previous command, the Department of the Ohio, and most of all his great admiration for the president made his appointment a personal honor, a feather in his already well feathered cap. During the "Secessionist winter," a term often used by historians to refer to the time between Lincoln's election in November 1860 and his inauguration on March 4, 1861, Pinkerton swore he'd saved the life of the president-elect when conspirators threatened to assassinate him in Baltimore as he traveled from Springfield, Illinois, on his whistle-stop tour that would take him to Washington.[8]

Pinkerton and his operatives Timothy Webster and Hattie Lewis, dubbed "Hattie Lawton" by Pinkerton in his book *The Spy of the Rebellion*, had embedded in Perrymansville, Maryland, and Baltimore to uncover secessionists. Pinkerton now decided that the threat to Lincoln was real, and he later determined that Lincoln was to be ambushed at Baltimore's Calvert Street depot by rabid would-be assassins who had vowed the president-elect would not live to see his inauguration. Lincoln, traveling from Springfield, Illinois, toward Washington, received the alert in Pennsylvania and reluctantly agreed to don a disguise—a cap and shawl. He was secreted in a "special train" with Pinkerton, Ward H. Lamon (Lincoln's bodyguard), and Kate Warne (the head of Pinkerton's female detective agency). After "determining . . . that the telegraph wires which connected Harrisburg" should be cut, Pinkerton later wrote, "the sleeping car . . . drawn by horses" whisked Lincoln safely through Baltimore to the Willard Hotel in Washington City. Some historians believe that this plot never existed (this author joins those who are convinced there is ample reason to assume the particulars are true), as Maryland's virulent secessionists throughout the city and Lincoln's refusal to let the state join the Confederacy are indisputable. According to Pinkerton, it was his warning to the newly elected chief executive, as well as his cloak-and-dagger operation to save his life, that helped to enhance Pinkerton's reputation, at least for a time.[9]

Soon after, McClellan gave the detective a plum assignment.

"By my own preference, as well as at his request, I accompanied him (McClellan) to Washington," Pinkerton wrote. "Among the first things the General did . . . was to organize a secret service force under my management and control," Pinkerton added, fully confident in the general's promise that the war would be easily won—with his help.[10]

Witness the capture of one of Pinkerton's earlier high-value targets on August 23, 1861: the sleek, black-eyed belle and Washington DC hostess Rose O'Neal Greenhow, the most cunning and beautiful rebel spy in Washington, nabbed by Pinkerton himself. At her home, with high-level government officials and Union officers calling at all hours of the night, breathless love notes, the letter W scrawled after utterances of undying passion (allegedly from the pen of Rep. Henry Wilson of Massachusetts), and Rose listening, memorizing, and then caching details of troop movements in her house, and in her courier's hair, after her lovers had left— all this was happening a scant two blocks from the White House.

It was rumored that, secreted in the long tresses of Rose Greenhow's courier, were battle plans sent straight to Confederate general Pierre Beauregard. The plans were said to detail Gen. Irvin McDowell's troop movements and his strategy for a great rebel rout. But that plan did not pan out at the initial Battle of Bull Run on July 20, 1861, when Lincoln's army suffered its first defeat. The humiliating skedaddle of Union troops after the battle was witnessed by celebratory picnickers perched on a ridge, providing a macabre entertainment for the champagne drinkers, cake sellers, sundries hawkers, and reporters eagerly penning details of the spectacle. As the war progressed and deaths piled up on both sides, the summer lark of that July soon turned to horror, as Bull Run was just the first of many bloodbaths. More defenses sprang up, and soldiers mustered and marched in a show that was sure to be spotted by the rebels through their spyglasses: the gleam of polished sabers, masses of blue uniforms not yet tattered or faded. It wasn't just Pinkerton and his men who were on the job. Federal police, the provost marshal general's forces, and State Department investigators were all certain that the innermost sanctums of the government had been infiltrated. The *Washington National Republican* newspaper helmed the hunt, seeking information on anyone "not true to the Union."[11]

• • •

As both sides of the shattered nation waited for an outcome, William A. waited for his orders. At first securing a boardinghouse room at 231 F Street, he is no longer blurred but a sharp image:

slender, of average height ("five foot eight and a half inches"), weighing 157 pounds; pale blue eyes, a trim beard, an "aquiline nose" that would droop and elongate as he aged; "round forehead, ordinary mouth, round chin, dark brown hair, healthy complexion and oval face."[12]

If William A. were soon to receive orders to proceed with Company M to the front, he would say good-bye to his beloved wife and son by letter or in person, ask her to give his love and regards to her father, and tell her to wait for him until the war was over. Maybe he would secure the paymaster's post or command his company in battles to come and fight his own relations if it came to that. Or die trying.

Perhaps he does not at first see the official dispatch as he combs through the mail he's picked up on the way to his lodgings. Or perhaps, as was previously suggested, he had already received his orders by the time he arrived in Washington City but had had not time to reply. When a military man received an order, army protocol required a prompt reply. William A. wrote immediately to Brig. Gen. Lorenzo Thomas, adjutant general of the army. Like William A., Thomas is a Mexican War veteran and Indian fighter, a stern, silver-haired old soldier already at war with Edwin M. Stanton, soon to be secretary of war but now serving as legal advisor to the corrupt and corruptible present secretary of war, Simon Cameron. Because Stanton is waiting to step in, step over Cameron, and run the war department himself and because he does not think Thomas is capable or competent, the adjutant general's future is uncertain. As is William A.'s. He must reply to the order. On November 22, 1861, he wrote, "I have the honor to acknowledge the receipt of a letter from the honorable Secretary of War dated October 14, 1861 informing me of my promotion to a Captaincy in the 3rd regiment of artillery." He then informed General Thomas, "I would respectfully state for your information . . . that I was transferred from my proper Company 'I' 3rd artillery now stationed at Alcatraces [sic] Island, Harbor of San Francisco, Cal, to Company 'M' and ordered to accompany the Battalion of the 3rd Artillery which left San Francisco for New York on the 21st of October by order of Brigadier General Sumner."[13]

In fact portions of Company M did remain on the front, engaging in battles throughout the war. Notably, in 1862 Company M was at "Newbridge, Mechanicsville and Gaines Mill."[14]

William A. asks the adjutant general if he has been assigned to the wrong company; he requests a delay until the situation is sorted out. He needs time and hopes there has been some great mistake. He waits and, unknown to him, while dining, sleeping, or walking about he is under constant surveillance. When Allan Pinkerton learned that yet another Winder had come to Washington, one of his priorities was to determine if *this* Winder could be trusted, for as Lincoln family friend Horatio Nelson Taft had written shortly before the war began, "Treason is rife in the city . . . we know not what a day may bring forth."[15]

Of course Pinkerton was well aware of William A.'s uncle, Charles H., whom he had interrogated and who was living a few blocks away from his nephew's boardinghouse at 168 North F Street. Pinkerton saw traitors everywhere: in the streets, in fancy hotels, across from the White House. And he vowed to find them all.

"I shall seek access to their houses, clubs and places of resort, managing that among the members of my force shall be ostensible representatives of every grade and society," Pinkerton boasted, adding, "Some shall have entry to the gilded salon of the suspected aristocrat traitors, and be their honored guests, while others will act in the capacity of valets, or domestics of various kinds. . . . Other suspected ones will be tracked by the 'Shadow' detective, who will follow their every footstep, and note their every action."[16] No one would be safe. Not even a Union Army captain.

The days crawl along. By December 1, 1861, William A. is still alone in Washington, without an assignment and not knowing that he was under surveillance by Pinkerton's "shadows." He still doesn't know if he is to remain with his company at the front or be sent back to California.

Also in early December President Lincoln delivered his State of the Union address to Congress, summing up the first year of war and the rebel insurgency that began it all. "A disloyal portion of the American people have during the whole year been engaged in an attempt to divide and destroy the Union," he stated. His anguish was apparent as he alluded to and warned against a war with England: "A nation which endures factious domestic division is exposed to disrespect abroad, and one party, if not both, is sure sooner or later to invoke foreign intervention." And then came a shot across the bow to France as well: "I am quite sure a sound argument could be made to show them [foreign nations] that they can reach their aim more readily and easily by aiding to crush this rebellion than by giving encouragement to it."[17]

By December 3 McClellan's artillery chief, William Farquhar Barry, had answered a request from Winder to delay his departure to California. Barry wrote to McClellan, referring to "Special Orders no. 315, Hd quarters U.S. Army, November 27, 1861, Captain Winder, 3rd Arty to join his Co. in California. Captain Winder is now in command of 2 Companies 3rd Arty consolidated as a Battery now just being mounted, and with both of which there is only one other officer—a Lieutenant. Cannot Capt. Winder be permitted to remain here until the Capt. of these Companies expected on the next steamer from California arrives? Yours truly, William F. Barry."[18]

William A., of course wished to remain in the East. He waited. The winter days grew longer and colder.

• • •

Some two hundred miles away, at the Confederate capital in Richmond, Virginia, snow is falling on Ligon's Warehouse and Tobacco Factory at the corner of Twenty-Fifth and Main Streets. The incoming blizzard has dampened the already rotting rafters of the porous building. Gen. John H. Winder was busy confiscating and converting the rest of the tobacco warehouses: Harwood's, Gwathmey's, Palmer's, Barret's, Scott's, Grant's, and Smith's. The reason the Confederate government took possession of those structures was to house Union pows arriving by the hundreds on trains and wagons.[19] Eventually the warehouses and other buildings would be known by archly grand names, in stark contrast to the dungeons they'd become: Castles Godwin and Thunder would house Union spies, soldiers, and political prisoners. Many of their inmates would never leave. More prisons were to come, bigger and better ones, for the South would pile up victory after victory. For that was the belief of many Richmond citizens, at least those who had not been jailed on false charges by General Winder's detectives. He also employed a trusted courier who was tasked with carrying rebel mail and personal communications across enemy lines, from Richmond to Baltimore and the nation's capital.

On the night of December 23 the courier slipped into the darkened streets of Washington City. He'd ridden hard and fast, avoiding the Yankee soldiers who guarded the bridges looking for anyone without a proper pass. On his way past President's Park—a cluster of stately wood and marble buildings, including the Departments of War, State, Treasury, and the White House—a few idle Union soldiers, unlucky enough to pull an all-night, frostbitten shift on sentry duty, might raise a rifle or two, think better before committing to a chase, and grumble back to camp.

Making sure he wasn't being followed, though only fools or harlots would be out on a frigid night like this, the courier rode on to his boss's headquarters to deliver the correspondence he'd carried from Richmond. He would brief and be debriefed by Allan Pinkerton. The initials "T.W." appear throughout Pinkerton's field reports when referring to his esteemed spy, the pride of his detective force, "a man of great physical strength and endurance, skilled in all athletic sports and a good shot . . . whose boldness and ingenuity was of incalculable value to Union officers," he wrote.[20]

At almost forty, Timothy Webster, an English immigrant turned proud American patriot, was tall and stocky, with wide-set gray eyes, a long, uneven nose twisted slightly to the right, and a high forehead with a spill of jet-black hair curling long at the neck. A brawler, a barrister, or zealous Confederate, depending on the mission, he was a different kind of soldier in Lincoln's army, for he was waging a secret war in cellars, rebel camps, statehouses, saloons, and would-be assassins' hotel rooms. This type of work was far preferable to his prewar career: nabbing crooks on the streets of Chicago. And it was far, far, preferable to a languid life with his faithful wife, Charlotte, in a cozy frame cottage in sleepy Onarga, Illinois. His "work behind enemy lines included multiple trips to the Confederate capital . . . acting as a courier for members of the Confederate army, and [he] received passes to cross enemy lines from the Confederate Secretary of War," wrote Corey Recko, Webster's biographer.[21]

According to another Pinkerton operative, Pryce Lewis, "Webster's usual plan was to bring the rebel mail bag himself into the office of the Provost Marshall [sic] [Andrew Porter] where the letters, one by one, were steamed open, and read and a careful record kept of the important ones. Then they were sealed up again."[22]

Always "successful at selling his cover and getting what he wanted," Webster would cross Union lines, snaking through the thickets and byways of the southern Maryland outback, all the while watching for adverse weather conditions, available river crossings, and the vigilance of the enemy. He was at great risk of capture, for which the consequences would be dire.[23]

Although it is not known how Webster was dressed that frigid December night, he may have changed into the full-on garb of a Washington gentleman: a top hat, plumped and spun-straight in his hand, a fur-trimmed frock coat, the pockets basted shut to conceal dispatches, ebony-black leather riding boots, and a derringer resting in his right hip pocket. It was the look of a high-stepper out on the town or, if anyone asked, a late-night patron of fallen angels, the women of the red-light districts, sludge-filled and crime-ridden. Should his mission go as planned, he would unmask another traitor to the government of the United States.

Webster headed east, toward a row of townhouses packed cheek to jowl on a block so dark only a rider who knew the city like a blind man's guide could find his way. Midnight, and the bone-chilling cold had shuttered the neighborhood. When war descended on the capital, dozens of Confederate spies, sympathizers, and saboteurs began arriving or were already in place; they were as much of a threat as the Confederate troops waiting for the first thaw to strike from across the Potomac in Virginia. In addition, a good number of businessmen, cotton brokers, and Southern families seeking proper comforts away from the cigar-choked hotels sheltered there.

It was at an innocuous, respectable location where Webster's quarry, Capt. William A. Winder, had lodged as he anxiously waited for his future to be decided. Pinkerton, using his wartime alias "E.

J. Allen," wrote to General McClellan on December 27, 1861, detailing Webster's encounter with William A.: "Captain Wm Winder of 3rd US Artillery [was found] at his residence or boardinghouse, on H. Street 296[,] Washington—kept by Mrs [Salome] Hutton, to which place he had been fully traced and with which . . . he had been permanently identified by a most thorough and rigorous 'shadowing,' with my operatives, from Nov. 30th to the 23rd . . . inclusive . . . and my operative saw Capt. Winder alone," Pinkerton wrote.[24]

Picture Webster pausing before walking up the boardinghouse steps. With ready facts stored in his head, he will quickly remember his briefing and William A.'s service record in some detail, as though reading from an unseen page.

William Andrew Winder: civilian paymaster in the Mexican War; organizing a ragtag bunch of civilians to repulse an assault by Mexican soldiers at the Battle of Buena Vista; rewarded for bravery with a second lieutenancy in the Third Artillery in 1848; subsequently a first lieutenancy promotion. A soldier moving from post to post: Newport Barracks, Kentucky; Jefferson Barracks, Missouri; Fort Constitution, New Hampshire; Fort Preble, Maine; and Palatka, Florida, where he attempted to locate Seminole Indians after the Second Seminole War. Brilliant and practiced as Webster is, he cannot see the past—the younger William A. Winder fighting alligators and slogging through the swamps when most of the Seminole had been dislocated, fighting illness and leeches in an effort to find malingerers, never killing or injuring a single man, woman, or child. This man Webster could not know. But he did know that after the wreck of the *San Francisco*, William A. was sent to California, to the remote outback of San Diego, to the Mission San Diego de Alcalá, then detached to Fort Yuma, California, finally leaving from San Francisco, arriving in New York City to begin recruiting service for the army, then posted to Alcatraz. From there he came to New York on the *Champion*. That was the sum of the captain's record, the sum of the soldier from whose possession Webster has been sent to determine William A.'s true loyalties and give verbal communications from his father, Confederate general John H. Winder.[25]

Going straight to Winder's room, he announced himself. Webster gave his real name, not an alias. He used one when he needed to but often depended on his ability to transform at a moment's notice. Given Webster's practiced southern drawl and a curl of the lip, a hiss, or a curse at the mere mention of a hated Yank, he became a trusted courier for targeted secessionists, rebel officers (especially Gen. John H. Winder), their detectives, Confederate secretary of state Judah Benjamin, and Richmond's elite; they all gave him letters, dispatches, packages, and medicine to transport. And now Webster, having gained admittance to William A.'s room, "fully satisfied the Captain of his entire reliability," Pinkerton wrote, and then Webster gave an "account of his interview in Richmond with Genl. Winder (the Captain's father.)" To further enhance his credibility, Webster spoke of the "great and essential aid," he rendered to Winder's close friend and bunkmate, a former Third U.S. Artillery assistant surgeon, Dr. James C. Herndon, when he deserted the U.S. Army shortly after the *Champion* docked in New York City. Webster told William A. Winder that he had "accompan[ied] Herndon in making his way to Virginia, by way of Leonardtown, Maryland."[26]

Pinkerton related, in a later letter to General McClellan, the difficult and often dangerous route to Richmond from Washington that Webster had taken: "via Leonardtown, MD . . . crossed Potomac at Cobb Neck . . . to Cuckhold Creek . . . to Fredericksburg, Virginia" and on to Richmond.[27]

William A. would have known of Herndon's desertion, but the fact that Webster presented a letter of introduction vouching for Webster (which Herndon had given to General Winder) and related the particulars of Herndon's flight appeared to convince William A. that Webster was who he said he was: his father's courier.

And there in the Pinkerton report was this, with italics for emphasis: "that he [General Winder] wished my operative to tell his son . . . that his father wished him to resign his commission if he *could not find the means of certain escape* by desertion, and come south."[28]

And then came this demand: "that his Father had much rather he should resign and, if it must be so, lay in jail until the close of the war, or if it should be demanded, that he would rather his son should *suffer death of the most ignominious character*, than continue to hold his commission and be made to serve the United States in this War against the South."[29]

Resign, be jailed, or die: this from a father to a son. And does William A., hearing his father's orders, curse the day he became a soldier?

He was not the son his father wanted him to be. No, this kind, artistic boy who painted and sketched in light-studded lands when at his posts in California—or wherever he was—was this whelp who humiliated him by six failures to get into West Point from "1840 to 1845."[30]

Even though the Winder name alone, his grandfather's shame, and his father's thuggish reputation among West Point's cadets might have spoiled his chances, this son with a pressing need to study medicine and heal others, this son who slipped sideways into the Mexican War as a civilian paymaster and then trudged dutifully into the family business of warring, this son, the father demanded, must join the other Winders. Or desert, be jailed, or die.

What then must William A. say to this rebel courier who landed at his boardinghouse like an errant nighthawk? With the room filled by the unseen presence of his father, a small man in gaudy general's garb, an old man with the power to singe a son from a distance of two hundred miles, was there a pause, an intake of breath until William A. told Webster what he knew his father wanted to hear?

"The Captain, further, told my operative that when he returned to Richmond," Pinkerton wrote, he should tell his father that "all his sympathies were with the South, that his relations and all he held dear were there, and that if he had the means, he would go South the very first chance he could get," that his father "might rest assured that he would never fight against the South . . . that he had met with General McClellan and had told the General his feelings, and had obtained from him the offer of returning to duty in California," but that "his pay, as Captain in the United States Army, was his only means of support for his wife and son."[31]

It is not difficult to imagine John H. Winder's face purpling with rage when he heard this upon Webster's return to Richmond.

William A.'s father knew full well that his son had married into a wealthy and aristocratic New Hampshire family. The U.S. Army his only means of support? Of course his son would be salaried if he joined the Confederate forces and would likely be promoted to the rank of major, or even general. This excuse, this rationale must have been unbearable for General Winder. And yet there was more from William A., reported Pinkerton. "In no possible event would he draw his sword against the south," Pinkerton stated, for William A. had indicated that he'd already sent his wife back to New Hampshire to join their son. "He would upon Webster's return tell him what choice he had made" and "would be ready to leave for Virginia the first chance, as all his hopes and prayers were with the South."[32]

So ended the interview, but not the final paragraphs of the report from Pinkerton to McClellan, which were replete with more emphasis, and if one views the original document, Pinkerton's hard, angry scrawl builds, scorches, until we can almost see the outraged detective clamping down hard on his ever-present cigar, puffs of smoke filling the room, choking the air:

> In Conclusion, General . . . I am not sufficiently acquanited [sic] with Military rules and law, to know if there be any power which can be exercised in the case of Captain Winder; but that a man, who, for *bread and butter* will continue to hold his commission and receive the pay from the *country which has been his benefactor*, while, at the *same time*, he *intends to act the traitors part*, can find *no parallel short of Benedict Arnold*, if indeed, his crime be not yet deeper dyed. . . . If there be no military rule far-reaching enough to touch his case, that at least, he be requested to *subscribe* to and *swear allegiance to the Country*, not that I have much *confidence* in the *saving power* of such *an Oath* . . . but for the purpose of testing whether Captain Winder will *add perjury to the crime of Treason*. I am, General, Your obet. Servt. E. J. Allen.[33]

The meeting ended. Webster rushed down the stairs of the boardinghouse and went straight to Pinkerton's headquarters to report word for word his disturbing conclusions. He'd found yet another traitor: William A. Winder.

According to William A., however, after the courier departed, he immediately rode two blocks to the Department of State, roused a dozing clerk, and reported his late-night encounter. While no record of this report has been found, there is this: many years later he wrote a letter mentioning the incident to his old friend from his early Third Artillery days at Jefferson Barracks, Lt. Gen. William Tecumseh Sherman. "I was on various occasions called on by parties claiming to be spies of the Confederate Government who urged me to cross the lines with them. . . . After reporting one of these and finding no notice was taken of it . . . with suspicion visited on me," Winder wrote, "I concluded that it was a plan to test my loyalty." Worse, "all my applications for service in the field were rejected. . . . I called on the President, and after stating my case, which by the way he appeared to understand perfectly, [was] satisfied."[34]

Although the Abraham Lincoln Papers in the Library of Congress are replete with daily logs of his appointments and chance meetings, no record of Winder's visit has been found. The absence of such a record is probably not unusual as so many people came to the White House seeking pardons or favors, so it is very likely that William A. did make the visit he recalled. The visit might have assured President Lincoln that he could be trusted to defend the Union. Perhaps that was enough. Perhaps.

On December 27, the day Pinkerton wrote his furious missive to General McClellan, a clearly desperate William A. Winder also wrote to McClellan's adjutant, Col. Albert V. Colburn, requesting a leave *"rendered necessary by urgent personal business."* He wrote that he'd tried to see General McClellan "on this subject," but he was "too unwell to receive me." Winder indicated that he went to Secretary of War Cameron, who "told me he knew of no objection and advised me to see the Adjt. Gen. [Lorenzo Thomas]. This I was not at all disposed to do, as he is unfriendly to me. I therefore submit the application directly to the Commanding General." This was a highly inappropriate and precipitous move, as Winder was breaching military protocol by going over Thomas's head. When Thomas learned of this, according to William A., he told him he "will regret it." This direct threat is foreboding, especially know-

ing that Winder's perceived disloyalty might well reach McClellan. A new year was threatening, or beckoning.[35]

• • •

William A.'s movements in the first weeks of 1862—as he anxiously awaited what the army had in store for him—are unknown.
The whereabouts of his uncle, William H. Winder, at the time
are well documented. He had been transferred from Fort Lafayette to Fort Warren Prison, "a two Story pentagon shaped fortress of heavy granite built on Georges Island . . . at the entrance
of Boston Harbor."[36]

William H. Winder complained of the harsh durance, of having
no chairs and "nothing but bare floors to lie on . . . some few perfectly raw hams, in the open air . . . were distributed, and some of
the prisoners thus got something to eat."[37]

But on January 11, during the fifth month of his incarceration,
it seemed freedom was at hand. Assistant Secretary of State Frederick Seward sent an order to Fort Warren's commandant, Col.
Justin Dimick. "Let W. H. Winder be released on taking the Oath
of Allegiance to the Government of the United States, stipulating
that he will neither enter any of the states in insurrection against
the United States," Seward wrote, "nor hold any correspondence
with persons residing in those states" and do nothing "hostile"
while at liberty.[38]

On January 14 William H. Winder wrote, "I was offered release
on condition of taking the oath of allegiance."[39] In extremis and
fearing he might fall victim to a typhoid epidemic sweeping the
prison, he listened to the moans of the dying and the infernal
grinding of the single pump that furnished water for the entire
population; he could barely hear the words of the guard or read
the paper they thrust at him through the bars of his cell. Freedom is yours, they told Winder—his once round face thinned
and hardened by months of confinement—freedom will be imminent if, and only if, he'd finally swear loyalty to the United States
of America.

He refused. Clearly outraged, Assistant Secretary of State Frederick Seward, informed of this refusal, wrote to Colonel Dimick:

Department of State, Washington, January 17, 1862.

Col. Justin Dimick, Fort Warren, Boston

Colonel: Your letter of the 15th instant reporting that William H. Winder refuses to take the oath of allegiance has been received. In reply I have to request that you hold Winder in custody till further orders from this Department.

I am, sir, very respectfully your obedient servant,
F. W. Seward, Assistant Secretary[40]

William H. would subsist on raw ham and soda crackers if he had to, as that was common fare. He'd write again to his brother Charles in Washington, and to the newspapers, damning Lincoln, the Union, and the abolitionists as "lunatics with Negro on the brain."[41] With no stove nearby, and no fire to stoke, he'd keep writing. It warmed him to write.

• • •

In Washington, his brother Charles H. Winder was taking an oath and making promises he was loath to keep. But unlike his brother, he is conditionally free.

WASHINGTON, February 1, 1862.

I, Charles H. Winder, of the city of Washington, D. C., do voluntarily agree and pledge myself in having this my parole extended to honorably fulfill the stipulations hereinafter set forth, to wit: That during the existence of the present rebellion I will not visit any insurrectionary State or Territory without permission from the Secretary of State and that I will not render to the enemies of the Federal Government any aid, comfort or information of any nature whatever. It is hereby understood that this parole extends until the 1st day of March 1862, upon which day I will report myself at the office of the provost-marshal of this District.[42]

As for William A. Winder, by January 14 it seemed that word of his meeting with Timothy Webster and Pinkerton's furious letter to McClellan had reached Assistant Secretary of State Frederick Seward's desk.

Department of State, Washington, January 14th, 1862

Brig. Gen. Andrew Porter, Provost Marshal, Washington

General: I inclose [sic] herewith and invite your attention to a memorandum laid before the Department relative to one Captain Winder, a son of the insurgent General John H. Winder, who it is alleged has given utterance to expressions that place him under strong suspicions of disloyalty. Will you please cause inquiries to be made into the matter and adopt such proceedings as in your judgment are proper and report to this Department.

I am, general, very respectfully, your obedient servant,

F. W. Seward
Assistant Secretary[43]

It is unclear as to whether General Porter acted on this alarming memo, as by January 15 President Lincoln had appointed Edwin McMasters Stanton to be the new secretary of war. It is entirely possible that during this transition, for Stanton did not officially take up his position until January 20, the Seward-to-Porter correspondence went astray amid the bureaucratic tangle of orders and documents transferred between the Departments of State and War. Perhaps government authorities—hugely distracted by the capture at sea of James M. Mason and John Slidell, two Confederate diplomats on their way to London, in the so-called Trent Affair that nearly led the United States into a war with Britain—dropped the allegations against William A. If there was to be any future action taken against him, the U.S. Army had perhaps unwittingly removed the threat to him for the time being. Or so it seemed.

• • •

On January 21 the *Champion* left New York City for California. Among the many passengers facing the arduous voyage was a family of three: a husband, his wife, and their eleven-year-old son—the William A. Winder family. As the buildings and spires of New York fade into the distance, no doubt young Willie is thrilled at his first sea voyage, his new adventure, for he has been a protected child tucked under the wings of a large adoring family, the son of a father who loves him but must spend months and years away from home. His mother is leaving her family's mansion on Islington Street in Portsmouth, New Hampshire, where she is the eldest and most relied-upon child of her parents. She is leaving her father, Ichabod Goodwin, her mother, Sarah, her sisters Hope, Sadie, Georgette, and Susie, and her brother, Frank, to stay by her husband's side. She is sacrificing everything to live among uniformed strangers, to go to this far-flung place. This is not what she planned. Her husband might have been a paymaster, close to home or at the front. Not a combat soldier, but holding an important position with the Union Army where even as a paymaster—he was a trained soldier after all—he would be in uniform and ready to fight should an attack come. Nothing had come of her effort to get him a good position. She had tried to help. At least now they were together. On a ship. Off to war. What then?

The *Champion* docks at Aspinwall and will return to New York. Its passengers must board a train across the isthmus to Panama City. All was not quiet there. Riots and a major fight were going on between the militia and the police. Willie Winder, so far from anything familiar, might have thrilled to or perhaps feared this part of the long journey. At Panama City the steamer *Orizaba* was waiting in dock for the railroad passengers to come aboard. By February 15 the San Francisco *Daily Evening Bulletin* was reporting "Capt. Wender [sic] & family" were on the *Orizaba* passenger list.[44]

Ahead is Alcatraz, their destination. Company D was William A.'s command. In spite of all his efforts to prove that he belonged on the front and his interview with President Lincoln during which he vowed that he could be trusted, he is after all and will always be a Winder. Absent real proof that he was a traitor to the Union, the order that sent him to California was clear. But who issued the order? An article in the *Milwaukee Sentinel* on April 12, 1889, reported, "During the Civil War he [William A.] was desirous of going to the front, but fell under suspicion of disloyalty because his father was Gen. Winder, an officer in the Confederate Army. Although President Lincoln was satisfied upon the assurances of (Captain) Winder as to his loyalty, Secretary Stanton insisted on his being sent to California."[45]

Stanton did not officially become secretary of war until January 20, 1862. Until then he had been legal advisor to the outgoing secretary of war, Simon Cameron. However, Stanton was notorious for investigating and prosecuting Union officers whom he suspected of having ties to the South. So who did order William A. to Alcatraz? Follow-up correspondence from Pinkerton to McClellan, written on January 24, is filled with Pinkerton's complex and lengthy details of Timothy Webster's spying. Pinkerton wrote, "My operative saw General Winder before leaving Richmond, and learned from him that his son, *Captain Winder* of the U.S.A. had been sent back to *California*, as he supposed for the purpose of getting him out of the way, as he (*Captain Winder*) was not to be *trusted* here in Washington, by *Genl* McClellan on account of his Southern sentiments."[46]

• • •

Not trusted. Gotten out of the way. The Winder name became increasingly and publicly synonymous with treason. It was almost immaterial at this point whether or not Capt. William A. Winder's unwanted post was a punishment from higher-ups beset by rumors of his disloyalty but unwilling or unable to act against him. The real question was if Alcatraz would become as much his prison as his command.

3

Of Toil, Treason, and the Golden Land

While William A.'s ship was heading north to San Francisco, he may well have mused about the times when he was young and untainted, when he first came to California, to San Diego. In the late spring of 1854 he'd toiled in the dust and hot sun when as a first lieutenant he had "landed at La Playa [at the tip of San Diego] from the steamer *Sonora* with two companies of the 3rd Artillery."[1]

Getting off the ship in San Diego, mounting up, and climbing a hill past the ruins of the old Spanish presidio, then down along slashes of browned ground, sand, and mud, Winder would have seen a road of sorts that drifted to a plaza where an American flag billowed. It hung on a pole plunged into the dirt on July 27, 1846, when John C. Fremont's California Battalion took the town from the Mexicans on his way to capturing Los Angeles. After the Treaty of Guadalupe Hidalgo, which ended the Mexican War, wanderers, failures, and health seekers, along with adventurers, merchants, outlaws, and land grabbers with bulging pockets or nothing at all, had streamed to California to hang their futures on a hardscrabble life far from home. They came on trading ships, many inspired by Richard Henry Dana's elegiac *Two Years before the Mast*, a paean to the working sailor that told how he, a Harvard dropout with eye problems and a sickly constitution, went to sea aboard the *Alert* on a long voyage to California. After traveling up and down the coast, he finally landed at La Playa, the center of a booming trade in cattle hides. His labors at the hide houses included scrubbing and cutting the flayed remains of cattle, curing the hides, storing them in barrels, then hefting them onto ships that arrived to take the valuable cargo to Boston. In return for the hides, the ships traded luxury goods and much-needed necessities of daily life to San Diego residents hungry for the tastes, smells, and silks from the Northeast. Of all the places he roamed Dana would most remember Old Town, the Spanish-Mexican settlement, the lighthouse at La Playa, and the "little harbor of San Diego," and he fondly recalled the warmth of the families who welcomed him. In 1835 he wrote, "We were always glad to see San Diego; it being the depot, and a snug little place, and seeming quite like home to me."[2]

Not yet seeking the snug little place of Dana's dreamy idyll, William A. would land at La Playa twenty years later as a soldier-passerby. The hide houses were gone, the cattle stock depleted, but he would meet and come to know the pioneer settlers who had come to California as new dreamers seeking warm air and a comfortable climate. When they arrived in the early 1850s, some were soldier-surgeons to the missions—bone crackers wielding scalpels and tinctures of laudanum to numb pained bodies. Sedate and sedating, they eschewed the Indian remedies and drifted to Old Town. William A.'s mining associate with whom he briefly partnered in 1857 was a Massachusetts-born merchant named Ephraim Morse. Morse had first voyaged north to the gold fields but was foiled by the "shine" that was no shine but merely bits of sun-bleached rock in the pans, so he drifted south to San Diego. Dr. David Hoffman, a graduate of Toland Medical College in San Francisco, came to San Diego as "a ship's surgeon with the Pacific Mail Steamship Company." He ignored the other ports of call—San Francisco, Monterey, San Pedro—and came to Old Town in 1853. The place beckoned to him, "hidden in the crook of the river, remote, asleep, forsaken, a place of oblivion."[3]

Hardly a lost soul, but seeing an opportunity as the lone physician in Old Town, Hoffman stayed and thereby met William A. The Old Town they saw was a village of long, thick-walled adobes that kept occupants cool in the heat. These structures had been built by proud landed gentry from Spain, Peru, and Mexico—the José Estudillos, the Juan Bandinis, the José Altamiranos, the Don Miguel de Pedrorenas, the José Serranos—they and their children often marrying Americans and speaking a mix of Spanish and English. There were Prussian émigrés among the settlers too,

35

German-Jewish merchants and entrepreneurs—Louis Rose, Joseph Mannasse, and Marcus Schiller. Yankees were well represented too—the venerable and venerated Old Town storekeeper, Ephraim Morse; the New Yorker who built the first brick home in the area, Thomas Whaley; the Pennsylvanian and Old Town mayor, Daniel Brown Kurtz, known as "D.B."; and the judges from Ohio, Oliver Witherby and James Robinson. Among the southerners who found their way to San Diego were George Pendleton, from Virginia, and Cave Johnson Couts, from Tennessee. From Ireland came Joshua Sloane, George Lyons, and Philip Crosthwaite. Wooden buildings, rough-hewn houses, and hotels like the Exchange were scattered around the plaza, where often, right in front of the courthouse, rough justice prevailed amid bullfights, bear baits, gunfights, duels, and a hanging or two. Such activities were commonplace, as were the *bailes* (balls), the festivals, the music, the Mexican food with chiles, beans, spiced beef, and corn tortillas—new tastes, new smells. Five miles away was New Town, a tattered little outpost, an attempt at a new settlement, the creation-turned-folly of developer William Heath Davis meant to draw investors to a "32 square block area" with the promise of fine dwellings and "better shipping" opportunities closer to the water. Few investors came, dreams failed. In defeat "Davis gave some land to the US Government for an army post, the San Diego Barracks."[4]

One of the hopefuls who dipped quickly into New Town and very briefly graced the place in 1851 with a newspaper, the *San Diego Herald*, was John Judson Ames, a giant of a man who came down from the gold country to tell the literate among the residents what news was news—there is a stage line from Los Angeles; there will be, God willing, a railroad, an overland mail route—and what was not. Seeing New Town as an utter failure, he quickly vacated to Old Town.

William A. Winder, a first lieutenant on the way to his post at the mission, would not forget the ragged Cahuilla and Kumeyaay left begging in the dirt of the plaza, driven off their lands by the white immigrants who wanted them gone forever. With the horrors of the shipwreck of the *San Francisco* still raw, William A.— thankful for solid earth—and the survivor-soldiers of the Third

U.S. Artillery marched about five miles to their post, the Mission San Diego de Alcalá, founded in 1769 by Father Junípero Serra. Thought by many to be unnecessarily brutal to his neophytes, while others proclaimed him a saintly Franciscan, Father Serra ultimately ruled over twenty-one missions that dotted the present-day state of California from San Diego to Sonora. By the time Winder arrived, the San Diego mission had been partially rebuilt after a damaging revolt by some of the natives. The Dieguenos, many of whom were Kumeyaay—one of the tribes dislocated to work at the missions—were ruled by a succession of priests who'd gone about the task of converting the natives to Christianity.

Winder, during his time at the mission with the occupying army, wrote two extant letters expressing his concern that the Cahuilla and Kumeyaay who called the mountains around the wild scrublands home were being ill treated and endangered by the white settlers. From his post at the mission William A. wrote to Bvt. Maj. William Whann Mackall, the assistant adjutant general, at No. 61, Dept. Pacific Division at Benicia, telling him that "Thomas, the principal Captain of the Santa Isabel Indians, together with thirteen of his Captains, came into this post some two weeks since, and complained that Mr. J. J. Warner (Sub-Agent for these Indians) had informed them of his intention to take all animals, having no brands upon them, in the hands of the Indians, from them as his property." William A. also told Mackall that "as many of these Indians own mares, which have had colts, and which are not branded for the reason that they have no brands, this proceeding would be manifestly unjust." The injustice prompted William A. to tell Thomas, the captain of the Santa Isabel Indians, to "bring the animals here in case any attempt was made to take them, and I would endeavor to secure his property for him." Again William A. addresses "one of the many cases of injustice practiced upon these Indians, and by the very men whose duty it is to protect them, and I presume my action will be reported as 'an interference on the part of the military' with the duties of an agent." But William A. is willing to risk his reputation and the possible consequences of such interference. He has taken it upon himself to "report the case, in order that the Commanding General [John

Ellis Wool] may be made aware of the characters of the persons making such reports."[5]

An earlier communication again gives evidence of William A.'s concern for the plight of members of the Cahuilla tribe. That letter he wrote to the commander of Mission de Alcalá, Capt. Henry Stanton Burton, a wise young officer and good friend. William A., unlike so many army men who saw the Indians as disposable nuisances, or worse, worthy of massacre, wrote on April 29, 1856, "I proceeded to the Rancho of San Jacinto, in the vicinity of San Gorgonio. On my arrival there I sent for Juan Antonio, the principal Capt. of the Cawilla (sp) Indians, from whom I learned that the Whites were encroaching upon the lands now occupied by the Indians." William A. then writes that Juan Antonio "complained that the commissioners had promised to send him farming utensils, and told him to live on this land where he would not be disturbed, neither of which promises have been fulfilled." Due to the failure of their crops, "the greater portion of the tribe was almost entirely destitute of the means of subsistence. . . . The whites were in the habit of taking the gardens or other lands from the Indians without paying them for either crops or improvements." And here William A. explains that "for many years these Indians have been in the habit of cultivating their fields without fencing, but at present the cattle of the whites overrun and destroy their crops and they have no means of redress. The foregoing facts will, I think, show the absolute necessity of adopting at an early day some means for protecting the Indians from the Whites."[6]

This evidence of the advice verging on a dictate given by Lieutenant Winder to his ranking officer was at once bold and a window into his thinking as he became a passionate advocate of fair treatment of Native Americans. For the rest of Burton's short life (he died suddenly in 1869, after a storied career as a West Pointer and heroic Union Civil War general), William A. remained friends with Burton and his wife, María Amparo Ruiz de Burton.

María was born at La Paz, in Baja California. Brilliant and eventually fluent in English, she married Henry Burton in 1847. María's writing talent (she wrote and directed plays for the soldiers to perform), and especially her later novels in English, brings her a measure of fame. And for William A. she becomes a devoted and lifelong friend. Both were artistic and in many ways out of place—he a gentle soul forced into soldiering and she a Californio, a Spanish land grantee of noble stock but regarded by some as a foreign interloper in her American husband's world. William A. and María were like-minded and generous. The two would endure struggles: she would fight to keep her land, and he would fight to keep his honor.

The first recorded example of William A. the artist working at what would become a passionate lifelong avocation was noted by Judge Benjamin Ignatius Hayes—"elected . . . in 1852, the first Judge of the Southern District of California, including Los Angeles and San Diego Counties"—as he traveled with his son through Old Town to the Mission de Alcalá. There he "found Lieutenant Winder painting in watercolors two views of the Mission. Several portraits there by him of different persons. A delightful quiet reigns around this post," he wrote in his diary.[7]

The delightful quiet and the painting were interrupted in early March 1855 when William A. was sent to Fort Yuma, at the junction of the Gila and Colorado Rivers. Scorching hot in summer, with the temperature sometimes reaching 130 degrees, the fort was tasked with protecting the ferry that crossed the Colorado from attack by the Yuma Indians or by volatile new settlers who feared the Indians and sometimes forced themselves on Yuma women. William A. is also trying his luck at mining—the fickle game that drove men to madness or made them poor and hopeless, middling drunks, or millionaires—and allying himself in that endeavor with the wealthy rancher Rufus King Porter, Ephraim W. Morse, and Capt. Henry Burton. In signing a contract with Mexican landowners, the three Americans made sure the agreement was binding, official and inked, ready and final. The San Antonio mine had rock ledges glinting with copper. From his post at Fort Yuma, William A. wrote to Morse and Porter that if the San Antonio mine could be properly managed—and this would be a common refrain—a great fortune awaited. But a windfall did not await. Here begins a pattern, one of almost-riches at the next mine and the ones after that.

But again William A. must move, leaving with another officer to follow the Mojave River on a survey for the Southern Pacific Railroad. The railroad: always planned, always awaited, as capricious and heartbreaking as the mines. Next William A. went to the Arizona Territory, once a slavery-riddled prize of the Confederates until it was pried away from New Mexico. In later years William A. will look back on his stint in the Southwest as the time when he was young, when he experienced all the colors, all the sights and sounds, all the pitfalls and disappointments. He will look back especially to San Diego, as did Richard Henry Dana when he pondered his lost youth. "The past is real," Dana wrote, mourning the "light hearted boys who are now hardened middle aged men, if the seas, the rocks, fevers . . . have spared them."[8]

The sea has spared William A. again and again. He will fear it, war with it, and struggle in its vastness and finally, eventually, find safe harbor in California after the war. Like a Circe in gossamer or in army blue, California will call him back to a state whose vicissitudes and loyalties will try him anew.

• • •

As the nation was divided, so was the state of California, threatened by sedition and talk of separation. The state that beckoned forty-niners, made ordinary men rich beyond their dreams, or sent them, desperate, into deserts or saloons, was also home to proslavery advocates of Southern birth. They were especially prominent in the Los Angeles area, in both the city proper as well as in towns such as El Monte, Sierra Madre, and Visalia, among others. Henry Hamilton's *Los Angeles Star* and the Democratic "Chivalry" (proslavery) wing of the party throughout the state repeatedly denounced emancipation, abolitionists, and "Black Republicans" and urged the creation of a separate "Pacific Republic." Many loathed, feared, and ridiculed the president of the United States. The *Visalia Equal Rights Expositor* described Lincoln as "the cadaverous, long shanked, mule countenanced-rail splitter from Illinois."[9]

Lincoln and the rise of the Republican Party in northern California and the crowded, enthusiastic, and defiant "Union mass meetings . . . convinced many Southern sympathizers to leave

California for Dixie."[10] The *Sacramento Daily Union,* "the political conscience of California," according to the historian Robert J. Chandler, rarely changed its loyal stance, declaring, "Secession is revolution." The newspaper condemned the institution of slavery and endorsed the Lincoln administration. Church pulpits became bully pulpits for both sides. "Jefferson Davis was no more traitor than George Washington," the Reverend William Anderson Scott of San Francisco's Calvary Presbyterian Church (now the site of the St. Francis Hotel) declared to his congregation, inciting riots and necessitating a call for Federal troops to quell the crowds.[11]

Taking up the opposing view, the Unitarian minister and orator Thomas Starr King "bolstered the weak-hearted" to stand for the Union and called for the use of black troops. He also said that "abolitionism" should no longer be considered a dirty word. Although "during the Civil War, civil authorities, by inclination, the ballot box, and presidential proclamation, smothered any secessionist threat to the three hundred thousand Californians," resistance was real. There were local armed militias and not-so-secretive cliques like the treasonous and seditious Knights of the Golden Circle. Already active in the Northeast, the group had infiltrated parts of California to ready their bands for a takeover of San Francisco in the Civil War.[12]

According to the historian John A. Martini, in this period "San Franciscans never felt more isolated." There was also "the real possibility that Great Britain might ally herself with the . . . Confederacy." Should that happen, "the Royal Navy's powerful Pacific fleet might try to capture San Francisco." These were real threats both foreign and domestic.[13] For protection and shows of strength, the U.S. Navy's Pacific Squadron, comprising six small wooden "sloops of war"—the uss *Lancaster, Saranac, Wyoming, Narragansett, St. Marys,* and *Cyane*—were at the ready as urgent warnings about "secessionists gaining a foothold, abounded." These ships plied the coasts of Mexico and California for the "protection of the mail steamers and their heavy shipments of gold."[14]

The Bay of San Francisco was guarded by Fort Point, Lime Point, and Black Point—also known as Point San Jose—none of which was as well armed or as well situated as Alcatraz. And the Navy

Yard at Mare Island, twenty miles away at Vallejo, California, not to mention the Benicia Arsenal, might well become rebel targets. Because of the threats, the immediate defense of Mare Island became paramount. The Kentucky-born general Albert Sidney Johnston, commander of the Military Department of the Pacific, was regarded with suspicion in the lead-up to the war.

Johnston was accused of abetting Confederates who wished to take over all the forts in the Bay Area and the all-important arsenal at Benicia, commandeer steamers to invade the Golden Gate, raid the gold stores, and create a separate nation, the Pacific Republic. Johnston, however, was never a party to any such cabals. "I have heard foolish talk about an attempt to seize the strongholds of government under my charge," he wrote. "Knowing this, I have prepared for emergencies, and will defend the property of the United States with every resource at my command, and with the last drop of blood in my body. Tell that to our Southern friends!"[15] When the war began, however, Johnston resigned from the Union Army to fight with Confederate forces. His loyalties apparently lay with those of his adopted state of Texas.

Gen. Edwin Sumner, who replaced Johnston as commander of the Department of the Pacific, well knew the profound and pressing need to defend San Francisco. In addition, there was the threat from Confederate privateers and marauding British raiders who might slip unnoticed through the Golden Gate, where "tens of millions of dollars of gold went east" from the harbor, so the question facing Sumner was, "How could it best be protected?"[16] "From 1861 to 1864, more than $173 million passed though the Golden Gate from the California mines and the Comstock Lode of Nevada," much of it having been housed in the U.S. Mint that was located in San Francisco, after passing through "Mare Island Naval Shipyard, and Benicia Arsenal." One "capture of a single gold steamer" would have helped the Confederacy. The immediate defense of Fortress Alcatraz was paramount.[17]

4

A Godforsaken Fortress

Alcatraz Island was a craggy perch surrounded by frigid winds, mists that stung the eyes and chilled the bones, fog in summer, rain in winter, and an occasional welcome blaze of sun and blue sky; there was always the endless slap of waves gnawing at the island, the swoops and cries of gulls, terns, and pelicans, their droppings streaking the rocks white. In this foreign and forbidding place there was much history. Perhaps, to pass an evening around a welcome warming fire, William A. might tell his son the tales, myths, and truths about the island.

Known officially and finally as Alcatraz and noted by the historian John Martini as the "island of many misspellings" (e.g., Alcatras, Alcatrazaz, Alcatrose, Alcatrus), the tiny island was discovered by Lt. Juan Manuel de Ayala from the *San Carlos* on August 5, 1775. Sighting the rocky outcropping in the bay and taken with the flocks of large-billed birds nesting there, Ayala called the place La Isla de Los Alcatraces (Island of the Pelicans).[1]

According to the National Park Service, which now oversees Alcatraz, "after the U.S. government took control of California from the Republic of Mexico in the late 1840s, it identified Alcatraz Island as a place of great strategic military value."[2]

By 1852 the island had become a fortress guarding the Bay of San Francisco. Of the climate on the island, Union general James "Birdseye" McPherson—unlucky enough to be posted there—wrote that Alcatraz was a godforsaken place that "beats all countries for wind I ever inhabited."[3]

Alcatraz was also in the sights of Lt. John Charles Fremont, the explorer, soldier, abolitionist, and ready scout. Upon reaching San Francisco at the peak of the gold rush, he took good, clean breaths of the salt-misted air and announced that now that the United States had captured California, it must be occupied and readied for war. Part of making ready for the conflict was a survey and then construction of buildings on the island. Alcatraz soon sprouted cannons, casemates, and the Citadel, a three-story stone-and-brick building looming over the island. According to one account, "the first or basement level was below ground level and was surrounded by a dry moat, which the army termed a 'ditch.'"[4]

The Citadel, which was the army barracks, was a forbidding structure with narrow rifle-slot windows looking down on the ever-moving water. It seemed impenetrable, with only one access point, from a road that wound around from the pier to the sally port—a secured entrance. "Alcatraces Island" and "1857" are inscribed atop the arch of the sally port.

Shortly before the Civil War began, with a clear warning to any enemies of the Union, the *Sacramento Daily Union* boasted, "Alcatraz Fort is one of the strongest in the United States. It has now one hundred and seventy-five guns mounted—some of them of immense calibre—being Columbiads, which throw shot weighing 120 pounds. Alcatraz [as] . . . 'the Sumter of California' . . . [is] capable of resisting any force that could be brought against it. . . . San Francisco need fear no enemy while that giant fortress is in the hands of men loyal to the stars and stripes."[5] Further historic observations indicate that Alcatraz bristled with guns "ranging in size from . . . 24 pounder howitzers . . . mounted on the island's guardhouse . . . and in the masonry towers . . . to the large smooth-bore guns, the Columbiads." Able to blast invading ships with heated "hot shots" (cannonballs from two furnaces that could send fiery red balls flying), the well-armed fortress was a world unto itself.[6]

And it was William A.'s world. The Alcatraz roster of officers records him as commander of Company D of the Third Artillery. His dear friend Capt. Henry S. Burton, who'd served with him at the old San Diego Barracks in 1854, was overall commander of the island. When Burton left for the front, we can be sure Winder wished to follow, but he was then legitimately commander of the entire island. William A., Abby, and Willie would occupy the first-floor officers' quarters, a dining room, and an adjacent parlor in the Citadel. Reasonable accommodations, to be sure, but it is possible that Abby enrolled young Willie at a school in San Francisco, although in many cases children were taught on Alcatraz.

At the time the Winders arrived, a tour of San Francisco would have revealed a boisterous, bawdy, roaring city, a place where society's immensely wealthy dined, gambled, and avoided the fragile shanties that clung to hillsides and dotted filthy streets. Whorehouses and gambling dens abounded in the Barbary Coast district, where drunks and failed forty-niners told tales of fools' gold and the fools it made of them. San Francisco's "many streets are made up of decaying, smoke-grimed wooden houses and the barren sand hills," wrote the young Mark Twain to his mother from the opulent Lick House Hotel.[7]

As gold strikes were fading, silver, the new star metal, promised fresh wealth, and businesses like the Colorado Silver Mining Company offered shares to those who dared not venture below ground to stumble through darkness hoping to see the glint of silver, a pursuit that might well cost them their lives. The *San Francisco Bulletin* was awash in ads for entertainment. Some advertised minstrelsy; the rhythms of *tambos*, the rattling of bones and strumming of banjos, the shuffling caricatures of happy plantation slaves portrayed by white men in blackface always drew large crowds. Or if Shakespeare was your joy, you could spend an evening at the glorious American Theatre on Sansome Street, where the eminent star "Mr. Charles Dillon will commence with the tragedy of Othello, The Moor of Venice." Private boxes went for "three and nine dollars," cheap seats for twenty-five cents, and "the circle exclusively for colored persons" had tickets for fifty cents each. Platt's Music Halls touted a "Grand Concert and Irish Evening." Eye doctors like Dr. Pilkington promised miracle cures for blindness.[8]

The cries of hawkers and hucksters plying wares and water cure schemes abounded. Imagine young Willie Winder amid all this, in the city and at Alcatraz, a very short boat ride from land but a world away, where there was also much to explore. A little garden atop the water cisterns just outside the Citadel was tended by the families who wished for green and growing things. If Willie walked about the island with his father, he would see the North

Battery, the North Caponier (one of several "two story brick towers for close-in defenses"), the parade ground, the Guardhouse, the lighthouse, the South Battery, the South Caponier, the West Battery, and the Engineer Building. Likely he marveled at the "cannon . . . from the small twenty-four pound howitzers up through the ten inch Columbiad" that belched smoke and fire as his father's men drilled again and again, dutifully obeying their commander in spite of the whispers, of the press reports of the disloyal Winder rebels far away.[9]

What did the boy see and hear, separated as he was from his New Hampshire family and his Grandfather Ichabod Goodwin, who was so firmly against human bondage that he traveled to an encampment occupied by former slaves to teach them to read? So little is known about Willie as a child. Was he frail, hardy, curious? But for now he is in a new world with parents who love him and will try to protect him. Much later Willie would come to know the ocean, to make his mark on the ocean, but now he was only eleven, and whether he was in a mainland school or on the strange windswept island, the endless fogs, rains, and frigid, choppy waters were unforgiving. As was the war.

• • •

To California came packet steamers bringing news of the mounting dead on the front. Two thousand miles away from his enemy-nephew in California, his plight now familiar to many readers, William H. Winder was continuing to wage his own determined war. Of defiance. From prison.

Although William H. Winder was offered release, he was determined to stay in durance until pardoned. He wrote to Secretary of War Edwin M. Stanton on February 22, 1862, saying he has been five months in confinement and asking if Stanton would consider his arrest illegal and investigate his case once and for all.

"I am to this hour in ignorance of the cause of my arrest and detention," he wrote. "My release was tendered me on condition of taking the oath of allegiance . . . a second time release was offered." His refusal backed by Seward, Winder states that support of the Constitution did not include, necessarily, support of the individual members "of the Executive." Winder is a clever man and insists that he in fact will support the Constitution but not the Union. Why should he not be favored with amnesty and parole? "If there be any charge of crime, I am ready to meet it," he states.[10] He denied that he was a traitor. His pleas went unanswered.

• • •

In Richmond, W. H. Winder's brother John was hungry for more space to house a growing prison population as Union POWs over-flowed their filthy, disease-ridden quarters. By March 1862 citizen Luther Libby's riverfront brick warehouse was wrested from its owner and confiscated by General Winder "for government use." It was larger than the other tobacco warehouses but just as unclean and overcrowded. Except when there was bright daylight, it was all darkness and cold. Winder "arranged for flat-iron bars to be installed over the windows." Any inmate who did not obey the order to stay three feet away from the windows would be at the mercy of guards who "patrolled with their guns cocked and end-lessly watched the windows for a chance to shoot" Yankees. There was a hunger to punish the bluecoats. For good.[11]

But for many of the ordinary Richmond denizens wearied by General Winder's treatment of prisoners and citizens alike, tired of jeering and cursing the exhausted soldiers dragged through the streets on their way to hell, deprivation tamed bloodlust, for there was real hunger. Food prices were skyrocketing, and the Union blockade of Southern ports made it hard for all but the wealthy to purchase foodstuffs, clothing, and other necessities. To combat gouging, "Winder laid a tariff of prices on all articles of domes-tic produce," wrote Richmond diarist Sallie Brock Putnam, "but did not legislate . . . groceries, liquors and articles imported from abroad." Given the difficulty in obtaining sufficient foodstuffs, with "meats so indifferent as scarcely to be fit for food," Putnam described how "the crowd pressed around the fish market was so dense that many were compelled to leave without anything for din-ner . . . the market men declared that people might starve." It was bad enough that many Richmond authorities were hoarding pre-cious foodstuffs, stealing, and brawling. With the fear of Winder's police force arresting with impunity, residents were bitterly aware that a once easy, languid life in an easy, languid city had ended. However, for a few hours at the close of April a grim spectacle sent hungry crowds racing to the fairgrounds to see a traitor die.[12]

• • •

William A. would not learn of the fate of the spy who brought him his father's orders until the following month, but on April 29 Timothy Webster was hanged at Camp Lee in the old Richmond fairgrounds. Gen. John H. Winder, after learning that his trusted courier was a Pinkerton agent, ordered Webster tried by court-martial, which convicted him of "being an alien enemy and in the service of the United States . . . lurking about the armies and fortifications of the Confederate States in [and] around Richmond," among other charges. Webster was swiftly sentenced to "suffer death by hanging," a sentence carried out in full view of jeering Richmond citizens. In an article wanly headlined "Local Matters" in the *Richmond Dispatch* of April 30, 1862, the particulars of Webster's suffering on the gallows were deemed fair and well-deserved justice, as the rope broke, whereupon he was thrown to the ground, then hauled back up the gallows, and finally hanged.[13]

Before he met that fate, however, Webster's final mission and his disappearance had for a time been a mystery. After he left for his fourth trip to the Confederate capital with Pinkerton detective Hattie Lewis posing as his wife, the Pinkerton spy was incommunicado. Due to his unusual absence as well as McClellan's reliance on the intelligence he brought back to headquarters, a worried Pinkerton sent operatives Pryce Lewis and John Scully, posing as cotton brokers and "ardent secessionists," to locate Webster.

After inquiring as to Webster's whereabouts—their cover identities gave them entry at first—and because Webster was successfully embedded in Richmond and so fully in Winder's confidence, they learned Webster was at the Monument Hotel, "suffering excruciating pain, confined to his bed" with chronic rheumatism, his wife by his side.[14]

Lewis and Scully visited Webster several times and reported to General Winder that his courier was still very ill, even fabricating a warning that Webster was being watched by Federal detectives. On one occasion when Lewis and Scully were walking on the street, members of a secessionist family then in Richmond recognized Lewis and Scully as Union detectives whom Pinkerton had ordered to search their home in Washington DC to find evidence of their disloyalty. They reported their suspicions to Winder's chief detective, Samuel McCubbin. An interview with Winder and others in his detective force followed. Unmasked, arrested, facing death, Lewis and Scully revealed that Timothy Webster was a Pinkerton detective. Winder's subsequent fury and the hasty trial that followed sent Webster to the gallows. Condemned to be hanged, Lewis and Scully remained jailed in spite of pleas from Pinkerton and Stanton to spare their lives; they were finally were released in 1863. Hattie Lewis, aka Mrs. Webster, was jailed as Webster's accomplice/wife but never exposed as a Pinkerton agent or tried. She pleaded with President Davis, claiming she was a loyal Southern widow, but Winder recommended against her release. Hattie lingered for eight months in two harsh prisons: Castle Godwin and Castle Thunder.

The latter was an infamous warehouse-turned-prison for accused spies and deserters. It was under the command of Gen. John H. Winder and run by his assistant provost marshal, Capt. George Washington Alexander, a black-bearded, pistol-and-knife-toting brute who was also a preternaturally cruel exhibitionist. At his whim or for reasons of insubordination, prisoners were bucked and gagged (a stick forced between their jaws and hands tied under the knees), shot, hanged by the thumbs, whipped, and starved, as well as routinely abused and tortured by Alexander and menaced by his giant Russian boarhound, Nero. So infamous was Alexander's reign that on April 11, 1863, a special committee of Confederate congressional representatives was convened to hear testimony about Alexander's brutality from other Confederates associated with the prison. After weeks of witness statements Alexander was exonerated, the judgment rendered. He was just following Winder's orders and had to impose such measures to keep order. The majority report based on three of the five committee members found Alexander's actions "justified" and stated

5

Treason at Alcatraz

W hen William A. returned to Alcatraz, the same kind of deserters and Union soldier-misfits he'd left behind before he was posted to the front were now in his keep. The *Sacramento Daily Union* reported on May 3, 1862, that at Alcatraz, "six members of the Fourth Regiment" were found guilty of desertion "and threats to kill officers." They were sentenced for a period of a few months to a year of hard labor, the worst offenders being made to drag about a "twelve pound ball and chain" and subject to having their "heads shaved upon discharge."[1]

The *San Francisco Bulletin* of June 12, 1862, expressing pride in the splendid and well-armed island, reported, "There are in garrison at Fort Alcatraz about one hundred artillerymen, and the Island is well stocked with ammunition and cannon. Upon the top of the Island are two eight-inch siege guns, the longest on the coast. There are also two ten-inch Columbiads, which are the largest on this side of the continent, and any number of smaller cannon of various denominations. One of these big Columbiads points at the Golden Gate, the other at Angel Island."[2] Soon secessionists would have more to fear than the forbidding sight of cannon in the distance. On August 8, 1862, the president ordered the secretary of state to suspend the writ of habeas corpus and thus allow army officials and chiefs of police to arbitrarily arrest people for "any other disloyal practice." The orders came by boat and did not reach San Francisco until September 8.[3]

Gen. George Wright, the reluctant commander of the Department of the Pacific, which "merged the military departments of California and Oregon," hungered to go to the front and was bitterly disappointed to learn he would command the department and remain in California. He wrote to his brother-in-law, General Sumner, however, that he could not "decline . . . this appointment without sacrificing all my future prospects. I love my country . . . I love the Union." And in a portentous echo of what would befall William A. if he abandoned his post, he wrote that there was "no personal injustice . . . or victimization" that would cause him to decline his new position.[4]

When Wright received his appointment, he was nearing sixty and had a thirty-nine-year career as an infantry officer behind him. He had entered West Point at the age of fourteen and later evolved into a brutal and infamous Indian fighter in the Pacific Northwest, his campaigns "devolving into a bloody and vindictive march featuring hangings, [the slaughter of seven hundred horses], burned villages, lies and coercion." His actions "did permanently suppress the region's native people, and settlers appreciated his effectiveness."[5]

Defense of the Union was now his mission. He vowed to purge California of civilians deemed probable and known secessionists-turned-supporters of the Confederate cause.

• • •

The Confederate cause was of course active, vocal, and persistent and deadly in William A.'s own family. On August 9, 1862, his cousin, Gen. Charles S. Winder, was killed in the Battle of Cedar Mountain while leading the famous Stonewall Brigade. He was proclaimed a hero despite his reputation as a martinet hated by his own men. There was even a rumor of assassination by his own troops when he was killed instantly. On August 14 the *Sacramento Union* reported that the "rebel general Winder" had been killed.[6]

Confusion sometimes reigned in press reports, as there were in fact two rebel General Winders: John H. and Charles S. And there was also William A.'s civilian uncle, Charles H. Winder. But this time there was no mistake.

After lying in state in the Confederate capitol building in a closed coffin, as the condition of his body was not fit for the many mourners to view, "*the remains* of the late Brig. Gen. C. S. Winder, commander of the Stonewall Brigade, were interred yesterday evening in Hollywood Cemetery," the *Richmond Dispatch* reported. "Up to 4 o'clock they were deposited in the old Senate Chamber of Virginia, the coffin being enveloped in the flags of Maryland and the Southern Confederacy."[7]

Perhaps William A. mourned the man he'd known from childhood, once a friendly sort whose prewar diaries read like weather reports—gleeful in describing sunny mornings or morose when rain threatened so many of his days aboard one ship or another. Now the two cousins who had survived the wreck of the *San Francisco* and were commended for their valor aboard the ship would never see each other again. But because the violent tear in the family fabric was becoming larger and more permanent, it is impossible to say with certainty if the death of William A.'s cousin was a personal trauma or nothing more significant than any other enemy casualty of war.

• • •

But William A., whether mourning his cousin or not, had a job to do, an island to protect, and rebels to punish. With summer bleeding into early September, by the eighth day of the month, with speed and determination even though it was not yet officially mandated as to how to handle seditious civilians, General Wright ordered the erection of a prison at Alcatraz Island to house Confederate sympathizers and "further allowed such persons to be brought before a military tribunal without habeas corpus."[8]

General Wright exulted that "open-mouthed traitors" were now beyond the reach of civil authorities.[9] Winder agreed and urgently recommended the construction of a separate prison building, as seen in his well-reasoned and urgent letter of September 10 to Maj. Richard Coulter Drum, the assistant adjutant general of the army.

"In view of the existing difficulties at home and the threatening aspect of our foreign affairs," Winder, as commander of "this all-important post," wrote that the caponier "at the entrance of the fortification, defending the approach from the wharf[,] is occupied by guards and prisoners."[10] Worse, "the earliest prisoners found themselves confined in the bare basement cell room of the guardhouse . . . and had to be housed in one of the howitzer rooms flanking the sally port." They were beset by illness, cold, insects, lack of sanitation, and no running water, "sleeping head to toe on pallets on the stone floors of the dungeon."[11]

Sympathetic to the plight of the prisoners and concerned about security, William A. said the overcrowding made it impossible to properly mount the howitzers so vitally needed for the defense of the island.

Drum, however, seemed unconcerned about prisoners and fully focused on his official orders: "The order of the President suspending the writ of habeas corpus and directing the arrest of all persons guilty of disloyal practices will be rigidly enforced. Those of them who are leading secessionists will be confined at Alcatraz."[12]

With no need to produce a living body to face charges before a court, Wright's Pacific Department had new powers never before granted. The "open-mouthed traitors" he'd earlier promised would be met with swift prosecution were now legitimate targets. The *Sacramento Daily Union* edition of September 13 elaborated: "General Wright . . . at his earliest opportunity will appoint a military Commission, to consist of three officers, who will take cognizance of all cases of arrests for disloyalty under the recent orders from Washington, which are intended particularly to meet the case of rebels who have lately emigrated from the Atlantic States. The decision of the Commission will be without appeal to the Courts."[13]

That same day the *San Francisco Daily Evening Bulletin* ran a story with much the same information, saying that there would be "immediate construction on Alcatraz Island of a prison for political offenders," and "if stringently enforced [the order] would make disloyalty in California . . . shrink into retirement." Wright's "great power rests in judicious hands," the article stated, before dropping a news bombshell. Offering no explanation for its precipitous scoop, the *San Francisco Daily Evening Bulletin* reported that "Captain Winder of that post [Alcatraz] has been relieved, and is succeeded by Captain Black."[14]

Proof of that news is the letter that Drum wrote to Lt. Colonel Caleb Chase Sibley, the commander of the Ninth Infantry, at his headquarters at the Presidio on September 12. He also ordered "a true copy" delivered to William A. that same day. Because Drum did not write directly to William A., the news was a great humiliation, without any associated explanation. But it was an order—to Sibley, not William A.: "Sir: Captain Black's company (9th Infantry) will be in readiness to embark from Fort Point Wharf tomorrow at 11 O'clock a.m. to proceed to and take post at Alcatraz Island; the command of which Captain Black will assume."[15] This meant that William A., an artillery captain, would be superseded by an infantry captain who was ordered to take command of the island away from him. Capt. Henry Moore Black, originally commander of Fort Vancouver in the Washington Territory, was in the wings, "at garrison in San Francisco, awaiting orders."[16]

It is likely that this assignment would have baffled Captain Black. Alcatraz was strictly an artillery post. What could have prompted this hasty, demeaning, and disturbing order?

The *Sacramento Daily Union*, clearly privy to information from an official unnamed source, had an answer: "San Francisco, Sept. 13th. Captain Winder, late of Fort Alcatraz, is under the ban of suspicion as to his loyalty, though it appears no charges have been made against him."[17] No charges but a ban of suspicion. The meaning was unclear. No explanation was given.

By sunrise the next day Capt. Henry M. Black's Company G of the Ninth Infantry had arrived at Alcatraz to take command of the post. Outraged, William A. wrote to Assistant Adjutant General Drum on September 14, 1862, about the extreme action taken by General Wright: "I have the honor to enclose herewith a slip cut from the *Sacramento Union* of the 13th, instant [referring to the ban of suspicion], the result of the position in which I have been placed by the act of the General commanding [Wright]. If there is any truth in the statements contained in this paragraph," William A. wrote, "I respectfully request that the matter may be fully investigated before a *military tribunal*—if not, I am compelled to request an unqualified denial of it." With anguish apparent, he continued: "I cannot believe, for an instant, that it is the intention of the Commanding General to place an officer who has proved his loyalty to the entire satisfaction of the authorities at Washington, from the President down, in so cruel and false a position without even an investigation[.] I *earnestly* request immediate action in this matter. I am sir, your obt svt Wm A. Winder Capt. 3. Arty."[18]

This was no faraway shipwreck, no near drowning, no gasp-ing for air as an angry sea nearly washed him away when he was much younger. These were the storm clouds hovering, near to bursting, that had followed him from New York along the Atlan-tic, into the Pacific with his family in tow, with no sailor's red sky warning, no sound of thunder.

No record exists of any military tribunal or even a formal military investigation. Again a newspaper appeared to settle the issue. "Dis-loyalty Disproven," the *Daily Alta California* bulleted. "As is generally known, Captain Winder has lately been superseded as Commander at Fort Alcatraz, by Captain Black. Thereupon the correspondent of the *Union* hinted at the disloyalty of the supplanted officer." And there it was again—the inescapable taint: "It is known that Cap-tain Winder is of Southern birth, but his earnest cooperation, in so far as we have been informed, has hitherto been relied upon by the Federal Government in aiding the suppression of the rebellion."[19]

Guilty of southern birth, and the qualifying "so far as we have been informed." What did that signify? Fortunately for William A. and the many readers of the *Daily Alta California*, there was more. "In relation to the question of disloyalty," the article stated, "we herewith subjoin a copy of a communication addressed by the Assistant Adjutant-General to Capt. Winder." The text of the let-ter was as follows:

Headquarters of the Department of the Pacific.
San Francisco, Cal., Sept 15, 1862.

[To] Capt. Wm. A. Winder. 3d Artillery through Commanding Officer, Fort Alcatraz.

Sir: Your letter of yesterday, enclosing a slip from the Sacramento *Union*, stating that suspicions are entertained as to your loyalty to the General Government, having been submitted to the General Commanding the Department, I am entrusted to say, in reply, that so far as these Headquarters are concerned, no such suspicions have been entertained.

Very Respectfully, Your ob't serv't,
Richard C. Drum, Asst. Adj.-Gen.[20]

Somehow the newspaper had gotten hold of and copied out this official communication from Assistant Adjutant General Drum to William A. In all probability it should be assumed that William A. got the letter the same day the *Daily Alta California* did. Many official reports and letters came to Alcatraz from San Francisco, but in order to get the letter straight to William A. at Alcatraz, a messenger from the Department of the Pacific taking the one-and-a-half-mile, roughly fifteen-minute boat trip straight to the island to deliver the missive is a likely scenario.

Drum's profession of faith in William A. Winder's loyalty might have given him some comfort. But the damage was done, his lot unchanged. He was still frozen in place, superseded by Captain Black.

General Wright would proffer an explanation, a tepid excuse that devolved into a defense of William, but it was not given until 1864 and did little to help William A. during the summer of 1862.

"In the summer of 1862," Wright wrote, "there was considerable talk in the city of San Francisco in relation to Capt. Winder, growing, I apprehend, out of the fact that his father was in the Rebel Army; and as I wished to increase the force on the island I sent Capt. Black with his company of the 9th Infantry, as he ranked Capt. Winder. I did this with a view to quieting the public mind." And he added this all-important sentence: "In all the period of Captain Winder's command of Alcatraz I had never a doubt of his reliability as a faithful officer."[21]

Reliable and faithful indeed but not at the front. On the day William A. was perfunctorily absolved of disloyalty, he was a bystander to a most important event. Just before he had lost his command on September 10, he'd made an official request for a much-needed new prison building. From the start of the war, inmates at Alcatraz were confined in harsh and crowded conditions in the guardhouse and were kept in dark basement dungeons, pressed together, sleeping toe to toe on lice-infested straw mattresses, with illnesses spreading, hardly any food, and almost no exercise. It couldn't last. William A. expressed concern about the conditions at the guardhouse, as well as the safety of the island, in a letter to Assistant Adjutant General Drum. The "caponier . . . defending the approach from the wharf is occupied by the guard and prisoners," William A. wrote, stating that this impossibly crowded area was threatening the defenses of the island: "The howitzers have never been mounted. . . . I would therefore urge the immediate erection of a building suitable for that purpose."[22]

On that very day, completely unknown to William A., and as he was no longer the ranking officer on the island, Assistant Adjutant General Drum addressed an order to Captain Black stating that the "General Commanding the Department [Wright]" had directed that any political prisoners on Alcatraz Island would not be allowed to receive any visitors "unless authorized by the General Commanding." In addition, "the General commanding the Department directs that you will make immediate arrangements for constructing on the Island of Alcatraz, a building (wooden) suitable for the confinement of political prisoners. All must take the oath of allegiance."[23]

This order was exactly what William A. had asked for, but it would be several months before a structure was put in place. Outraged and humiliated, frozen in place, unable to fight at the front or take back his command at Alcatraz, William A. wrote to Assistant Adjutant General Drum. The letter remained stiffly formal. He was an officer, not a belligerent private. It must have been painful to write.

> September 28, 1862
> Alcatraces Island Cal
>
> Sir
>
> With great reluctance I find myself compelled to appeal from a decision of the General commanding the Department of the Pacific, but a sense of duty to my corps and to myself demands it—I therefore respectfully submit my letter of remonstrance addressed to him, with his endorsement to the General in Chief for his decision. The departure of Major Burton 3rd Artillery for the East, left me in command of this post and according to the customs of service, and all former discipline, I believe myself entitled to retain the command.[24]

He tries all manner of reasoning, even while Captain Black's men are fixed in place—no infantry men are needed on the island; in fact their sheer numbers force Winder's company to sleep in tents. There are "many infantry stations," so why are there infantry troops on the island? They don't belong. His position is unjust, "a great personal injustice—and that which has cursed him"—being southern by birth—"the act of the General Commanding, at once gave the impression to the citizens of California that my loyalty was doubted." He encloses the *Sacramento Union* squib saying he was "under a ban of suspicion" (quickly retracted, in fact) and cites the "very cruel position in which to place an officer who has given every proof of his earnest desire to support the Government." He invokes individual rights and demands, "all palpable encouragement to officers of the Army."[25]

This letter forms part of a package Winder sent first to Wright, who then forwarded William A.'s correspondence to Lieutenant Colonel Drum along with William A.'s request that he "forward the above to Brigadier General Lorenzo Thomas."[26]

• • •

As William A. agonized over his plight during the months of September and October, rebel supporters became outraged by Lincoln's preliminary Emancipation Proclamation of September 22, which stated that "the States [in rebellion] . . . may voluntarily adopt . . . immediate or gradual abolishment of slavery." Emboldened after the Union victory at Antietam—a grim tally of twenty-three thousand dead, wounded, or missing on both sides over a single day—Lincoln had even more reason to demand that the rebels end the fighting and that Wright immediately order the roundup of his so-named "open-mouthed traitors." Wright had yearned to arrest California secessionist politicians— self-declared colonels and majors who'd made active threats, spouted treasonous sentiments, or headed local militias—and send them to Alcatraz.[27] The *Daily Alta California* on September 16 trumpeted, "First Arrest for Treason in California." The article stated that "Major R. I. [W. R. Isaacs] Mckay, a notorious secessionist" and former state official, was arrested in Benicia for publicly voicing treasonous sentiments and refusing to take the loyalty oath. "He will be transported to the healthful but breezy atmosphere of Alcatraz Island . . . and chew the bitter end of treason."[28]

"This obese man," the *Santa Cruz Weekly Sentinel* reported, "was arrested at Benicia, and "loses no occasion to vilify the country which gave him bread." He refused to take the oath of allegiance, "declaring he would rot in jail first," and was sent to Alcatraz "to ruminate on the bitter fruits of treason."[29]

During September and October there were suppressions of various newspapers known to be overtly secessionist. The *Daily Alta California*, calling Wright's decision "a proper subject of publication congratulation," listed the newspapers that were "excluded from the mails and Express." That list included the *Stockton Argus*, *Stockton Democrat*, *San Jose Tribune*, *Visalia Post*, and *Visalia Equal Rights Expositor*, as well as the *Los Angeles Star*. "Of course, there will be a howl from the Secessionists about the 'liberty of the Press.'"[30]

More arrests followed: "George P. Gillis, Democratic State Central Committee representative from Sacramento . . . E. J. C. ('Colonel') Kewen," *Los Angeles Star* editor Henry Hamilton, "and state senator Thomas Baker from Visalia."[31]

The *Daily Alta California* of October 11, 1862, announced another arrest, detailing with a bite the "early salt-water trip" to Alcatraz of Maj. John S. Gillis, ruing the fact that "the only regret that loyal men will feel in his case is, that he must now be kept alive at the expense of that Government which he has so long vilified . . . and in a manner that puts to the blush the treasonable tirades of the scurviest soldier in an Arkansas rebel regiment."[32]

The *Sacramento Daily Union* on October 16 announced that, by order of General Wright, Thomas Baker, "Senator elect from Tulare and Fresno counties, was arrested yesterday at San Francisco, for treason, and will be sent to Alcatraz to-day."[33]

Several days later the *Sacramento Daily Union* provided its readers with a discussion of the sentiments that did and would send disloyal men to Alcatraz: "Is it treason to rejoice over rebel victories, to denounce the Administration, to curse the Union, and call every man a d—n Yankee Abolitionist who is in favor of sustaining the Government and defending the national flag?"[34]

On November 22 Secretary of War Edwin M. Stanton issued an order allowing the release of all prisoners in military custody who had taken the oath of allegiance. By December 20 the last political prisoners had left Alcatraz. As one historian notes, "Most took the oath of allegiance quickly, while [anti-Union] newspapers suspended briefly or resumed publishing under new names."[35]

• • •

The same order freed William A.'s uncle, William H. Winder, from Fort Lafayette on November 27. Even as he was several days away from walking out of the prison, he was still railing against the "monarchy, despotism, abolition, or any similar outrage" of the Republican Party and the preliminary Emancipation Proclamation. "The sins of this war are already a sufficient stench in the nostrils," he wrote. "Shall this country, by adoption of the proclamation . . . attach to itself an inextinguishable odor of infamy?"[36]

William H. Winder remained free for the duration of the war, but "none of his personal possessions were ever returned." Nor did he ever see his nephew William A. again.[37]

• • •

William A.'s spirit, will, and patience were sorely tried in 1862, and he remained frustrated that he could not fight for the Union. Lincoln's patience with General McClellan was similarly tested, and running out. Mary Lincoln, in a letter to her husband on November 2, 1862, spoke for many who feared an unending struggle and an absurdly intransigent commander who, when his Army of the Potomac had the chance to crush Robert E. Lee's forces, did not. Mary Lincoln wrote, "They would almost worship you if you would put a fighting general in place of McClellan."[38]

By November 5 McClellan was out. Gen. Ambrose Burnside was now in charge of the Army of the Potomac. Rumors that McClellan was no true friend to the Union but a pawn of the Peace Democrats had abounded.

6

A Rebel Cell

Once William A. was back in command at Alcatraz, he immediately had to contend with rumors of rebel schooners, often used for blockade running and privateering, lurking in the waters around San Francisco. Might invaders arrive via the Golden Gate, the waterway to the city? In the busy harbor would ships loaded with gold bullion be commandeered and delivered to the enemy?

There came on the night of March 14, 1863, just such a threat, one that William A. would have to handle head on. Suspicious activity had been detected on and around the *J. M. Chapman*, a ninety-ton schooner docked at the Jackson Street wharf. Men were steadily going aboard and coming from the vessel—dockworkers, thieves, no one knew just who they might be. Burly strangers were busying themselves, loading boxes, then scurrying—if a burly bunch could scurry—into the darkness. But it was the wharf, and strangers made strange night forays. But this night the men along the wharf had been under surveillance for months. And a raid was imminent.

At first light only two men remained on the deck of the *J. M. Chapman*, one of many schooners in port. It was later learned that the vessel's captain, W. C. Laws, had gotten cold feet and stumbled into a saloon, allegedly spilling details of a plot to anyone who would listen. Just as the *J. M. Chapman* slipped from the wharf, moving slowly toward the bay and open water, city detective Isaiah Lees, along with revenue officers, customs house officials, and Federal soldiers from the *Cyane*, a revenue cutter ship, clambered aboard, weapons drawn. They rushed below toward the hold and found not "an assorted cargo of innocent merchandise including machinery bound for the Port of Manzanillo, Mexico," according to the bogus manifest filed by the absent Capt. W. C. Laws, but an arsenal of "vast quantities of powder, shells, and ammunition."[1]

Three men, hunched in the darkness, were dragged to their feet. Scattered about them were torn bits of paper. One of the captured was attempting to chew and swallow the papers. Once the salvaged documents were examined, incriminating evidence emerged: a Confederate captain's naval commission, a letter of marque signed by Pres. Jefferson Davis, "whereby a government can authorize a private individual to prey on the shipping of another government . . . consistent with international law," to protect the perpetrators should they be captured.[2]

Behind a false door in the hold crouched fifteen other men, "armed with navy revolvers, loaded and capped," and brandishing Bowie knives.[3]

It is worth a good look at the ringleaders of this invading force—in modern parlance, the rebel cell orchestrating this planned attack. Among them was Asbury Harpending, a wealthy, hair-trigger young Confederate fanatic from Kentucky who with a cabal orchestrated by the Knights of the Golden Circle had at the start of the war tried and failed to recruit Gen. Albert Sidney Johnston.

A year later Harpending traveled to Richmond and, according to him, had an audience with Pres. Jefferson Davis and Secretary of State Judah Benjamin about the immeasurable value of a takeover of California. "Had this isolated state on the Pacific joined the Confederate States," he wrote in a self-aggrandizing but mostly accurate account of his life, "it would have complicated the war profoundly." That may have been true, but he was captured. Harpending's effort to smuggle munitions out of San Francisco on the *J. M. Chapman* may have been foiled, but the cocky compendium of zealots waiting to grasp riches and glory and to extend slavery into Mexico was still alive: the Golden Circle and its insurgent dreams, which were in turn the stuff of Union nightmares.[4]

Captured along with Harpending was the *J. M. Chapman*'s buyer, a rich, like-minded Confederate sympathizer and fellow Kentuckian named Ridgely Greathouse. Yet another was British citizen Alfred Rubery, a constituent of the famous abolitionist, parliamentarian, and philosopher John Bright. Harpending, Greathouse, and Rubery—no Dickensian inventions here—all used their real names. Their plot *was* the stuff of Wright's nightmares. The "efforts made in smuggling materials of war into Mexico . . . and [to] clear vessels for southern ports . . . to use as privateers under the employment of the Confederate states" were also real.[5]

The prisoners were taken to Alcatraz in irons, and William A. immediately began their interrogation in the prison building.

The *Marysville Daily Appeal* of March 20, 1863, reported the particulars:

> From the Custom-house authorities we learn that the examination of the prisoners taken from the *Chapman* is being made, under the authority of General Wright, by Capt. Winder of the forces at Alcatraz, who holds a military court. The prisoners are being examined separately, and are kept in solitary confinement, no person being allowed access to them, and no papers, either written or printed, can be passed to them without especial permits . . . though the particulars of the examination cannot now be made known, yet the result of the same is to place beyond any doubt the criminal designs of the prisoners to commit piracy upon the United States commerce.[6]

William A. duly warned the prisoners that what they say might be used against them as evidence in a civil trial. According to Harpending, he was "locked in a lath and plaster room" in the prison building. He boasted that, when captured, he'd concealed a derringer "in a specially prepared pocket inside the right cuff of my coat." Allegedly this weapon was still with him at Alcatraz. When Captain Laws, who had betrayed the rebel band to the authorities and had just been arrested, tried to speak to him through a hole Harpending had bored in the plaster of his prison cell with a penknife he claimed to have, Laws escaped death by derringer as William A.'s men dragged him away for questioning. It is questionable that the weapon was on Harpending's person throughout his durance at Alcatraz, in spite of his boast.[7]

William A., in charge of Harpending and his partners, was for once and for a painfully short time not the object of suspicion.

Until he was. Very quickly a new assault on Winder's character was made by the *San Francisco Morning Call*, which accused him of "feeding the rebel prisoners held there [Alcatraz] on the fat of the land and . . . from silver plates."[8]

Because members of the *J. M. Chapman* rebel cell were in Winder's keep and under military interrogation, it is not a leap of logic to see just how much some fearful Unionists wanted a man named Winder gone. Imagine his distress and discomfort, not just for himself but also for his family. And would he succumb, resign, or seethe and stay in place and do his job, which was at that moment to examine and determine the guilt of the rebel raiders locked in solitary confinement?

On March 24 Winder sent the damning squib from the *San Francisco Morning Call* to General Wright.

A reply that had to be of some small comfort came almost immediately. Not from General Wright but from Assistant Adjutant General Drum:

Headquarters Dept. of Pacific
San Francisco CA March 27th, 1863

Sir

The General commanding [Wright] read your letter of the 24th instant enclosing a slip cut from the "Morning Call" and desires me to say that scurrilous attacks against officers have no influence whatever at these Headquarters, the General has the most implicit confidence in your ability and zeal, and feels confident that you will look to the safety of your post,

> Very respectfully yr obt sevt
> Richd C Drum. Assist Adj gen
> Capt Wm. A. Winder
> 3rd Arty
> Comdg Alcatraz[9]

A letter to William A. from Wright arrived on the same day.

San Francisco, March 28, 1863

Captain,

Give yourself no uneasiness about what the papers say. I have
full confidence in your ability and will to take care of the fort and
everything confided to your care. Yours very truly,

G. Wright[10]

After William A.'s interrogations of his prisoners were completed, Harpending, Rubery, and Greathouse were transported to
the jail on Broadway in downtown San Francisco on October 2 and
were tried in the U.S. Circuit Court by Judge Stephen J. Field and
Judge Ogden Hoffman. On October 17 it took the jury four minutes to reach a verdict. The three were convicted of high treason,
sentenced to ten years, and fined $10,000 each. The fifteen crew-
men found hidden in the *J. M. Chapman* were released after they
claimed they didn't know what the mission was but that they'd
simply been hired on as guards. All were ordered to take the oath
of allegiance to the U.S. government. Greathouse made bail, and
Rubery was eventually pardoned by Abraham Lincoln at diplomat
John Bright's request. Only Harpending remained jailed because,
according to the papers seized on the *J. M. Chapman*, he "held a
commission in the Confederate Navy."[11]

• • •

With Harpending still in durance and William A. witnessing the
war from afar at Alcatraz, a May spring rustles to life on the island.

Then from across the ocean came a notice, elusive and temporary, a bolt of hope that might have thrust Winder willingly into
battle. According to one small paragraph in the *Sacramento Daily
Union* of May 28, 1863, "The Governor of New Jersey has tendered
to Lieutenant Winder (now in command of Fort Alcatraz) the Colonelcy of the First Regiment New Jersey Volunteers. He will accept,
with General Wright's permission."[12]

It would be an escape for William A., a legal escape from Alcatraz. But nowhere except for the brief item in the newspaper is
there any mention of this offer or of Wright's pending permission. Perhaps there was a request conveyed to New Jersey gover-

nor Joel Parker by William A.'s father-in-law, Ichabod Goodwin. Maybe it was a favor, something owed, or just a hope, a way to extricate this family and enable Captain Winder—erroneously called lieutenant—to be the warrior he wanted to be. And it does not happen—the colonelcy will go to Maj. William Henry Jr., of the First New Jersey Volunteers, who led the infantry regiment after the battlefield death of Col. Mark Wilkes Collet on May 3, 1863, at Chancellorsville. Henry was a hero, an on-the-spot hero. He has glory. He has a colonelcy. William A. has Alcatraz. He was still being kept isolated from the fray.

Loyal Unionists wherever they were learned that a bloody July had brought trouble for the Confederacy. Vicksburg was besieged and fell to Grant. The last guardian of the Mississippi River was now in Union hands. Gettysburg, a cataclysm of death and fierce fighting during a brutal three-day battle as Lee's invasion of Pennsylvania, meant to storm to the center of the Union and ultimately overtake Washington City, was stopped, with tens of thousands dead. But Lee was not defeated; he merely backed away, his forces readying for more advances, more lunges. More war.

• • •

There was trouble of a different kind for William A. Family trouble. His half brother, Capt. Sidney Winder, his father's adjutant in Richmond, was threatened with execution. The news sent William A. scrambling to help.

It is worth the telling, the story of how a man called Winder, this time a Confederate Winder, became headline news—and not for presumed atrocities against his father's prisoners. The strange tumble of fact and misinformation began with Gen. Ambrose Burnside's order of execution for Confederate captains William F. Corbin and T. G. Mcgraw, who'd been caught out of uniform in the divided state of Kentucky while recruiting for the rebels. Union authorities claimed they were spies and summarily executed them. Confederate authorities demanded immediate retaliation, with Gen. John H. Winder issuing Special Orders No. 160 on July 6, 1863. "At the Libby Prison yesterday

(July 7th)," the *San Francisco Bulletin* reported, two Union captains from among the packed prison, thinking they were summoned for exchange, were to be shot in retaliation for the deaths of Corbin and Mcgraw. Huddled around a hat filled with black and white beans (or a box filled with slips of paper, depending on the reports), the men were to reach in and pick out the symbol of their fate: a white draw meant life, while a black one meant death. "Amid a silence almost deathlike the drawing commenced."[13] Capt. Henry Washington Sawyer of the First New Jersey Cavalry and Capt. John Flinn of the Fifty-First Indiana, were the "condemned men . . . sent to Winder's office," and they were allowed to write to their loved ones, as they were to die in a matter of days. Upon hearing of her husband's fate and his request to see her and his children one last time, Sawyer's wife raced to Washington and, with the help of a New Jersey congressional representative, was able to see Lincoln. With one day left, the president conferred with Maj. Gen. Henry Halleck and recommended that "two Confederate officers in our hands would be immediately selected for execution in retaliation for the threatened one of Sawyer and Flinn."[14]

W. H. F. "Rooney" Lee, who was Robert E. Lee's second son and who had been wounded at Brandy Station and captured by Federal cavalry two weeks later, was the first hostage. Lee was taken to Fortress Monroe. Capt. R. H. Tyler, already an inmate of the Old Capitol Prison in Washington, was ordered to stand with Lee and face the same fate as Sawyer and Flinn.

A storm of desperation, high drama, and inexplicable error began. Capt. William Sidney Winder's name was mentioned over and over as the hostage taken along with Rooney Lee, though there was never any information to back up the capture of General Winder's son. Reading of this—and it was impossible not to read of this—with great alarm on August 7 at Alcatraz, William A. sent an urgent telegram to a Lincoln cabinet member, Postmaster General Montgomery Blair:

Via San Francisco, 7 Aug
Alcatraz Island

To Hon Montgomery Blair

I ask the release of Capt. Winder held as hostage.

W. A. Winder
Capt 3rd U.S. Artillery[15]

William A.'s plea is the only mention in any known primary source material of his concern for any Confederate relation. But he is pleading for a life. In that brief moment there is a window into Winder's humanity and concern for a half brother. For an enemy.

On August 8 Blair forwarded the telegram to President Lincoln: "Sir, I submit the enclosed from Capt Winder of our service on behalf of his brother [illegible, *demanding*?] this. I hope we may not be compelled to execute the hostages."[16]

• • •

The news traveled fast. Having just heard of his nephew Sidney Winder's impending fate, William A.'s uncle, William H. Winder, wrote to Secretary Stanton from New York: "Sir, I learn from the papers that Captain Winder [is] held with Capt Lee as hostages for Capt Sawyer and another Federal officer in Richmond. [He] is the son of my brother Gen Winder of Richmond." W. H. Winder goes on to say their detention is "unjustifiable" and that he would "procure a substitution of myself for Capt. Winder . . . that he is young and has a family, [whereas] I have not long to live." He excoriates the "terrible evils which this administration is multiplying for the succeeding generations." He further adds that if he is substituted for his nephew, Stanton will be "availing himself of an implacable opponent who deems the entire course of the administration unadulterated treason."[17]

The rumor of Captain Winder's capture and impending execution was untrue. His life was never at risk, and it is not clear as to why word of his incarceration was carried in newspapers throughout the country. The Confederate hostages were in fact Robert E. Lee's second son, "Rooney," and Capt. Robert H. Tyler of the Eighth Virginia Infantry. Why the great error? Because the story concerned two generals' two sons? Because the newspapers wanted sensational headline fodder?

William A. would still be worried about his half brother, as the mistaken identity of the hostages was not publicly rectified or clarified until February 1864, when Lee and Tyler were released and returned to their regiments. When Winder knew of this is not known. A letter, perhaps? A quick word overheard? A message from San Francisco? There is no trace of any letter or message. Absent relief, or plagued with concern, did he wonder if his telegram had averted a disaster for his half brother or if it had been ignored? Was there breathing space for William A. at last? The answer was no, because he nearly caused an international incident that might well have vastly complicated the war.

7

Invasions, Arrests, and Cannon Fire

In the predawn hours of October 1, 1863, the darkness is tinged by a shard of moonlight on the horizon, the air is unusually still, and no breeze is blowing through or around the island when a mysterious, heavily armed frigate enters the harbor. Steady on it comes, towed by rowboats, not dropping anchor, steady on toward Raccoon Straits, a highly unusual direction, it seems. Benicia and the massive arsenal are that way. What was it? A Confederate vessel? A foreign ship? The city and harbor are and have been on edge since the *J. M. Chapman* affair. And why was there no sign of the side-wheel steamer, the *Shubrick*, assigned to the Revenue Cutter Service? Naval regulations mandated a cutter for harbor patrol. According to one historian, "At one hundred and forty feet and eight inches long . . . weighing 339 tons, carrying a crew of thirty-five, made of live and white oak, she carried a single-expansion steam engine. Fleet and well-armed, but small."[1] Revenue cutters were the equivalent of today's U.S. Coast Guard patrol ships, but remarkably the *Shubrick* was the sole vessel tasked with patrolling and protecting the harbor, not just from Confederate "raiding cruisers" like the *Alabama*, responsible for "damaging the Union maritime trade" in the East, and the *Sumter*, a stealth rebel ship. Rumored to be prowling the waters as well were "privateers fitted out in French-occupied Mexico or British Columbia."[2]

Thus this open, badly guarded bay that was the main approach to the city was in the hands of a small cutter, its guns, and its crew. Enemies were thought to be circling like sharks, and many residents of San Francisco were fearing the worst. But there were friends, of a sort, who were in the area as guests of the United States: the brave, bold, swaggering, colorful Russian navy men and their ships—firm allies, defying their government's mandate of neutrality and defying England and France to declare allegiance to the Union in the Civil War. The arrival of Adm. Andrei Alexandrovich Popov's fleet—exotics, heralded, gawked at, admired—was both spectacle and hoped-for aid, or at least comfort, should the enemy come.

But in the haze and stillness of that morning, the first of October, no Russian ships, no revenue cutter, only the huge mystery frigate breaching the Golden Gate. Had the *Shubrick* been in the area, it would have approached the frigate, signaled, examined it, and determined its purpose. But the *Shubrick* is nowhere to be seen, having rushed to the aid of a Russian corvette, the *Novic*, aground in pieces on a sandbar at Point Reyes, miles away from Alcatraz.

It is just William A. and his men on Alcatraz, and they are tasked with the defense of that island, the bay, and the city. On this windless morning the mysterious frigate's flags hang limp, its nationality indiscernible. As the vessel nears, Winder watches, his men watch—where is it headed? And he acts. Precipitously, perhaps. He fires a warning shot at the frigate. Rear Adm. John Kingcome of the Royal Navy is furious that the HMS *Sutlej*, the flagship of the British squadron stationed in the Pacific, has been attacked. And the port authorities should have been well aware of its arrival. The *Sutlej* is the "leviathian [*sic*] of the fleet, 4,060 tons . . . [actually 3,066] . . . with a crew of five hundred and fifty men," the *Marysville Daily Appeal* reported, with "engines of five hundred horsepower. . . . On her main deck she carries four 110-pound Armstrong guns, and twenty-two 68 pounders," more than fifty guns in all.[3]

From the time of the capture of the *J. M. Chapman*, Thomas O. Selfridge, captain of the *Cyane*, had been asking General Wright to have a "man of war [the *Cyane*] . . . anchored in those waters to cooperate with the forts under attack, and to afford protection to that part of the city lying behind the range of the fort's guns." Selfridge's letter of February 10, 1863, indicating the need for the cutter to be at the ready and on call, was reinforced on the same day in another letter to Wright, in which Selfridge adds that "the collector [John Taylor McClean] of the port of San Francisco [should] have all inward bound steamers boarded . . . this would effectually preclude the possibility of any steamers getting in under false colors."[4] False colors? The ship flew no visible colors at all. When the frigate gave no response and no sign of stopping, Winder fires a blank shell at the vessel. It lands perilously close to the bow of the *Sutlej*. Rear Admiral Kingcome and his crew don't know the shell is a blank. The tow ships stop, the frigate stops. What next? Is the United States trying to provoke a major incident? After all, Britain sided with the Confederacy and, though it was not widely known, was supplying guns in exchange for cotton. But the rear admiral thinks better of a fight with the cannons of Alcatraz, and he fires—one, two, three—and keeps firing. And firing. The count is up to nineteen, twenty, finally, twenty-one. A twenty-one-gun salute, an acknowledgment that this frigate bristling with guns on every deck is not the enemy. But in the smoke, in the chaos and cacophony, the cannons of Fort Point join in thinking this is indeed an invasion. A barrage of fire, loud and long, booming across the water. The *Sutlej* does not venture any farther. The incident seems over. It isn't.

On the morning of October 7 an urgent message arrives at General Wright's office. Rear Admiral Kingcome demands an explanation. Couched in abundant, pro-forma politeness—"I have the honor," et cetera—but seething with indignation, Kingcome writes, "When her majesty's ship *Sutlej*, bearing my flag, was about to drop anchor at this place . . . a shotted [loaded] gun was fired from the batteries on the island of Alcatraz in the direction of the ship, and that the shot fell within three hundred yards of her." Kingcome went on to say that "there was no other vessel in the line of fire. . . . I am forced to the conclusion that the shot must have been directed toward the ship." He goes on to demand that, though the shot must have been a misunderstanding, Wright should "institute inquir[i]es into the matter."[5]

Wright answered almost immediately. He understood that Kingcome had asked for an inquiry and will demand that Winder give one. But he must explain the rules. Although Kingcome will feign ignorance, it is surprising that this high-ranking naval officer is unaware of these harbor mandates. Wright tells him that "the port regulation adopted by the Government of the United States for the harbor of San Francisco require[s] that all vessels shall be brought to, and inspected by a Government steamer from her usual position on the outer harbor. . . . The orders of my government require that all vessels of whatever character be examined before being permitted to pass the forts." Wright goes on to say that in the absence of the *Shubrick*, the island commander bore responsibility for the decision to fire on his ship.[6]

William A. had his orders. He must "bring to all ships entering the Port in order that their character must be ascertained before being allowed to approach the city." Even so, Assistant Adjutant General Drum demands an explanation from Winder. He must "make a special and full report as to the matter of firing certain signal guns from Alcatraz on the arrival of her Britannic Majesty's ship *Sutlej* in this harbor."[7]

On October 6 Winder sent back a reply and a recounting with all his strength summoned. His report of the incident on that uneasy morning when booming guns shattered the dawn quiet is his own shot across the bow for everyone who'd questioned him. He is in the right. This time there can be no suspicion. He has followed orders. He had no other choice. The message is terse, stating that because the *Shubrick* was otherwise occupied, aiding a wrecked Russian corvette (a small warship), and that the mystery frigate's flag "fell in folds," even when he presumed that the *Sutlej* fired the salute "to our flag," he kept his men at the ready as the *Sutlej* was enveloped in the "smoke from her guns." When he learned from a "boatman that the U.S. flag was flying at the masthead when she fired," he returned the "national salute of twenty-one guns," but not before. And then Fort Point joined the action with loud cannon booms. "I have only to add that I should consider it my duty to bring to any ship pursuing so unusual a course," William A. continued, adding, "I trust that my action may be approved by the commanding general."[8]

It is as though the past months, so wearying and so painful for William A. Winder, are not any longer to be endured. Back and forth the communications between Kingcome and Wright went until Kingcome admitted he had misunderstood the rules and did not mean to be in error, though he believed two hours had passed for Winder to ascertain the nationality of his ship before firing. He added in an appeasing tone, "Had I known port regulations I most certainly should not have attempted to infringe [on] them in any way."[9]

The historian John Martini has elaborated on the event: "By all appearances it looked like the *Sutlej* was deciding on her own anchorage site." The rear admiral offered the excuse that visiting warships often dropped anchor at what was then known as the Rancho Saucelito. As for whether the ship's approach would have been noted, Martini adds, "a semaphore signal atop Telegraph Hill would announce the ship's approach to downtown merchants and waterfront businesses . . . all kinds of small craft would then head out to meet the ship to offer various services." He concludes, "Perhaps the *Sutlej* crew rowed out and towed the frigate or previously arranged for tugs to meet the ship."[10]

Without specific first-hand witness accounts, it may never be known just how or why the ship went unnoticed until it was almost too late.

Without knowing the *Sutlej* had departed, by October 15 Wright had once more written to Kingcome, responding to his letter of October 7, again asserting that "it has been the usual arrival of foreign ships in the Harbor of San Francisco that the commander [Winder], should communicate the fact to my headquarters." With a measure of obsequiousness, he made a final effort to keep and strengthen the "bonds of friendship" between the two governments. Ruffled feathers and misunderstandings notwithstanding, not to mention relief that an international incident was finally averted, Kingcome did not respond. The affair was over. Kingcome's "leviathian" was gone.[11]

With William A. in the clear after the *Sutlej* incident, might he finally be free of suspicion? Or better yet, has he permanently cleared his name and thus is forever separated from his enemy-kin in the minds of the public? Perhaps he could believe so, if he read no newspapers and spoke little if at all to anyone on the island or in the city.

• • •

If William A. were to secure a post on the front, be captured in battle, and find himself a prisoner of war among the souls trapped in his father's keep, he could be severely punished for his betrayal or be spared. He might see other prisoner-officers exchanged and paroled. And if he survived, he would witness the abject cruelty and torture of black soldiers and their white officers. After Lincoln's Emancipation Proclamation went into effect, the Union began recruiting black troops in 1863. This move was anathema to the Confederacy. Then came the issuance of laws of conduct for troops in the field and the first codified rules of war, which forbade discrimination based on skin color if a soldier was captured. These new rules, known as General Orders No. 100, compiled for the Union Army by Francis Lieber, a German immigrant and humanitarian, contained one article that stated, "The law of nations knows of no distinction of color, and if an enemy of the United States should enslave and sell any captured persons of their army, it would be a case for the severest retaliation, if not redressed upon complaint."[12]

In fact, even when exchanges were permitted under the Dix-Hill Cartel, created by Union general John A. Dix and Confederate general Daniel H. Hill and stipulating one officer in exchange for an officer and a like number of privates—the Confederate government eventually refused to treat black soldiers as POWs but instead treated them as mere chattel and deemed their officers worthy of execution. When the Confederacy refused to abide by these rules and vowed never to exchange any black troops or their officers, an outraged General Grant eventually shut down the program on August 18, 1864.

The historian Arch Blakey writes that before the exchanges were stopped "the Confederacy viewed the Emancipation Proclamation as an attempt by Lincoln to incite servile insurrection, the worst form of treason."[13]

Maltreatment of black and white captives in Richmond grew worse as hundreds of new men stumbled into the hell of Libby Prison and into the island camp called Belle Isle in the James River at Richmond. With scant food rations and little to no medical care, many men at both prisons died of exposure and disease each day. Horrified Northerners and Southerners saw photographs of men reduced to skeletons.

Charges of deliberate extermination were made. John H. Winder, though not wholly responsible—provisions were scarce in the city, scarcer yet in the prisons—was blamed. And blamed. And excoriated. It was now literally impossible for most in the country to escape the news from Richmond. Included in an article head-lined "Horrors of the Libby Prison at Richmond–Belle Isle" and leveling a hard blast of blame and disgust at William A.'s father, the *San Francisco Bulletin* reported that Libby Prison was "under the supreme control of Gen. Winder . . . a man of middle height, or slightly under it, rather stoutly built, hair quite white, florid in complexion, with a red nose and a cold, cruel gray eye; and his acts from the first prove clearly that he is precisely what that eye indicates to the observer—cold, cruel and vindictive."[14]

With literally no more space to house the captives—Richmond residents feared their escape or liberation at the hands of Yankee invaders—Robert E. Lee urged the Confederacy's secretary of war, James A. Seddon, to ship Winder's prisoners south from Richmond.

Meanwhile Gen. John H. Winder, W. Sidney Winder, and another relative, Richard Bayley Winder, were ensconced in the Confeder-ate capital. Union authorities wanted to rein in the Winder fam-ily, and unless and until those in Richmond could be captured and punished, those authorities satisfied its urge by rounding up another family member then at large in the East.

• • •

On November 21 William A.'s eighty-four-year-old grandmother, Gertrude, the widow of W. H. Winder of the Bladensburg deba-cle, was arrested in Baltimore. The *Baltimore Gazette* edition of November 23 spelled out the particulars.

"Colonel Fish's detectives went to the boardinghouse of Mrs. Hughes, No. 77 North Charles Street, on Saturday afternoon, and arrested Mrs. Gertrude Winder, a very old and feeble lady, mother of General Winder, Provost Marshal of Richmond," the article stated. Gertrude Winder was charged with "corresponding with persons in the South . . . several letters of a disloyal character were found in her trunks, all of which are retained by the military authori-ties and for other offenses of a grave character." She "was taken to the Provost Marshal's office, accompanied by her son, Charles H. Winder of Washington (who happened to be in the city upon professional business)." Gertrude Winder was interrogated, "which resulted in her being sent back to her boarding house where she remains under guard. It is very probable that she will be sent south, not to return during the war." Gertrude Winder "exhibited the most stolid indifference with regard to what was said or done in relation to her individual case; but when Colonel Fish intimated that it would be necessary to detain under guard the son who had accompanied her, she endeavored to dissuade him from such a course, and offer to do anything in her power to render his detention unnecessary." Charles Winder was not charged. "But for the extreme age and enfeebled condition of Mrs. Winder she would have been sent off at once." However, the authorities were "satisfied that she could not stand the fatigue of a trip South by way of Harper's Ferry."[15]

Gertrude Winder remained in her boardinghouse under surveillance, defiant and defending her Confederate relations to the end of her days. With this arrest, and with no way to capture the remaining Winders, would William A., the lone Union loyalist among them, survive a purge?

8

The Loyal Man and the Madman

During 1864 noble efforts are being made to get William A. away from Alcatraz. In the Arizona Territory the newly appointed governor, John Goodwin, a devoted Lincoln man (but no relation to William A.'s father-in-law, Ichabod Goodwin), is determined to protect the territory and requests that the captain from Alcatraz head a volunteer regiment. He fears that Arizona, ceded to the United States after the Mexican War and carved away from the Confederate stronghold of New Mexico with the Gadsden Purchase of 1853, is under threat from Confederates as well as restless Indian tribes. The territory is railroad-ready and thus ripe for a land grab, and it could be a Union stronghold. Governor Goodwin sends his request for Winder straight to the top. Writing to the president from Fort Whipple on February 8, 1864, Goodwin "respectfully recommend[s] that Capt. William A. Winder U.S.A., now stationed in California[,] be appointed Brigadier General of Volunteers and assigned to command in this territory." Governor Goodwin wrote that he is "intimately acquainted with Capt. Winder and know[s] him to be thoroughly loyal, when considerations of birth and position have influenced every other member of his family to the other side, and I believe that such devotion to his country and flag, as he has exhibited, should be recognized by you."[1]

Of course Abraham Lincoln, the recipient of this letter, more than likely knew a great deal about various members of the Winder clan.

"Of his qualifications for the position there can be no question," Goodwin wrote. "His services in the field are the best evidence. He has been for a long time stationed in this territory and is well acquainted with the different Indian tribes [of] their country, and [illegible] of comfort. As Governor of this territory, and honoring in [illegible] its future advancement and best interests I would strongly urge this appointment. Every other state and territory has received [illegible] military appointments and been in some way recognized and I would most respectfully request . . . this appointment of a gallant and patriotic soldier."[2]

• • •

While William A. perhaps entertained high hopes that Governor Goodwin's bold proposal would propel him to the rank of general, as post commander at Alcatraz, he must contend with a matter that on the surface, while tragic but not uncommon, has occurred on a windy afternoon a few yards offshore. On March 1 Horace Dearborn, a recently enlisted private in William A.'s Company D, drowned in a boating accident. With him at the time was Dearborn's close friend Pvt. Simon Kennedy, also in William A.'s company. This unfortunate incident will ultimately take on a life of its own as Private Kennedy descends into madness and within several months will see his commander, William A., empathetically and brilliantly act in a way he has never acted before. It will be without exaggeration his finest hour.

But until it is time for William A. to find this opportunity away from familiar suspicions, he of course remains in place at Alcatraz as his supporters mount passionate campaigns on his behalf. There are further petitions to Lincoln from California notables for a change of command. For a few months it seemed possible. Sworn statements and endorsements of Winder's unwavering fealty to the Union echo through the correspondences as requests—impassioned pleas—are made to Lincoln and Secretary of War Stanton. Here was a chance, a real chance at both a promotion and a final cementing of Winder's loyalty. But do not think he will find succor, even in promotion, even with letters like this:

April 12, 1864

To the President,

The name of Captain W. A. Winder having been presented to you by Governor Goodwin and others, with a strong recommendation that he be appointed Brigadier General of volunteers and stationed in Arizona Territory, we desire respectfully to add our emphatic endorsements of that recommendation and in a like spirit to urge the requested appointment. Captain Winder to our personal knowledge has at all times since the commencement of the present rebellion stood staunch and true in his loyalty to the government, alone among all his kith and kin, proved by pure motive of patriotism, valuing that as the highest and most sacred impulse of the human heart, in the [illegible] of an American citizen to his country and his flag. So far as his soldierly qualifications are concerned, his past record as an officer of the United States Army need only to be referred to satisfy the departments in that point. We believe him loyal, honest, capable and true, well fitted by past experience for service in Arizona and hence we join Governor Goodwin and others in recommending him for the appointment which it has been asked, may be bestowed upon him.

Very respectfully,

Delos Lake, Ogden Hoffman [Judge], Port Surveyor John T. McLean, U.S. Attorney, William H. Sharpe, and others[3]

Apparently Lincoln saw the letter and knew just who William A. was, but he unfortunately passed it to Stanton on July 7, 1864. Too late, it seemed. What was the delay? Was this promotion, this change of venue, ever considered or was it quashed by the secretary of war, who would not ever trust him?

His father-in-law certainly trusted him and showed his trust in the middle of a family tragedy.

On February 24 Ichabod Goodwin's beloved daughter Georgette "Georgie" Cumming Goodwin Bradford died of consumption at the age of twenty-nine, leaving her husband, U.S. Navy lieutenant Joseph Bradford, and their two-year-old-son, Fielding, to mourn her. The little boy would be raised in the Goodwin mansion with the indispensable Abby at hand. In the midst of mourning Ichabod Goodwin was somewhat preoccupied with thoughts of Abby's husband, William A., a man he admires for the stand he took against his blood relations and the pain inherent in that choice. Ichabod Goodwin thus writes to Lincoln, "My son-in-law Captain William Winder at service of the 3rd Artillery U.S.A now in command of Fort Alcatraces . . . has been recommended by his friends in California and Governor Goodwin of Arizona to be appointed a Brigadier General of Volunteers and assigned to the command of the territory of Arizona. . . . Captain Winder is desirous of the position." Ichabod Goodwin adds that Winder is "among the most faithful, loyal, efficient and accomplished officers in the service. . . . I should [illegible] this appointment a personal favor."[4]

Although a post in remote Arizona was far from the front, it would be a valuable promotion and a point of honor. But these testimonials that William A. is more than worthy and loyal are met with silence. There are no reasons given for the denial of these requests by very prominent people on behalf of a man who was so highly regarded. Absent any correspondence from his commanding officers about the much-desired Arizona post, the public record is silent.

As yet another disappointment besets him, William A. will in the coming months find a strange comfort in defending a soldier in his company, a murderer. Pvt. Simon Kennedy slaughters a fellow soldier, Pvt. James Fitzgerald, an act that will preoccupy William A.

While still at Alcatraz, Pvt. Simon Kennedy repeatedly asked William A. for protection from what he believed to be threats of hanging by some members of the company, whom he claimed held him responsible for Horace Dearborn's drowning death at Alcatraz. Both men had enlisted with Company D of the Third Artillery a day apart in early February and more than likely had a relationship well before that, given the grief Private Kennedy expressed over and over at this loss. He also suffered from delusions, which worsened.

Even with the obviously mentally ill private being an object of William A.'s increasing concern, he faces yet another controversy for a seemingly heartfelt act of pride in the island fortress he has struggled to command with honor. In spite of his defenders and the past accusations of disloyalty being disproven, this new uproar made it seem that William A. might well prove a dangerous traitor, true to the name. He had made a sudden decision that would enrage the War Department.

On or about April 15, acting on his own initiative, Winder paid a visit to the opulent photography studio of William Herman Rulofson and Henry William Bradley on Montgomery Street in San Francisco and asked them to photograph Alcatraz and its fortifications. Apparently not suspecting the captain of treasonous intent—these were solid businessmen—but demanding far more money to do the job than Winder expected, Rulofson refused Winder's initial request. Four hundred dollars "in government greenbacks for a photographic survey of Alcatraz" was not nearly enough to interest the men. Bradley and Rulofson wanted at least $1,500. Finally Winder suggested that "the company [Bradley & Rulofson] would make up the cost difference by selling sets of the photographs to the public." Winder personally escorted one of the company's photographers and his "brassbound view camera" around the highly fortified island, "eventually exposing two thousand negatives," covering every battery, every cannon, the fortified Citadel, the guardhouse and prison, every gun, and the entire lay of the island.[5]

By July, with a catalog of the photos in distribution to the public at a price of $200 per set, all seemed in order. Then Mark Twain, a reporter for the *San Francisco Daily Morning Call*, went on a grand tour of the area's fortifications with "General McDowell, accompanied by his staff and many military officers officials and civilians." At "Alcatraces, under a thundering salute from the southern batteries," they undertook a "general examination of the whole island and its defenses . . . then a partaking of the hospitalities of Captain Winder, Commandant of the Post."[6]

In spite of the fact that large touring groups often saw every corner of the fortifications, the Alcatraz photographs he had ordered generated not just pride but also consternation and eventually serious trouble. Lt. George Elliot of the Corps of Engineers, who "oversaw the work crews who labored at modernizing and expanding the island's defenses," was not present when the photos were taken, but upon his return from Oregon he was pleased to see what Winder had done. He had moreover labored mightily to construct even more fortifications and update buildings on the island and "saw in the pictures an opportunity to document his most recent labors for his superiors in Washington."[7]

Writing to Brig. Gen. Richard Delafield, army chief of engineers, on July 8, Lieutenant Elliot stated, "I have thought that you would be glad to obtain copies to illustrate the condition and the progress [of the works so that he might be paid for these improvements] and append a list, and include two specimen copies." With the aim of trumpeting his accomplishments, he went on to describe the stereoscope photos in detail, even adding a list of "some other views [the batteries so named for notable officers like Halleck, McClellan, Rosecrans, etc.], which I would have suggested."[8]

Elliot's commanding officer, Delafield, was clearly agitated at this breach of security and telegraphed Elliot that such an act was prohibited: "You will immediately advise with Colonel De Russy to the end that they [the photographs] be instantly suppressed."[9]

A flurry of commands and demands—anger and worry apparent—begins and continues.

By August 1 the army chief of staff, Maj. Gen. Henry Wager Halleck, had written to Major General McDowell, commander of the Department of the Pacific, who had supplanted Wright: "It is officially reported that photographic views of the interior and exterior of the batteries at Alcatraz Island have been taken by permission of Captain Winder, commanding, and that their publication has been sanctioned by Colonel De Russy." Halleck adds that the "Secretary of War directs you to take measures to suppress such publication, and that you report to the Adjutant General whether or not Colonel De Russy and Captain Winder gave their sanction and permission as above stated."[10]

Sanctions and permissions notwithstanding, on August 4 the *San Francisco Bulletin* sounded an alarm with the headline "Fort Alcatraz Taken!"

Some two months or more ago, Bradley & Rulofson, photographers, were employed by some person or persons supposed to have the proper authority, to take photographic views of Alcatraz. The views, it was understood, were wanted for the use of the Quartermaster's Department. . . . Views were obtained from all points[;]

every battery was mirrored in picture a well posted enemy would ask no further information concerning Alcatraz, if he proposed to take it, or to run past it. The work was quite completed except that of mounting the pictures, and it had already cost the photographers some fifteen hundred dollars. Indeed, a single set, consisting of the thirty views, had been delivered to Captain Winder or General Wright.[11]

And then, the *San Francisco Bulletin* reported, came disturbing news: "At four o'clock p.m., yesterday, General Mason with a squad of soldiers dropped in at Bradley & Rulofson's gallery and producing orders from the War Department, demanded and received all the negatives, and all the copies of the pictures, and the names of all parties to whom any copies had been delivered." And here was perhaps a partial vindication of William A.: "We understand that General McDowell has satisfied himself of the antecedents of the photographers, and that they did their work in good faith at the request of parties having authority to order it. But it is evidently concluded at Washington that either somebody had blundered, or on a sober second thought it was deemed perilous to publish so circumstantial an exhibit of the strength or weakness of one of our principal harbor defenses."[12]

With this new storm hardly subsiding and with the War Department in an uproar over the blunder—bad judgment or yet again a potentially suspicious action on the part of William A. and others to allow the entire island to be photographed—the beleaguered William A. requested and was granted a transfer for himself and members of Company D to Point San Jose, a small battery perched at the tip of Fort Mason, a shout away from Alcatraz on a calm day. The site was formerly known as Black Point and often referred to as such, but in 1863 the Federal army commandeered the land, renaming it Point San Jose. Although William A. was furnished with a house overlooking the bay—with plenty of room for Abby and Willie—the post was not operating at the start of the war but was quickly garrisoned as further protection should another attempt at invasion by marauding Confederate privateers occur. In the "West Battery . . . there were six ten-inch Rodman cannons, and the East Battery had six 42 pound rifles." Point San Jose was not as wind-whipped, it was on the mainland, and it was not far from the center of San Francisco. It also had a newly built "post headquarters, hospital and barracks, clustered around a rectangular parade ground."[13]

Arriving at Point Jose on August 2, William A. assumed command of the post. Capt. Frederick Mears of the Ninth Infantry was already on scene. William A. must have known that beneath his feet once stood Porter Lodge, razed for the fort's expansion. It had been the beloved home of abolitionist luminaries, including Gen. John C. Fremont and his brilliant wife, Jessie, the Reverend Thomas Starr King, and others. It was Union ground—and the scene of a murder that occurred two days after William A. arrived. He was at this time in the thick of the outrage over the photographs he'd authorized to be taken of the Alcatraz fortifications and had barely unpacked when he was thrust headlong into a drama that grabbed headlines. What followed and William A.'s role in the events are a testament to his fortitude and his humanity.

• • •

It is shortly before 1:00 a.m. on August 4 in the pitch-dark blackness of the Point San Jose guardhouse, where privates of the Third Artillery and the Ninth Infantry are temporarily confined for various infractions: drunkenness, dereliction of duty, and petty crimes. They are asleep, unaware that Pvt. Simon Kennedy is delusional and convinced that among the sleeping soldiers are those who wish to hang him as revenge for the drowning of his friend, Pvt. Horace Dearborn. Although the drowning was an accident, Kennedy is beset with guilt. He has blamed himself. As he had done before he left Alcatraz, he has again gone to William A., the new post commander at Point San Jose, for help. Kennedy tells William A. that some of the men in the company are intending to kill him and have been digging his grave.

Picture now the silent guardhouse crowded with sleeping soldiers. Private Kennedy is wakeful, however, roaming the room and repeatedly striking matches until he spots his first victim. From a hook on the wall he grabs a bayonet left carelessly within reach by a day guard and aims the weapon at the heart of Pvt. Michael Condon. He misses and stabs the soldier in the arm. Condon kicks him away and screams for help. The night guard is nowhere to be seen. Kennedy leaps on his next victim, Pvt. James Fitzgerald, his friend. A good friend.

Over and over Kennedy thrusts his bayonet into Fitzgerald until he falls, bleeding profusely, on the wooden planking. There are cries of "Murder!" Panic, scuffling, screaming, and utter mayhem ensue. Finally the guard approaches.

"When the door opened and the light [was] brought in Kennedy was beating Fitzgerald on the head with the socket of the bayonet," Pvt. Timothy Moran later testified at the court-martial of Simon Kennedy for the murder of James Fitzgerald. The panicked soldiers had crowded the door of the guardhouse as Kennedy raced past them and fled into the night. Alone with the bloodied victim, whose head was bashed in and his body covered with stab wounds, Private Moran testified, "I felt Fitzgerald's wrist and put my hand over his heart. When I took it away it was covered with blood. He was there dead."[14]

Seizing on the lurid details and a chronology of events the next day was the San Francisco Morning Call's Mark Twain. His article, headlined "Soldier Murdered by a Monomaniac: Escape and Subsequent Arrest of the Murderer," breathlessly took his readers into a night that had all the elements of a penny dreadful: a madman racing from the crime scene, after which "Captain Winder turned out his whole force to pursue the killer Kennedy," a "bloody towel, abandoned under the bank near the Bensley Water Works," and Kennedy's flight in civilian clothes to his former confessor, "Father Cotter at Vallejo Street," who convinced him to put down his bayonet and surrender to the police.[15]

A bit calmer, but full of assorted facts, the Sacramento Daily Union relayed that "at an early hour this morning Chief Burke received a message from Captain Winder, commander at Black Point, informing him that one of his men, who was confined in the guard house with a number of others, had killed one of his companions, wounded another and made his escape."[16]

A coroner's inquest was held immediately. The Sacramento Daily

Union later summarized the case: "Some months since a recruit named Simon Kennedy, aged 29, a seaman by profession was bathing at Alcatraz where he was stationed, with a boy attached to the garrison, when the boy was accidentally drowned." The drowning "seemed to make a deep impression on the mind of Kennedy and from constantly brooding over the matter he became mentally deranged, complaining to Captain Winder and others that people were following him, threatening to hang him, and otherwise persecuting him." William A. confined him to the guardhouse for his own protection "and watched, in hopes that his insanity might prove only temporary." That was not to be. The mayhem in the guardhouse resulting in the slaughter of Fitzgerald ended any speculation that Kennedy would ever come to his senses.[17]

Before the court-martial began, Simon Kennedy begged from jail for William A. to be his defense counsel. Winder agreed, but not only did he have to study and prepare his defense brief, he still had to deal with the photograph scandal that might have resulted in his own imprisonment for having provided the enemy with critical information about Alcatraz. On August 5, the same day Mark Twain wrote about the murder, escape, and surrender of Kennedy, there is this:

Adjutant General U.S. Army [Lorenzo Thomas]

In compliance with the orders communicated by Major General Halleck by telegraph on the 2nd instant, I have to report having suppressed the publication of the photographic views of the batteries of Alcatraz Island. The provost marshal general has all the negatives and all the copies, except those Captain Elliot sent to the Engineer Department. Captain Winder reports, in answer to the inquiry directed to be made, that the pictures were taken in compliance with circular orders from the Quartermaster General, and that to save expense he gave permission to sell some of the detached views as [they] would be of no particular use in the hands of improper persons; that the proofs were all submitted to Colonel De Russy before this permission was given. Colonel De Russy reports that some small photographs of different parts of the works on Alcatraz Island were sent to him by Captain Winder, then commanding at Alcatraz, to know whether any objections could be made to printing them, and that on examination he said there was no impropriety in those he saw being printed.[18]

Although a later statement by Rulofson in a letter to Secretary Stanton concurred with Winder's claim that he had official approval for the photographs and that "after we had undergone all this labor . . . and had received from individuals orders for between 4,000 and 5,000 dollars," Rulofson's demand for compensation in the amount of $2,500 was never paid. But as a token of his belief in Rulofson's seeming innocence in the security breach, Brig. Gen. J. S. Mason, the assistant provost marshal general for California and Nevada, deemed him "a true and loyal citizen, who might be injured in the minds of parties not conversant with the facts in the case."[19]

This confluence of events, dizzying and demanding, was occurring alongside the "Proceedings of a General Court Martial convened at Point San Jose by virtue of the following orders . . . on Friday, the 9th day of August." Serving as court president was Lt. Col. Caleb Sibley, Ninth U.S. Infantry. Others named were officers from the Third and Ninth Artillery. Lt. George M. Wright, Third Artillery, was appointed judge advocate, and various witnesses from the guardhouse—men who had heard Simon Kennedy ranting and acting paranoid, as well as those who had seen the murder—along with doctors, surgeons, a police officer, and a priest were sworn to appear in the coming days.[20]

By August 20 Winder was in the courtroom as Kennedy's defense counsel when Kennedy was arraigned on the following charges and specifications:

Charge 1st. Murder . . . that he did assault with a deadly weapon (a bayonet) Private James Fitzgerald of the same Company . . . and did inflict a number of wounds upon the body of the said James Fitzgerald which caused his death. All this at Point San Jose on or about the night of the 4th of August, 1864.

Charge 2nd. Assault with intent to kill. Specification . . . that Simon Kennedy did assault with a deadly weapon, intending to kill

Private Michael Condon of the same Company and Regt and did inflict a severe wound upon the person of the said Condon, all this at Point San Jose . . . (Signed) William A. Winder Capt 3rd Arty.[21]

Through Winder, Simon Kennedy pleaded not guilty to all charges against him.

William A. began to question witnesses. Most if not all speak to Kennedy's paranoid state before the crime, his belief that he must act in self-defense as the men were out to hang him; those called to bear witness to the attacks on both privates tell much the same story. Kennedy was not a known drinker and appeared to grow more and more obsessed with the death of his friend Horace Dearborn. They related that the guilt and trauma from what had occurred that day on the water left Kennedy in a state of perpetual grief leading to delusion, finally believing he would be blamed for the tragedy, for the death of Horace Dearborn.

The question before the court-martial was this: Was Kennedy insane at the time of the murder, acting on a mad impulse—his behavior both erratic and hysterical as he flailed and stabbed wildly in the darkness—or were the deeds premeditated, calculated, and done while he possessed his reason and faculties?

On August 26 Winder made his final impassioned defense of a man who'd come to him for help and protection as voices in his head drove him to kill. His defense brief is prescient and compassionate and defines the particulars of the nature of temporary insanity as the cause of the bloody rampage. The ultimate penalty is hanging. Winder must save Kennedy's life and educate the court-martial participants in what he believes will be a grave injustice should they find him guilty of the charge of murder. In his own hand and read aloud to the court is this statement:

1st. Insanity is divided into two grades. 1st there is melancholy accompanied by delusion. In this case the party may be regular, his mind apparently bright, but yet there may be an insane delusion by which the mind is perverted.

2nd. Where a person is totally insane. In either case, if a party is insane at the time of the commission of the act, he is not held responsible; if he becomes insane after the commission of the act, but prior to trial—or if he becomes so after the judgment in each and all of the cases mentioned, he is relieved from the penalty because he is irresponsible, incapable of making defense, and it would be inhuman to punish a man who knows not the difference between right and wrong.[22]

William A. argued that "the punishment of crime is not intended to gratify revenge upon the offender, but to warn others from similar acts; therefore to punish a man for the commission of a crime while insane, is to perpetrate a great wrong upon human infirmity."

He said that "the accused was laboring under some great mental excitement; this combined with the fact that he often applied for protection, under the apprehension of being hung by his comrades, clearly shows that his insanity" was caused by melancholy accompanied by delusion, "especially since the accused was a good and sober man, and always lived upon terms of friendship with the deceased. . . . His conduct must be attributed to delusion . . . in obedience to a blind impulse; madness is the result of certain pathological conditions of the brain. . . . To constitute murder, it must be shown that there was malice, there was premeditation. . . . It has been shown here . . . that the indispensible [sic] constituent of malice is wanting." William A. goes on to say that "the accused was present when a favorite boy of the company was drowned to whom he was tenderly attached, that there was superinduced [sic] by that occurrence a melancholia which beyond all doubt is the source and cause of his insanity."

He begs the court not to punish Kennedy with the scaffold and admonishes them to "save a human life." And then comes this claim: "In the books relative to courts martial, a single authority cannot be cited where the plea of insanity has been made in a capital case, so far as I am informed this is the very first [case] that has been presented in the United States to a military court." Again he pleads that "you give him the benefit of all the doubts," and he calls upon the court to "commit him to the care of these institutions which human charity has dedicated to just such human frailty." This brief, though much longer, resounds with a similar theme: save Kennedy from the death penalty and pity his afflicted state. "Let not man's vengeance follow God's visitation," he concludes.

Judge Advocate George M. Wright for the prosecution opened his argument with a compliment to William A.: "The counsel for the defense has not overestimated the gravity and importance of this case." With clear, blunt language he outlined the evidence against Private Kennedy. To wit: his victim died from the wounds he inflicted, and "the counsel for the defense has presented a plea of insanity." Wright will "endeavor to show to the court from the evidence . . . that the prisoner has no valid excuse for his act." This was the prosecution's claim of apparent premeditation. He intended to show "reasonable doubt in the mind of the court of the insanity of the person, as the proof of committing the act ought to be to find a sane man guilty . . . whether the prisoner knew at the time right from wrong . . . according to Common Law, that if there is a partial degree of reason," the prisoner should have been able to "restrain his passions which produced the crime . . . and distinguish the nature of his actions." Since the offense is proved, "the judgment of the law must take place." Reasonable doubt, "beyond a shadow of a doubt," the judge advocate wrote, "must prevail." Did the prisoner know at "the time right from wrong?" It was in fact a reasoned argument, one that might well stand. Wright concluded that the prisoner's crime was premeditated, as was his escape.[23]

Pvt. Simon Kennedy was convicted of manslaughter, not murder, and found guilty of the second charge of assault with a deadly weapon. He was returned to Point San Jose to await final sentencing. It was not until November 22, 1864, that Maj. Gen. Irvin McDowell rendered the final judgment that buttressed William A.'s defense and saved the life of Simon Kennedy. "The crime therefore, if any, could not be manslaughter of which the court finds him guilty, if any was committed it was that of murder," McDowell wrote. "The proceedings, findings, and sentence of the Court are not approved . . . as there is abundant evidence to show that the acts were committed whilst the prisoner was insane: he will be held in confinement till he can be sent to the insane asylum."[24]

William A.'s defense carried the day.

• • •

Kennedy remained a prisoner until February 14, 1865, when he was committed to the State Insane Asylum at Stockton, California. He joined a varied and pained population of men and women— common criminals, murderers, habitual and violent alcoholics— suffering from various forms of madness caused by "dementia, monomania, melancholy, suppression of menses (change of life), uncontrolled masturbation, or hallucinations." Some stayed a week, while others remained for months or years, or died there. Simon Kennedy, of the "mania class" for which there was no treatment ordered, died at the asylum on July 27, 1868, of diarrhea.[25]

• • •

With the Kennedy court-martial behind him and apparent vindi- cation in the photograph incident, William A. remained at Point San Jose. But as he did in younger, brighter times when gold and silver strikes were just over the hill, in a stream or under a bridge, he resumed his side business: mining. At first it was copper min- ing in Baja California, notably at La Paz, "the principal port and territorial capital of Baja, California," which drew thousands of Anglos. Winder's mining ventures, labors, and hopes will con- sume him as he is turning away from his military career, away from lost honor.[26]

Absent any glory, in large part defended by his superiors, but surely wearied and worn by his years of struggle, William A. again looks to his mines, his investments. He looks away. He must do something. From the spring of 1864 onward he has again formed an association with Ephraim W. Morse, the Yankee pioneer Winder knew from his mission years in San Diego. An upright, solid man known for his honesty and fairness, Morse had fled the New England cold and come to San Diego in 1850 with a head full of gold dreams, and he did well in the warm, dry air of Cali- fornia, especially that of San Diego. With Winder's full-throated pledges of big strikes and big dollars, a match was made. Morse supplied all manner of foodstuffs and equipment from San Diego to the mines through the prominent San Francisco firm of Breed

& Chase, owned by brothers Daniel N. Breed and D. C. Breed along with Morse's cousin Andrew J. Chase. The firm of "Jobbers and Wholesale dealers in Groceries, Provisions and Case Goods" suffered and succeeded with the vicissitudes of the various mining enterprises they supplied.[27]

Winder and Morse formed a company that would work with the Mexican "owner [of] the mine near La Paz," in Baja, thus allying with men who were already in place but without usurping their sovereignty and yet making sure a legally binding contract was signed. It was an uneasy and often contentious mix of ham-fisted miners, assayers, lode haulers, squatters, and absentee owners like Winder who tried hard to make sure there were fair deals made.[28]

Because William A. is still at Point San Jose and must not rely on speculators, short of going to the mines himself he has no choice but to send an expert assayer, a Professor Blake, "a gentleman of high standing in New York," to either sell or "carry the work through surely to our profit and satisfaction." Although he must have assurances that "the facilities can be granted . . . money is in abundance and will be in my hands," Winder promises. Eventually Winder and Morse will own shares in at least four copper mines in Baja— the San Antonio, Santa Rosa, El Venado, and Delphina. The mines were not without risk as investments, and ultimately they offered no immense returns, but they became an impending burden for Winder as he tries to redeem himself in his own eyes, in Abby's, Willie's, and Ichabod's eyes, and in his commander's eyes, against all odds.[29]

• • •

In early December there finally came both a condemnation and a defense of Winder: a final and peculiar effort to both beat and bless him for his actions in allowing Alcatraz to be photographed. If he saw any of these communications, and there is no guarantee that he did, was he at best comforted? Or was it too late?

Headquarters Department of the Pacific
San Francisco, December 3, 1864

Maj. Gen. H. W. Halleck,
Chief of Staff, Washington City, D.C.:

General: I have the honor to report as follows in compliance with your instructions of August 11 in the matter of the conduct of Capt. William A. Winder, Third Artillery, in allowing photographs to be made on Alcatraz Island "for sale of batteries showing their exact condition, number of guns &etc."[30]

Here came a pronounced criticism. Here came the condemnation: "I do not think Captain Winder was authorized under the circular of the Quartermaster-General you sent me to make or suffer others to make for sale photographs of batteries. Batteries do not belong to the Quartermaster-General's Department, but it could not reasonably be inferred that the Quartermaster-General was interfering with affairs so well known to be under the charge of another branch of the service. So far as that circular is concerned, it clearly gave Captain Winder no authority."

And here came this: "As to the motives which actuated Captain Winder I do not believe them to have been in any degree whatever of the character imputed to him. He is an officer of intelligence and would not, if he intended to be disloyal[,] have acted so openly and undisguisedly as he did."

What of Winder's motive? He saw it as one

of pride and interest in his important command and a desire to have himself and the community have pictures of the place. He referred them to the engineer in charge of the work, Captain Elliot, and to Colonel DeRussy, senior engineer officer in the harbor. They found nothing objectionable in his having them taken and made public. I quite agree with them. I see nothing in any of them that I have seen that would be of any comfort to an enemy. . . . I take the occasion to say I do not question the loyalty of Captain Winder.

And this: "I have relieved him from the command of Alcatraz and stationed him at Point San Jose at his own request. I have the honor to be, very respectfully, your obedient servant, Irvin McDowell, Major General Commanding Department."

Here again is an endorsement of William A.'s loyalty, and though he would gladly escape his watery fortress and finally and forever redeem the family name as a Union defender, it is too late. Over

William A.'s trying and painful summer, into the fall, and on to a piercing winter, a tragedy of immense proportions has been unfolding deep in Georgia that will finally and forever associate the Winder name with unspeakable suffering and death. The site of infamy is a camp for Union captives known as Andersonville, a place Robert Scott Davis has called "the world's first modern concentration camp and the Civil War's most notorious prison facility."[31]

If what happened there over fourteen months was planned starvation, a deliberate attempt at genocide, a medical laboratory used to study the effects of deadly diseases, or, in a less punitive scenario, simply the lack of food for Confederate troops, never mind the prisoners of war, or the fault of a stew of Confederate government officials at Richmond unwilling or unable to help ease the horrific conditions, the ultimate responsibility for more than thirty thousand Union POWs rested in the aging hands of William A.'s father, Brig. Gen. John H. Winder.

9

A Slog to Hell

By late 1863 and into early 1864 starvation was stalking Union prisoners and citizens alike in the South. "Food was scarce, fuel was scarce . . . our soldiers in the field were insufficiently supplied with shoes and blankets. . . . Oh, Lord, how long, how long?" an agonized Sallie Brock wrote as she witnessed the dire conditions in Richmond.[1]

A good number of men and women once plump and in fine fettle were reduced to utter desperation—eating rotted foodstuffs, rioting for loaves of bread, robbing neighbors, or finding themselves with no choice but to beg in the streets. They blamed John H. Winder's damnable rot holes of prisons and the damn Yankees trapped there for their miserable circumstances. To ease the catastrophic situation, and while still under the ever-present threat of invasion by Union troops, General Winder must empty his bulging prisons and send his captives away. And fast. But where was a place big enough to house thousands of Union POWs? On November 24, 1863, John H. Winder's son Capt. Sidney Winder received orders issued that very day by Secretary of War James A. Seddon. The order came from Adj. Gen. J. W. Pegram of the Department of Henrico at Richmond and stated that "a prison for Federal Prisoners shall be established in the State of Georgia" and that he should "proceed without delay . . . to a town . . . between Macon and Andersonville."[2]

After consulting as ordered with Georgia governor Joseph E. Brown, Gen. Howell Cobb, and others, Sidney Winder homed in on a remote whistle-stop of the Southwestern Railroad known as Anderson Station, which had a "depot that consisted of a dozen log and plank buildings." This sparsely populated backwater—later called Andersonville—was a good find, because Sidney Winder, as he traveled deeper into the Georgia countryside, was turned away several times by landowners who feared the proximity of Yankee prisoners.[3]

Finally, the historian Richard Scott Davis writes, "Benjamin B. Dykes persuaded Winder to lease land owned by Deputy Sheriff William Wesley Turner on a tributary of Sweetwater Creek in Sumter County—less than thirty acres—for thirty dollars a month."[4]

A short distance away work on the parcel that was to become the Andersonville Prison stockade—originally called Camp Sumter—was begun, as had protests from Sumter County residents who "voiced fears about potential mass prisoner escapes, bloody slave revolts and the looting of their farms by hungry guards."[5]

Although orders from Richmond gave Sidney the ability to commandeer "whatever labor and materials he needed . . . and at the government's prices," supplies were delayed or nonexistent. John H. Winder's cousin Capt. Richard Bayley Winder would serve as quartermaster. He would oversee the building of the camp and eventually provision it. Winder cousins Richard and Sidney "found that their needs ranked at the absolute bottom of both Confederate and Georgia priorities." This seeming indifference was puzzling.[6]

When the Winders learned that prisoners would soon begin arriving, it became obvious that great speed in preparing the site would be necessary if any captives were to be safely housed and kept from escaping. Close to one thousand slaves were immediately taken from plantations and put straight to work felling the large stands of pines that covered the area, the cut timber eventually forming the walls of the stockade. Lacking any shade, the sun-scorched prison pen—deadly and pestiferous in the summertime Georgia heat and without shelter from winter rainstorms and cold—was to enclose many, many thousands of Union prisoners of war. With a scarcity of ready timber, save for stumps and fallen branches, or, as it was rumored, because William A.'s half brother Sidney had purposely ordered the grounds left barren, no shelters were built. Sidney's order was reportedly, "Make a pen here for the d—d Yankees, where they will rot faster than they can be sent!"[7]

With the prison expected to hold no more than nine thousand captives, on February 3, 1864, the first five hundred men were taken by train from Richmond, being "packed in freight cars like sardines," wrote Andersonville survivor Charles Ferren Hopkins of the First New Jersey Volunteers.[8]

Prisoners were sent from Richmond "by way of Raleigh, North Carolina, and Columbus, South Carolina."[9]

While the old cars rattled along and the stench of cattle manure hung in the air, many of the prisoners, sick, pained, and wasted from their durance at Libby and Belle Isle, had heard the rumor of prisoner exchanges as they lay dreaming of home, imagining bountiful meals, then catching the scent of pines and the rush of fresh water as the train headed south. Throughout March and into April thousands of Union POWs poured in to Andersonville, men captured on battlefields, in swamps and cornfields, men from the Northeast, men from the regiments serving Gen. Benjamin Butler and who had never been south before the war.

"The people told us that we were going to Andersonville, but they said it was a fine place," wrote Andersonville survivor Alexander Angus McLean, a corporal in the 117th New York Infantry. "They represented it as a pleasant shady grove, with a fine stream running through it, with barracks enough to accommodate all of us," he stated.[10]

As McLean and other prisoners approach the tall, wooden gates of the camp, they are forced into the stockade and their possessions commandeered. Of course they were promised all would be returned. It was a fever dream pocked with falsehoods; many of the men are ill, and there is no salvation in sight. As the stockade gate swings open, they are pushed inside. Alexander Angus McLean describes the sight that met him and his fellow prisoners:

> It beggars the description! There were men with nothing to cover their bodies but poor remnants of drawers. . . . Some had ragged old blankets for tents, some had holes dug in the ground, in which they vainly sought shelter, others had nothing but the burning sun by day and the cold blue heavens by night; the latter class was by far the largest; there they were wallowing in their own filth. The

ground was literally alive with maggots. Near the gate was a long row of dead, lying with their ghastly faces upturned to the glaring sun; many of the bodies were entirely uncovered except by the patches of ravenous flies.[11]

Prisoner, diarist, mapmaker, and watercolorist Robert Knox Sneden, a private of the Fortieth New York Volunteer Regiment, was resident at Andersonville as of February 24, having traveled from Richmond to Petersburg, Lawrenceville, Virginia, to Roanoke and Salisbury, North Carolina, to Macon, Milledgeville, and Savannah, Georgia, "packed sixty to seventy in cattle cars . . . in a filthy state, and the manure was some inches deep . . . over twenty were so sick and feeble that their companions had to lift them out . . . and lay them on the ground."[12] Willing himself to live through this nightmare and record most of what he saw, Sneden was one of the very few artists to sketch the prison, the men inside, and the outbuildings—hospitals, cookhouses, swamp, and guard camps.

• • •

Into this morass and with great reluctance, on June 17, 1864, William A.'s father, Brig. Gen. John H. Winder, now commander of all prisons east of the Mississippi River, arrived at Anderson Station after a six-hundred-mile journey. He'd been ordered to "report to Americus, Georgia with the assumption of the command of the . . . prison post at Andersonville," the *Richmond Examiner* reported, "hoping for . . . the best results."[13]

It was more than likely that General Winder's poor reputation in Richmond was one of the reasons he was sent to Andersonville, replacing and ranking the original prison commandant, Col. Alexander W. Persons of the Fifty-Fifth Georgia Infantry, an essentially humane man who tried to better the deteriorating conditions at the prison camp.

Picture John Winder peering at the stockade though a pair of binoculars: a weathered, grim visage, hard-set mouth, all framed by long straggling gray hair above a gray, bright-buttoned uniform and loose whiskers poking from his star-studded collar. He is at a safe distance from the camp, sequestered in his quarters across the railroad tracks. For fear of contracting a disease, he would rarely if ever venture inside the pen, where the stench of corpses, feces, and the gangrenous, rotting limbs of his prisoners filled the air.

Behind the stockade walls as commander of interior operations was Winder's close protégé, Capt. Heinrich "Henry" Hartmann Wirz, a Swiss-born former adjutant and prison keeper in Richmond. Faced with the growing mortality of the prisoners, not to mention their abiding hatred, as he was said to be cruel to many, a scapegoat to some, and to most a fearsome, profane specter on a white horse, his perpetually festering arm in a sling, Wirz was tasked with the impossible. Despite the knowledge that Wirz sent packs of bloodhound mixes—trained to track runaway slaves— after any men who dared to try to tunnel out to freedom, many prisoners did attempt escape. Few succeeded. Some even made last-ditch efforts by pitching themselves into the wagons that carted bodies to the trenches for burial.

For most, because of illness, starvation, or skin color, there was no chance of escape. John H. Winder would have called for particularly harsh treatment of black soldier-captives; their very existence was anathema to him and to the Confederate Army, which saw them not as fighting men but black demons who should be treated as slaves.

According to prisoner Warren Lee Goss, of the Second Massachusetts Heavy Artillery Regiment, wounded black soldiers were tortured and often subjected to "atrocious amputations" or outright neglect by rebel surgeons who figured the men would die on the spot.[14]

One of the victims of outright neglect was Cpl. James Henry Gooding, a poet and columnist for the Mercury in New Bedford, Massachusetts. Gooding was a member of the Fifty-Fourth Massachusetts Infantry, a unit of black soldiers already famous for their heroism and sacrifices at the assault on the South Carolina rebel earthwork at Fort Wagner. Corporal Gooding was captured on or about February 24, 1864, at the Battle of Olustee in Florida and dragged to Andersonville, having been severely wounded in the thigh. Doctors there ignored him as he lay near death, his wound festering until a massive infection finally killed him in July 1864.

Gooding's columns for the *Mercury*, printed as letters to the editor, appeared as weekly columns from March 3, 1863, until shortly before his capture.[15]

Gooding's letter to "Your Excellency Abraham Lincoln," of September 28, 1863, was written when black men were finally allowed to serve in combat. But Gooding protested the unequal pay of black soldiers versus white troops. Gooding asked, "Are we Soldiers, or are we Laborers?" It was not until after Gooding perished at Andersonville that "Senator Henry Wilson of Massachusetts introduced legislation for the retroactive equalization of pay. . . . The law was finally passed . . . in mid June of 1864." Three months later—and two months after Gooding's death—"the United States Paymaster distributed $170,000 in back pay to the men of the Fifty-Fourth Regiment."[16]

• • •

Yankee soldiers being paid while imprisoned was the least of John H. Winder's concerns. He is overburdened by the responsibility his government has placed on him. His orders are ill defined, and he is at times incapable of taking any action, even as he frequently requested help for what he could see was beyond help. He learned from his distant perch that by June 22 there were "24,193 prisoners of war and increasing daily . . . I ask nothing that is not necessary," he wrote. To control the masses of captives, he also requested an additional guard force of two thousand men after learning about "a tunnel . . . fourteen feet deep and from 90 to a hundred feet long."[17]

In fact there were never two thousand "spare" men in Confederate service. Desertions were common. Guarding Andersonville was never a realistic assignment. If the prisoners did attempt to escape, how could the guards who were present—older men and boys from the Georgia Reserves, the dregs of a rebel army that has run low on soldiers—and planted atop the stockade walls in sentry boxes, called "pigeon roosts," control twenty-four thousand captives?[18]

They were a ragtag, trigger-happy lot, hurling taunts at the prisoners while training their guns on them. They shot to kill. Often. Inside the stockade was a crude wooden railing running along the interior perimeter, a "dead line" ordered by Winder. Given his choice not to risk his health by visiting the stockade, Winder no doubt had never witnessed a starving man breaching his dead line by so much as a fingertip to snatch a piece of offal or a crust of bread and, half-mad with this brutal durance, be shot dead for the act of simply falling on or reaching through that low, rickety fence?

Or, as was alleged, had Winder promised the guards a bounty or a furlough for shooting a Yankee? With cries of "Halt!" or sometimes no warning whatever, they often fired a shot to the head or chest and watched as a prisoner crumpled to the ground.

As for food, rations were often raw; men were fed indigestible cobs, rancid meat, and cornmeal studded with maggots. There was also the horror of thirst due to the lack of water, the essence of life and survival for the captives. Between two hills above the prison a single stream called Stockade Branch flowed downhill from the officers' quarters, the overcrowded hospital building, the Confederate soldiers' tents, guardhouses, slaughter pens, dead houses, and cookhouses. The filthy, feces-filled stream served as a toilet and a place to wash and drink.

Hygiene was thus practically nonexistent. Throughout the summer of 1864 and into early fall, roughly one hundred men die of starvation each day, succumbing to dysentery, smallpox, scurvy, rickets, and other wasting illnesses. Chief camp surgeon Isaiah H. White could do little to help, as the hospital was bulging with the sick. When the emaciated prisoners died, if their corpses were noticed at all, they were carted off in wagons by prisoners or slaves and then pitched like cordwood into trenches and covered with dirt or nothing at all. The survivors lived packed together in an unholy mass, some in improvised shelters. Pieces of ragged cloth stretched atop thin, uneven wooden poles—forming a shelter called a shebang—offered some protection if the frequent rains did not make everything a stew of dangerous filth swarming with lice. Many men lay in holes in the ground, which they had laboriously scratched out by hand or dug with sticks of firewood, with nothing but dirt as cover.

For the still strong, or at least those strong enough to be resourceful, a society or city-within-a-stockade formed. Prisoners known as "Raiders" preyed continually on others. After so many vicious attacks—murder, beatings, and theft—fellow prisoners known as "Regulators" began to fight back against the murderous Raiders. Finally General Winder "formally authorized the prisoners to organize trials for the worst of the raiders." Six Raiders went to the gallows on July 11, 1864.[19]

Once a semblance of order had been restored among thousands of weak, diseased, and dying men, General Winder apparently began to contemplate what would happen if Union general William T. Sherman's forces attempted to liberate the camp. Seeming to disregard the possibility that the prisoners were physically too incapacitated to fight, Winder had a plan to counter the threat of liberation by force: an order.

Order No. 13
Headquarters Military Prison
Andersonville, Ga., July 27, 1864

The officers on duty and in charge of the Battery of Florida Artillery at the time will, upon receiving notice that the enemy has approached within seven miles of this post, open upon the Stockade with grapeshot, without reference to the situation beyond these lines of defense.

John H. Winder
Brigadier General Commanding[20]

Guard troops never opened fire on the helpless prisoners within the stockade, but doing so would never have caused Union troops to stop their advance, no matter how many prisoners were murdered. After Sherman's forces battled their way south to Atlanta, destroyed it, and ordered everyone out of the city before beginning their scorched-earth march to Savannah, many expected that Maj. Gen. George Stoneman's cavalry troops would try to liberate Andersonville and the officers' prison at Macon. Stoneman's cavalry troops were ordered to do just that, but there was no raid on Andersonville.

On August 4 General Grant sent an urgent dispatch to Sherman from his headquarters at City Point, Virginia:

Major-General SHERMAN:

Richmond papers of yesterday announce the capture of General
Stoneman and 500 of his party near Macon, Ga. The capture took
place the 31st of July. Have you heard anything of this?

U. S. GRANT,
Lieutenant-General[21]

Sherman answered immediately. The unthinkable had occurred.

NEAR ATLANTA, GA., August 4, 1864.

Lieutenant General U. S. GRANT, City Point:

General Stoneman had only 2,300 men; 900 have got in. I fear
the balance are captured as related in your dispatch. General
Stoneman was sent to break railroad, after which I consented he
should attempt the rescue of our prisoners at Andersonville.

W. T. SHERMAN[22]

"The last lingering illusions about imminent freedom crum-
bled on August 2, . . . when four hundred Union cavalrymen were
brought to Andersonville," and they reported to the prisoners the
truth of the rumor that "they, General Stoneman, and many more
of his men had been captured."[23]

As a high-ranking officer, Stoneman was not taken to Andersonville. He was instead detained at Macon's Camp Oglethorpe
and exchanged two months later.

As the first days of August scorched and killed at Andersonville, 33,006 men were penned in the stockade. Hearing reports
of the horrors at the camp, Richmond authorities ordered an
inspection of the prison. The man chosen by the adjutant and
inspector general's office was a Confederate assistant adjutant
and inspector general, Lt. Col. Daniel Thomas Chandler, a former
Union POW and District of Columbia native. His lengthy second
report of August 5—his first of July 5 was essentially ignored—to
Confederate colonel Robert Hall Chilton provided a full account
of the prison's conditions. It is meticulous in detail and gravely

damning, especially to Gen. John Winder. After detailing the particulars of the stockade and the dead line, he notes that a "small stream passes from west to east through the inclosure. . . . [It] furnishes the only water for washing accessible to the prisoners. Some regiments of the guard, the bakery, and cook-house, being placed on the rising ground bordering the stream before it enters the prison, render the water nearly unfit for use before it reaches the prisoners."[24]

Colonel Chandler then addressed the lack of medical care "furnished within the stockade . . . and the hospital accommodations are so limited that, though the beds (so-called) have all or nearly all two occupants each, large numbers who would otherwise be received are necessarily sent back to the stockade."

Chandler's report continued the bleak listing of horrors: "The dead are hauled out daily [by] the wagon load and buried without coffins, their hands in many instances being first mutilated with an ax in the removal of any finger rings they may have. The sanitary condition of the prisoners is as wretched as can be, the principal causes of morality being scurvy and chronic diarrhea. . . . Nothing seems to have been done, and but little, if any effort, made to arrest it by procuring proper food." As noted earlier, the prisoners received raw rations. In addition, "no soap or clothing has ever been issued. It is impossible to state the number of sick, many dying within the stockade whom the medical officers never see or hear of 'till their remains are brought out for interment. The rate of deaths has steadily increased from 37.4 per 1,000 during the month of March last to 62.7 per 1,000 in July. The supply of medicines is wholly inadequate, and frequently there is none, owing to the great delays experienced in filling the requisitions."

Chandler's report closes with this:

My duty requires me respectfully to recommend a change in the officer in command of the post, Brig. Gen. J. H. Winder, and the substitution in his place of someone who unites both energy and good judgment with some feelings of humanity and consideration for the welfare and comfort (so far as it is consistent with their safe-keeping) of the vast number of unfortunates placed in his control; someone who at least will not advocate deliberately and in cold blood the propriety of leaving them in their present condition until their number has been sufficiently reduced by death to make the present arrangements suffice for their accommodation, and who will not consider it a matter of self-laudation and boasting that he has never been inside the stockade, a place the horrors of which it is difficult to describe, and which is a disgrace to civilization; the condition of which he might, by the exercise of a little energy and judgment, even with the limited means at his command, have considerably improved.

Upon receiving Chandler's report, Colonel Chilton wrote to Secretary of War James A. Seddon on August 18: "The condition of the prison at Andersonville is a reproach to us as a nation." Chilton said that no more prisoners should be sent to Andersonville, and he recommended that Winder move the present occupants immediately.[25]

At that, Winder ordered mass evacuations. No matter their condition, save for the men too weak or sick to move at all—the dead and the near dead—the prisoners were sent to equally unendurable sites as Sherman's men—the "blue behemoth"—thundered and plundered along. Imagine then an army of POWs pushed and forced ahead, far too weakened to cause any real trouble. "The prisoners at Andersonville were divided into three groups in September 1864," writes the historian Robert S. Davis. "One group went to Camp Lawton at Millen, Georgia." Sherman came closer. Six long weeks later those captives were relocated to Blackshear, Georgia, and six weeks later they were moved again, to Florence, South Carolina, and Salisbury, North Carolina. The group was then divided into two. Off went the "second group to Savannah and later to an open-air island prison at Blackshear." What was worse, "those prisoners ended up back at Andersonville."[26]

According to John H. Winder's biographer, when the general finally read Chandler's report, "he branded the charges as false . . . he did not know of Chandler's charges against him personally and never saw that portion of the report."[27]

On September 24, 1864, Winder's subordinate, Henry Wirz, was sent Chandler's damning report, by Winder himself. In his response to Winder, his commandant, Wirz claims that he accompanied Chandler as he toured the camp, serving "as his guide.... I soon found however that he preferred to communicate with the prisoners themselves." Wirz is clearly uncomfortable and writes, "I saw very soon he would be made the plaything of cute Yankees." Wirz fears that the prisoners "would give him most horrible descriptions of their sufferings, short and uncooked rations, and unheard of outrages perpetrated upon them." Particularly egregious in Wirz's opinion were the "sympathy which his [Chandler's] looks indicated he had for them." After defending the indefensible, Wirz complains that Chandler's tour took three hours that "should have demanded one week's devoted attention." With a "very sympathizing look toward the Yankee prisoners," Chandler remarked to Wirz, "this beats anything I ever saw; it is indeed hell on earth."[28]

• • •

On February 6, 1865, John H. Winder collapsed and died as he was entering an officer's tent—a celebratory dinner was the occasion—at the Florence, South Carolina, prison. "The boys said it was a clear case of Death by Visitation of the Devil," prisoner John McElroy wrote years later. "It was always insisted that his [Winder's] last words were: My faith is in Christ; I expect to be saved. Be sure and cut down the prisoners' rations."[29]

Last words or not, true or not, McElroy's account of Winder's utterings as he died were recorded for all posterity.

John H. Winder's life thus ended on the dirt floor of a prison. His death was only the beginning of the descent of the Winder name into perpetual infamy and irretrievable darkness.

10

The War Criminal's Son

At Point San Jose there would be no telegraphic dispatch rushed by messenger to inform William A. of his father's sudden and abrupt end. The *San Francisco Daily Evening Bulletin* reported a major telegraphic service outage on February 9, 1865, thus depriving the city and all military posts throughout the state of news via the modern and already indispensable communication technology. William A. would not find out about his father's demise either by letter from the East—which generally took three weeks—or from the local press.[1]

Although the *Richmond Examiner* had received a dispatch from the Confederate War Department and noted on February 9 the "sudden death of General John H. Winder" down in Dixie, those who had access to the *Wilmington Journal* from North Carolina could have read this eulogy: "In every position in which he [Winder] has been placed his official conduct has been marked by strict probity, energy and promptness," and his "noble and genial nature" was cherished by friends and family.[2]

Readers throughout the Union would not read of Winder's noble and genial nature. The *Providence Evening Press* of Rhode Island instead reported on "this monster[,] whose death" would be welcomed by "our brave soldiers and loyal people everywhere."[3]

After word spread that John H. Winder had died of natural causes, there was an article printed in the *Beverly Citizen* of Massachusetts via the *New York Herald*, and many newspapers printed variations on it and other biographical sketches of the monster Winder, "the rough from Baltimore" who "like the devil's own had blighted and buried thousands. . . . It would be only just and proper . . . to know that he fell by the hands of some one or more of the prisoners whom he has so inhumanely treated. The grave is supposed to bury the faults of most men with them, but it cannot hide the crimes of such a monster as John H. Winder."[4]

"He was called 'Hog Winder,' owing to his brutal habits and avarice. . . . His name is synonymous with all that is cruel and vindictive," the *Milwaukee Sentinel* opined.[5]

On March 19 the *Daily Alta California* reported Winder's death "by apoplexy . . . John H. or 'Hog' Winder as he was familiarly called . . . had charge of the prisoners confined in the Libby, Belle Island, and Andersonville and Florence prisons." The article further described the origin of "the epithet of 'Hog' Winder given him at West Point, as expressive of his avarice. His selfishness made him notorious in the United States Army while his inhumanity to our prisoners captured in this war have made him hated by his own people and despised by the civilized of all races." Furthermore, the newspaper reported, "no officer to which the rebellion has given prominence sinks into his grave more generally hated than does this . . . inhuman monster Winder . . . He was about sixty-five."[6]

Absent any previous communication from anyone in the East, it is probable that William A. read of the death of his father during the daylong, much-heralded "Grand Military Review." He was spared any last-minute squibs identifying him as the son of "Hog" Winder. Or perhaps out of kindness to a man so many in San Francisco's rumor mill had once deemed disloyal, surely by now most if not all readers knew and even admired this son born to such a demon and who remained loyal to the Union.

Appearing in the same *Daily Alta California* issue of March 19, on the same page as the notice of General Winder's death, is a mention that William A. is part of a great celebration, the spectacle at the Presidio known as the Grand Military Review. Major General McDowell and staff reviewed the troops, and "over three thousand of . . . the State's stalwart sons . . . were paraded," the article stated. "Captain Winder of Black Point was observed" among officers and privates posted at the forts guarding the bay within the "immense crowd in attendance."[7]

The March 23 edition of the *Marysville Daily Appeal* reported that "the notorious rebel General Winder will never be able to repeat his evil deeds."[8]

And this from the *Sacramento Daily Union*: "When Winder the jailer of Libby Prison, Belle Isle," and of course Andersonville, was a sure "instrument of rebel barbarity . . . his apoplexy cheated the gibbet of a fitting victim."[9]

No matter his shock, grief, or relief, William A. must find a way forward—for himself, for his wife who'd endured so much by his side, for his son Willie, who was nearly an adolescent.

A friend once again tried to assist William A. in advancing his career. Shortly after the death of William A.'s father, Gov. John Goodwin of Arizona wrote Secretary of War Stanton from San Francisco:

Sir,

I would respectfully suggest the name of Capt. William A. Winder 3rd Artillery for a brevet.

Captain Winder has been true to the flag, and has rendered important and valuable service during the present war.

I earnestly hope that his services will be recognized. Your obt. servt,

John N. Goodwin, Governor of Arizona[10]

Perhaps Governor Goodwin doesn't realize that Stanton will not then, not ever recognize William A.'s service, no matter how many vouch for his loyalty. And William A. must forever view the events at Andersonville through a jagged prism, a glass distorted and endlessly reported. He cannot escape the taint of Andersonville or, in nightmares, hear the cries of the sufferers, and though he has longed from his teen years to be a healer, what could he have done to stop the deaths that mounted daily in faraway Georgia? Only in his mind could his troops, their artillery, cannons, and hot shots have bombarded, invaded, and liberated the caged and starving Union men. He is bound to his post; dutiful, surely wearied, and permanently estranged from what remained of his Confederate family.

At least William A. is now on the mainland north of the city, a small advantage as on occasion he travels a relatively short distance by carriage, or on horseback to visit the office of the merchandise and mining suppliers Breed & Chase. Talking of the mines and to Ephraim Morse and that he will pay the drafts owed for mining supplies must all somehow put him on a path forward.

"Capt. Winder was into the store yesterday," Breed and Chase wrote to Morse. "He said he believed Gen. McDowell was going down that way [Southern California] next week. If he visits San Diego, you must give him a proper reception and impress upon him the advantages of S. Diego as a military point, and the necessity of fortifications in case of a foreign war."[11]

There will be no war, foreign or domestic, for William A. or General McDowell to fight. By April 2 Richmond has fallen and hundreds of Union troops pour into that city. Amid the chaos of thousands of residents fleeing in panic—by horseback, in carriages, on foot—as the fleeing troops ignite massive conflagrations so as to leave nothing of use for the invaders and thousands of Confederate documents are pitched burning into the streets, Jefferson Davis and his entire government are in flight. Throughout the night trains leave the depot, the last carrying Davis and his cabinet to Danville, Virginia.

Sidney Winder was tasked with guarding a treasure train carrying Confederate specie—gold. The cars rumbled through the night, leaving behind a ruined city, the charred leavings of a self-declared nation that had warred with the United States for four long years. Although Sidney Winder received a portion of the gold, which he and his comrades had divided, making sure a portion of the money was earmarked for the Davis family, he fled toward North Carolina. Arrested and paroled, he returned to Baltimore. Grieving for his father and their lost cause and in a perpetual state of depression, he tried to resume his law practice.

Richard Bayley Winder made his way to his home in Accomack, Virginia. William A.'s uncles, Charles H. and William H., mourned and fumed as they witnessed the end of all they believed in. Now they must try and try again to defend their family, efface all excoriations, all shame.

With grief shading sunlight for the remaining rebel Winders, at least for William A. the war is over. On April 9 Lee surrendered to Grant at Appomattox. When the news quickly reached San Francisco by telegraph—which was up and running again—there were celebrations in the streets and the cannons of Alcatraz were fired over the water. When news of Lincoln's assassination reached the celebrants on April 15, the cheering stopped. Violence erupted in the streets as "crowds of Unionists sacked pro-Confederate newspaper offices in the city." The military ordered artillerymen from Fort Alcatraz into the city to maintain order. Confederate sympathizers throughout California who celebrated Lincoln's death were arrested and imprisoned on Alcatraz.

Again the island's guns sent out a "half-hourly cannon shot over the bay as a symbol of the nation's grief."[12] Winder's cannons at Point San Jose did the same. Would that he could tear into the streets, blast away all traces of the Confederacy, and find an elusive peace in a time of undeniable turmoil.

With all hope that he might soon leave the war far behind for a way forward with mining, he wrote to Morse, "I am striking for a big thing" and asked for a loan of $1,500 to own "a good sized tract."[13]

Perhaps peace will come to William A., perhaps in San Diego:

San Francisco, Apr 29, 1865

Friend Morse:

. . . Had quite a talk with Capt. Winder about San Diego. He is urging the Government to remove the depot to San Diego, and feels quite encouraged that it will be done. If the gov't depot were at S.D. & fortifications commenced there, you would see lively times. Hope it may be so soon. Breed & Chase[14]

• • •

While William A. may be entertaining fervent hopes that better times lie before him, the opposite is true for the defeated Confederates. Imagine his late father's horror if he had learned of the capture of his president, Jefferson Davis, in the vicinity of Irwinsville, Georgia, on May 10, 1865. Davis was taken to Fortress Monroe to be charged as an accomplice in the Lincoln assassination, and if that could be proven with the zealous efforts of the judge advocate general, Joseph Holt—bent on punishing to the fullest extent any and all former Confederates—Davis would be tried for treason. And if it could be proven that he helmed and abetted the Andersonville disaster as well, that would be added to his catalog of crimes. On May 7, 1865, John H. Winder's subordinate, Capt. Henry H. Wirz, was arrested at Andersonville Prison by a detachment of the Fourth U.S. Cavalry. He was taken to Macon, Georgia, then to the Old Capitol Prison to await trial for war crimes. On May 25, 1865, while at Annapolis, Maryland, Walt Whitman saw "the released prisoners of war . . . coming up from the southern prisons." Out of "several hundreds" unloaded from a large boat, he saw "only three individuals were able to walk. . . . Can those be men—those little livid brown, ash-streak'd, monkey-looking dwarfs? Are they really not mummified, dwindled corpses? . . . There are deeds, crimes, that may be forgiven; but this is not among them. It steeps its perpetrators in blackest, escapeless, endless damnation."[15]

Lurid accounts of Andersonville spread unchecked throughout the country, as did news of a shipwreck and the death of a man who had sprung to William A.'s defense amid the accusations of disloyalty. No doubt reviving old demons of death at sea for William A., his former commander, Gen. George Wright, drowned in the wreck of the steamer *Brother Jonathan*. On July 19 the schooner hurtled into sharp rocks near Crescent City, California, while carrying the general, his wife, and two hundred passengers to his new command, the Department of Columbia. Wright was widely mourned. California governor Frederick F. Low eulogized the general "to whose loyalty, fidelity and military ability the people of this state are so much indebted for the peace and good order."[16]

As part of the "good order" of a country now experiencing some semblance of peace, William A. and his artillerymen left Point San Jose for San Diego to assume command of the San Diego Barracks. Used as an "army supply depot for Southern California . . . it was in a lonely spot called New Town, hardly a town but a failed thirty two block venture of developer William H. Davis. After few want to live in Davis' Folly, as it came to be known," Davis donated the land to the U.S. government for an army post and the barracks.[17]

William A. and his family find themselves living just a few miles from Old Town, then "occupying but a few blocks of 45,557 acres of pueblo lands . . . donated by the King of Spain." Located along the San Diego River, the community had "not more than sixty-five structures . . . the population . . . evenly divided between Americans and those of Spanish and Mexican descent."[18]

Ephraim Morse's future wife, a Massachusetts schoolteacher named Mary Chase Walker, penned an account of her first visit to Old Town in July 1865, just at the time William A., Abby, and Willie arrived.

Eagerly awaited, this proper New England young woman was hired as the first schoolteacher at the community's first schoolhouse, just constructed on Mason Street. Promised a salary of sixty-five dollars a month, Mary arrived in the Bay of San Diego on July 5. "It was a most desolate looking landscape," she wrote. "The hills were brown and barren; not a tree or green thing was to be seen." She said of Old Town, "Of all the dilapidated, miserable looking places I had ever seen, this was the worst. The buildings were nearly all of adobe, one story in height, with no chimneys. Some of the roofs were covered with tile and some with earth."[19]

Mary wrote that on her first night at the local hotel

a donkey came under my window and saluted me with an unearthly bray. The fleas were plentiful and hungry. Mosquitoes were also in attendance. An Indian man did the cooking and an Irish boy waited on me at the table, and also gave me the news of the town. . . . I rented two rooms in the Robinson House for $2.00 a month. My school was composed mostly of Spanish and half-breed children, with a few English and several Americans. I aimed to teach [that] which was most meaningful to them; namely reading, spelling, arithmetic, and how to write letters. At recess the Spanish girls smoked cigaritas and the boys amused themselves by lassoing pigs, hens, etc. The Spanish children were very irregular in their attendance at school on account of so many fiestas and amusements of various kinds. For a week before a bull fight the boys were more or less absent, watching preparations, such as fencing up the streets leading to the plaza. . . . Through two glass doors that opened on a veranda . . . wild Indians, nude with the exception of a cloth about the loins, stalked majestically across the plaza, their long hair plastered up with paste made of grease and ashes.[20]

Mary's truant boys, too busy with bullfight preparations to go to school, didn't bother the townspeople, but some residents did take exception to her invitation to a female mulatto ship stewardess who'd helped her when she was ailing on the long ocean crossing. Some months after she began teaching, Mary saw the young woman eating alone and asked her to dine with her—in public, in a restaurant. According to Ephraim Morse's diary, "there seems to be quite a combination against the school teacher . . . none of the Californians will . . . send their children [to school] . . . the whole affair is a Secesh move. . . . A resolution was passed unanimously that Miss Walker be dismissed for the reason that a majority of the heads of families refuse to send their children to her any longer . . . the trustees agreed [with the exception of Morse and Robert Israel] . . . but admitted it was a Secesh move." Morse's well-known disgust at all things rebel is prominent in his diary entries. Mary was replaced by another teacher. Morse wed Mary later that year. It was a long and happy marriage.[21]

Another resident of Old Town at the time William A. arrived was the newly elected San Diego district attorney, Godfrey Adolphus Benzen. With a persistent cough that presaged a fatal illness, he was elected to replace the former San Diego district attorney and had fled the chill of San Francisco with his wife, Harriet, hoping the drier, milder climate of San Diego would cure his condition. At first he praised the "delightful, even temperature and climate. I feel I have to stay here or die," he wrote to a friend, San Francisco attorney Wellington Cleveland Burnett. But even though he was breathing warm air and basking in the sunshine, the sad little town was to him land's end. Old Town was a "lonely, hard and miserable place." He reported that the U.S. mail arrived once a week, "wind and weather and the state of rivers permitting," and that "the steamer comes here once a month, but she carries only Wells Fargo & Co. Express." Despite his own physical condition, he states that "sickness is hardly known here." Benzen, a

wry observer, notes that "the favorite and uniform way of sever-
ing the relations that bind men . . . is generally an ounce or two of
lead, or the insertion of a black or white handled bowie knife into
the party." Benzen laments the terrible conditions at the Exchange
Hotel, the "laziness and recklessness of the population, a mix-
ture of Indians and Cholos from Mexico, and refugees from justice from everywhere else. We have even no barber, no tailor, no
shoemaker, nothing but whiskey shops and Fandango houses." He
sees "hundreds of cows running around most of the time but not
a drop of milk . . . nothing here but beef, fresh and dried, beef in
the morning, beef at dinner and beef for supper." And he notes that
"if a man is arrested for murder or some other trifle as robbery,
etc., he is placed in the county jail by the sheriff, who calls on him
three times a day" and drinks with him at a saloon at night. The
misery and isolation of Benzen's wife haunts him just as they do
William A.'s Abby, though she is living at the barracks with her husband and Willie. Who, Abby might have thought, could ever live in
a place like this? Her husband saw a life there. She did not, could
not. Like Harriet Benzen, she wanted to go home. Godfrey A. Benzen died at the age of thirty-one in San Diego. His wife transported
his body to San Francisco, where he was buried on August 17.[22]

• • •

On August 23, 1865, a military tribunal convened at the U.S. Court
of Claims Hall in Washington DC for the trial of Henry Wirz,
by order of the president. Norton Parker Chipman, judge advocate general, served as chief prosecutor and helmed the proceedings. Orrin Smith Baker and Louis Schade served as Wirz's
defense counsel. Originally it was decided—and it was the fervent wish of Judge Advocate General Joseph Holt, who one month
earlier had concluded the trial of the conspirators in Lincoln's
assassination—that Jefferson Davis, confined at Fortress Monroe, be included in Wirz's trial as a co-conspirator in the Andersonville case." Much to the anger and disappointment of Holt
and Chipman, "his [Davis's] complicity and that of some of his
cabinet officers in the crime of Andersonville" was dismissed as
it was "undesirable for many reasons to furnish any pretext for

bringing the ex-president to the capital," wrote Chipman.[23] After much debate, the trial began in earnest.

The case against Wirz amounted to thirteen charges, including "murder, in violation of the laws and customs of war," customs that had been codified by Francis Lieber in General Orders No. 100. Article 71 of the orders states that "who ever intentionally inflicts additional wounds upon an enemy, or who orders or encourages soldiers to do so, shall suffer death, if duly convicted, whether he belongs to the Army of the United States, or is an enemy captured after having committed his misdeed."[24]

John H. Winder was posthumously charged with "maliciously, willfully and traitorously . . . between March, 1864 to April 10, 1865, conspiring with Richard B. Winder, Joseph White, W. S. Winder . . . and others unknown to injure the health and destroy the lives of soldiers[,] . . . starving the prisoners, [and] providing insufficient shelter to over thirty thousand men." Although prisoners and witnesses testified to John H. Winder's reputed cruelty and indifference throughout the trial, his death placed him beyond punishment, so it was Wirz—"who did permit to remain in said prison, among the emaciated sick and languishing living, the bodies of the dead"—who was blamed for "malicious intent" and murder.[25]

Among the 160 witnesses called were former Confederate personnel, doctors, Union officials, and surviving prisoners. The repeated claims of the ailing and belligerent Wirz that he was just following Winder's orders did little to convince the court. Henry Wirz was the only soldier from the Civil War tried as a war criminal for failing to adhere to the standards in General Orders No. 100, according to the historian Lawrence P. Rockwood. Judge Advocate Chipman "argued a theory of command responsibility," Rockwood writes.[26]

According to the prosecutor in the case, "a superior officer cannot order a subordinate to do an illegal act, and if a subordinate [does] obey such an order and disastrous consequences result, the superior and subordinate must answer for it. General Winder could no more command the prisoner to violate the laws of war than could the prisoner do so without orders . . . both are guilty."[27]

When Sidney Winder learned that the military tribunal had charged him with war crimes, he fled to Canada. Unable to escape the dragnet, Richard B. Winder was arrested, confined in the Old Capitol Prison, and eventually taken to Richmond, Virginia, to face more charges.

· · ·

The Andersonville trial lumbered on, with avid coverage by newspapers from New York to California. William A. meanwhile relinquished command of San Diego Barracks, per orders of July 22 from Washington, and on October 6 he left for New York City via San Francisco, with Abby and Willie accompanying him. While he was at sea there was constant coverage of the tribunal for Wirz and the trial-in-absentia of his own father. The *New York Times* reported that John H. Winder "was chief among the conspirators and the actual participators in the crime." One witness testified that well before Andersonville, "his role as Provost-Marshal was . . . a reign of terror" and that he had "unlimited control of the prison."[28]

"Another chapter of horrors!" the *Weekly Alta California* exclaimed as the daily testimony continued to be reported and excerpted in the press.[29]

William A., traveling at sea during the trial, would eventually hear that Wirz was found guilty of the most serious charges and hanged on November 10, 1865, at the Old Capitol Prison.

Ten days later, on November 20, William A. and his family arrived in New York City on the *Henry Chauncey*. Also aboard the ship was someone who had the potential to be his salvation: Maj. Gen. William Starke Rosecrans. Although it is not known how these two officers first met—one being the son of an infamous rebel and the other a flawed and controversial Union general fleeing a contorted and painful career, likely there was a shipboard conversation, some glad-handing, an invitation, an offer to make a fortune. Copper fever was spreading to so many, and although Winder was already deep in the game, he still needed an investor, a partner, despite the general having a tarnished reputation. During the war Rosecrans was initially extolled as the commander of the Army of the Cumberland, with victory after victory making him seemingly invincible. When he blundered in the execution of an order, however, shame and excoriation followed. His mistake allowed Gen. Braxton Bragg's rebel forces to outnumber Union troops at Chickamauga Creek. Rosecrans was blamed for the Union defeat and ultimately fired by Lt. Gen. Ulysses S. Grant. Rosecrans needed a new victory.

William A. Winder was overdue for a victory as well. The two men needed each other. But first William A. faced an unwelcome interruption when he was posted to Newburgh, New York, to engage in recruiting for Company D, a job with little to no reward. With so many men having been lost in the war and so many disabled, the job of recruiting men who had little reason to rejoin the army, even in peacetime, was a difficult task. Bounties were offered in an attempt to lure literally old and often disabled veterans, as well as new recruits. And there was corruption involved, as "substitute or bounty brokers positioned themselves as indispensable assistants to drafted men," fanning out across the Northeast to fill quotas. The whole enterprise created a "market in men." In January 1865, according to the historian Brian P. Luskey, agent George Northrup wrote to the New York firm of Fay & Dalton, saying, "Men is cheep here to Day. 3 years Sub[stitutes] 700 to 800 dollars." While there is no evidence to suggest that William A. was involved in such shady practices, a new life was calling so that he could remove himself from the recruiting effort.[30]

On December 12, 1865, William A. was ready to vault into that new life from his post in Newburgh. Perhaps Adj. Gen. Lorenzo Thomas would allow it:

General [Thomas]:

I have the honor to apply for a leave of absence for twelve months to enable me to attend to urgent private business.

I would respectfully state for the information of the Commander in Chief that I have had three months leave since 1848.

Yr. obt. Servt,

W.A. Winder, Captain 3rd Artillery[31]

The urgent private business was of course to firmly fix his mining interests. A leave of twelve months, though not nearly enough (considering the length of time it would take him to get to California, let alone start anew), might bring William A. a small measure of peace, perhaps even some reward, for this was for him at least a chance to leave the world of war and his blighted family behind. His urgent private business plea is a plea for freedom at the end of a furious, frenzied war that has left the president and at least 620,000 others dead. The former Confederacy lay in ruins; even the Wirz trial, ending with the hanging of John H. Winder's subordinate, has not silenced cries for vengeance and has not silenced William A.'s uncle, who has vowed to spend his remaining days attempting to clear his brother John H.'s name. Toward that end he has written to Secretary of War Stanton.

"The long continued and atrocious efforts to cast obloquy upon the memory of Gen. John H. Winder has been . . . persistently carried on, . . . suppressing truth and suggesting falsehoods & much of this under official authority," W. H. Winder wrote, suggesting that he himself be tried for his dead brother's crimes, with some conditions, for example, that such a trial would be conducted in a court "that shall consist of those members to be named and appointed by you" and that Robert E. Lee should be on the jury. "The court [should] appoint a judge advocate," as the trial would surely prove the Confederacy was unable to prevent the crimes at Andersonville because the Union government forbid exchanges. This position omitted the fact that the Confederacy had refused to consider black POWs to be legitimate prisoners of war. In addition, W. H. Winder wrote, the same Lincoln government was just as guilty of crimes against their Confederate prisoners. General Winder's efforts, he continued, "were first wholly to avert suffering . . . to protect them [the prisoners] from wanton injury or injustice." In offering to stand trial in his late brother's stead, W. H. Winder claimed, "I am perfectly willing that my life shall be at stake." He promised his nephew W. S. Winder would return from Canada if such a trial were permitted.[32]

There is no response. W. S. Winder does not return from Canada until well into the next year. To W. H. Winder, to his brother

Charles H., to his aunt and grandmother, William A. will always be the phantasm in blue, the unforgiven enemy, the traitor, the symbol of the Union's great injustices, and the final fatal wounding of the family name.

As for the much-desired twelve-month leave William A. requested, it was denied by Ulysses S. Grant. "Application not approved," he wrote.[33]

In desperation, on December 28, 1865, from Newburgh, New York, knowing he cannot have the twelve months' leave he really wants, William A. writes to Grant's assistant adjutant general, Col. Theodore S. Bowers. "I have the honor to apply for a leave of absence for six months, to attend to urgent personal business." William A. goes on to use the same wording of his previous request for twelve months, writing that he has had "three-months leave since 1848."[34]

Ichabod Goodwin made a final attempt to ask for his son-in-law's leave. Goodwin wrote to Secretary of War Stanton, telling him that William A.'s "interests in California . . . demand his presence in such a situation that his presence on the spot is required for successful development. If this leave is granted," Goodwin wrote, "I shall consider it as a personal favor to myself."[35]

Although Goodwin does not specify the length of the leave he is requesting for his son-in-law, he has tried time and again to help William A., always unsuccessfully. There are two days left before a year riddled with tragedies, victories, and vengeance ends. William A.'s future and his family's future must, he fervently hoped, be in faraway California, far from the wreckage of war.

11

Of Resignation, Railroads, and Exile

Despite Ichabod Goodwin's personal request for his son-in-law's leave to be extended beyond six months, on January 5, 1866, a curt and disappointing reply came from the Adjutant General's Office at the War Department and was forwarded to Lt. Gen. U.S. Grant.

"Approved," for six months, Grant wrote.[1]

Not realizing William A. Winder had already been granted the lesser leave, William M. Stewart, a U.S. senator from Nevada and mining magnate, also wrote to Secretary Stanton on William A.'s behalf on January 9, 1866. "I do not ask you to transcend any of the regulations" of the War Department," he wrote, all the while flattering Stanton by saying his is an "admirable and unsurpassed system." Stewart writes that he hopes Stanton might overlook army regulations in this case, but because William A. was refused a twelve-month leave by Grant he suggests that William A. "would be thankful for six months time." Importantly, Stewart adds, "If the refusal was caused by any charges which may have been preferred against Capt Winder will you be kind enough to inform me, as I do not think he is informed of them if there be any, and in order that he may have an opportunity to, as I have every confidence that he can entirely disprove them."[2]

It was not Stanton's call to make. It was U.S. Grant's. Surely Stanton knew full well that there were no charges against William A., but perhaps with the infamous Confederate Winders jailed, on parole, or indicted for war crimes, Stewart might have feared the worst for him. And rightly so. The suspicions that hectored and haunted William A. throughout the war have caused Stewart to say that at the very least, if any charges were the cause of the refusal

of a twelve-month leave, might he and William A. be informed?
As usual, there was no response.

• • •

William A.'s post as a recruiter in Newburgh, New York, ended.
He must head west once again, ride the tide, and catch the copper, and he needs to do so quickly if he is to bring his wife and
son back to California. This time it would be different. No more
disgrace, no more suspicions. On January 20 he left New York
for California with Samuel Storer, a Portsmouth lawyer who was
married to Abby's sister, Sarah "Sadie" Parker Rice Goodwin. Like
William A., Storer was seeking a new beginning, "as he had some
difficulty in establishing a lucrative practice in Portsmouth." For
a short time Samuel, Sadie, and their young daughter Mabel had
lived a hard prairie life in Peotone, Illinois. That didn't last. Sadie
was ill. With a small child to tend, she hurried home to Portsmouth, to her mother and father and her sisters.[3]

As for Samuel Storer, he was intoxicated by the sunlit promise
of California, and wasn't William A. going to make a fortune? Their
plans were to build homes for their families, bring them to California immediately thereafter, and live side by side. Abby would have
her beloved sister Sadie and her niece Mabel close by. Willie and
Mabel would thrive. It would be perfect. It should have been perfect.

• • •

William A. was eagerly awaited in California, as is evident in the
continuing correspondence from Breed & Chase to Ephraim Morse
in San Diego. However, high hopes expressed in the correspondence give way to concern and finally despair at William A.'s inability to pay for the supplies provided to him:

San Francisco, Feb 2, 1866

Friend Morse,

The N Y steamer arrived today but did not bring Capt Winder as
you expected Probably he was detained, and will be home next
steamer. Shall be glad to see him when he comes.

Breed & Chase[4]

On February 11 William A. and Sam Storer arrived in San Francisco to good press. "Captain Winder's Del Fino [*sic*] copper mine is progressing nicely and will soon be paying," the *Daily Alta California* reported.[5]

Breed and Chase agree. All seems well so far.

San Francisco, Feb 17, 1866

Friend Morse,

Capt Winder arrived by last steamer . . . and seems in good spirits & I think has his business in satisfactory shape. . . .

Breed & Chase[6]

A pattern was emerging. Winder was traveling from San Francisco, dipping in and out of Old Town to see Morse, assuring him that all is well, and then going to Baja to supervise their copper mines. "Will you or Capt. Winder write & say whether he is able to pay or not," Breed and Chase finally write.[7]

Despite William A. being in arrears with his debt to Breed & Chase, there was more positive press for his mines. He now has a partner. The San Diego correspondent for the *San Francisco Daily Bulletin* wrote, "Capt. Winder and another gentleman have just returned from the mines of the southern frontier. They report everything favorable, and intend returning to make a more extended survey shortly."[8]

The other gentleman, as the newspapers will soon trumpet, is Gen. William Starke Rosecrans, now a celebrity in California and the proponent of a railroad line, a great line that would link the East to the West, with a terminus in San Diego. With Gen. John C. Fremont's millions made in the gold fields at his disposal to buy up the "franchise and rights of the Kansas Pacific Railroad . . . the Memphis and Little Rock . . . and the Memphis and El Paso," he would be able to have a "great consolidated line running from Norfolk" to the jumble of pueblo lands, adobes, and shacks at land's end in San Diego. Although Rosecrans later aided in the formation of the San Diego Gila Southern Pacific and Atlantic Railroad Company, hopes were high, but disappointments, impassable roads, squabbling, and legalities collapsed the effort to bring travelers and settlers to where "dreams of greatness were being born of visionary railroads."[9]

Here again was the chimera of prosperity and promise, this time in the guise of the imagined whistle of a great locomotive, clacking and rumbling along. Rosecrans, with his dreamed-of railroads, and Winder, with his mines flourishing in his mind, arrived in San Diego. "The whole population got together, raised the flag under which he so gallantly and bravely fought through one of the most gigantic rebellions that the world ever saw, fired one hundred guns . . . [and] gave him [Rosecrans] the freedom of the city." The next day "he took his departure for the Delphina copper mine, in Lower California. The owner of the above named mine, Capt. W A Winder, Third U.S. Artillery, accompanied him. . . . I trust that the many and varied resources of this part of California will be speedily brought into notoriety."[10]

On April 27, 1866, the San Diego correspondent for the *San Francisco Daily Bulletin* wrote, "A party of eight men or more have gone down the country as far as the Serlado [Salada] mine—say 180 miles—to put the whole road in good order for hauling ore. Capt. Winder and Gen. Rosecrans are the prime movers in the affair."[11]

As a prime mover in this venture and still planning for Abby and Willie to come west to be with him, there was this announcement from the *Salt Lake Daily Telegraph*'s "San Diego Matters" column: "Some new dwellings are to be built here this summer by Capt. W. A. Winder, U.S.A. and Mr. Storer. Their families are coming from the East to occupy them as soon as completed." Also mentioned is General Rosecrans, "who will probably soon become a permanent resident of this place [San Diego]."[12]

With high hopes and good reason to harbor them, William A. wrote to Rosecrans.

"After careful examination of the Delfina Mine [Winder's spelling] made in company with yourself, [I believe] that the Delfina Copper Co., have it in their power to become one of the leading mining companies in the world." Winder suggested they take possession of other mines with promising lodes, such as "the Candelaria and the Capitano," and that the Delfina Company get "possession of, and working these mines for the sum of about ten thousand dollars, the Company will control one of the richest mining districts in the country." But he needs more time—a longer army leave—to make this plan work.[13]

Another of Winder's business partners, the wealthy New York merchant Anthony Gilkison, wrote to Secretary Stanton on Winder's behalf. "Capt. W. A. Winder now in California, is associated with myself and other gentlemen in New York in a mining property, and I respectfully request an extension of Capt. Winder's furlough till January 1, 1867 to enable him to complete our business," Gilkison wrote, offering to send Winder a telegram "so as to enable him to return by steamer."[14]

Perhaps Gilkison did wield some influence, for William A.'s leave was extended until October 1, as indicated by a telegram sent at the "order of the Secretary of War."[15]

• • •

But October 1 would be it. Thereafter William A. would have to be reposted. He remained in California for the time being. The local press paid close attention.

The San Diego correspondent for the *San Francisco Daily Bulletin* wrote,

> The *Pacific* brought down a large lot of freight for the mines in La Baja, and Capt. Winder, with some of the gentlemen who are interested with him in the mines at San Antonio and the Del Fino Mine [Delphina], which is near San Vicente [it was actually at Salada], has gone below by land. They intend to ship a large lot of ore and expect to make a great sensation. The roads have been extensively worked by Capt. Winder's company, so that between San Diego and San Vicente Mission, a distance of about 180 miles, there is a good wagon road.[16]

A San Diego reporter also writing for the *San Francisco Daily Bulletin* noted, "Capt. Winder has returned from below the line and goes up on the steamer to charter a vessel to take a cargo of ore from his mines near San Antonio and San Vicente. He intends to ship 500 tons."[17]

William A. could ill afford to stop his headlong dash to riches. He made a fateful decision.

San Francisco, Cal
September 10th 1866
To the Adjt Gen U.S. Army
Washington D.C.

General,

I have the honor to tender my resignation as a Captain in the 3rd Regiment of U.S. Artillery, to take effect on the 30th day of September 1866, and if accepted, I respectfully request the answer may be telegraphed to me at this place, care of R. H. Linton.

> I am Sir,
> Very Respectfully
> Yr obedient svt
> Wm A. Winder
> Capt 3rd Arty[18]

An inexorable process was set in motion. Not only was Winder's resignation letter received, it was submitted to and "approved by command of General Grant . . . and Secretary Stanton." There would be no Winders left in the service of any army.[19]

• • •

Less than one month later William A. sent a telegram from San Francisco to Brig. Gen. Edward Davis Townsend, the assistant adjutant general of the army.

At 1:30 p.m. his telegram of October 5, 1866, was received at the War Department.

To Gen E. D. Townsend, AG

I request permission to withdraw my resignation.

> Wm. A. Winder
> Capt 3rd Artillery[20]

• • •

If his resignation was successfully canceled, William A. would reclaim his captain's salary of $115.00 per month. Of course he would have been aware of army regulations in the matter of his resignation, regulations stipulating that as soon as an officer resigned, another officer of similar or lower rank would be appointed, but desperation trumped logic. On October 23 in a few short notes the assistant adjutant general, Lt. Col. John Cunningham Kelton, recorded William A.'s resignation as "successful" and forwarded Winder's telegram to E. D. Townsend. "Inform him," Townsend ordered.[21]

Winder was informed that his resignation was in effect, but he was not willing to accept his official resignation nor was he able to pay what he owed to Morse.

Breed and Chase insist that Morse—struggling with his mercantile business and with a great deal of money invested in the mines—must send them the money William A. owes.

San Francisco, Oct 5, 1866

Friend Morse,

Nothing new in regard to Capt Winder's business.

It seems now very uncertain when any money will be realized from it. All efforts thus far have failed. Capt is as full of promises as ever tho' I think not quite as sanguine. We have sent these goods which with previous amounts press very heavily on us. So we wish you to exert every effort possible to raise money. Remit to us every dollar you can collect, borrow or get hold of by return of steamer. And then keep collecting.

Very truly yours
Breed & Chase

P.S.

Don't pay out another dollar for the mines. Send all the money you can. B[22]

• • •

Without ill intent but in desperation William A. has broken their trust. He has tried and tried again to grasp and hold fast to the riches that are always just out of reach. Imagine him now, with the stench of failure trailing him through the streets of San Francisco, dropping in to reassure Breed and Chase that yes, he can be trusted, or avoiding them altogether, as he can only offer promises of payment. And on one of these nervous rambles it is probable that he has gone to his close friend, a San Francisco U.S. attorney and former judge who is a lusty, robust brawler and loyal to a fault to his friend Winder. Like so many others, Delos Lake believed in William A., stood by him throughout all his trials, went on record to affirm Winder's loyalty to the Union, and advocated his promotion and transfer out of California while suspicions swirled around him at Alcatraz. Now, with or without Winder's prodding, Delos Lake wrote to Stanton, "I have known Captain Winder for many years, and was fully cognizant of his official course and conduct during the war. I always regarded him as an excellent officer and a loyal gentleman." And there it was again—the story so often told of a loyal man, as though this very loyalty could trump all legalities, all regulations. "He is highly esteemed in this State, and especially in San Francisco where he is well known," Lake writes. "His restoration to the Army will be gratifying to the entire community."[23]

Although Delos Lake assured Stanton that the entire community would be gratified, that community surely did not include Breed and Chase. With a good measure of anger, they again demanded money from Morse:

San Francisco, Nov 30, 1866

Friend Morse,

. . . Nothing further from Capt. Winder.
<u>Send all the money you can by return of steamer.</u>

Very truly yours,
Breed & Chase[24]

William A.'s family situation now bears a question mark. With Abby surely aware of and pained over her husband's misfortunes, she does not come to him. Willie and Abby remain in Portsmouth. Any communications between husband and wife that might illuminate the decision to remain apart—perhaps about his unsuccessful attempt to return to army service or his fears that he will not be able to support them, given the unprofitable mining ventures—are no longer extant. The houses William A. and Storer planned were never built. Separated from his wife by a great distance, William A.'s marriage fractured. The year ends. He must try harder in the next.

• • •

As the new year of 1867 begins, poverty overshadows William A., like a circling raptor he cannot shoot or banish or pray away. From San Francisco on January 15, 1867, he writes to Pres. Andrew Johnson, telling him he had been "appointed a 2nd Lieutenant in the 3rd Artillery in 1848 for services rendered during the war with Mexico and continued in the service until the 18th of last October when my resignation was accepted."[25]

William A. perhaps wrote to President Johnson because he knew the president couldn't abide Secretary of War Stanton. President Johnson wanted to fire him but was met with fierce resistance from the more radical abolitionists, who wanted to see the former Confederacy punished further.

It was well known that Johnson wanted to go easy on the former rebels. Perhaps William A. believed that the Winder name would not fill the president with disgust. William A. boldly continued: "My resignation was tendered while under the impression that the Hon Sec of War was unfriendly toward me. I now respectfully request that my record may be examined by yourself, and if found to be satisfactory I may be permitted to recall it and be restored to my former place. Very Respectfully, Yr. Obdt. Sevt, Wm. A. Winder."

President Johnson was warring with Stanton and the Radical Republicans who wanted no easy reconciliation with the former Confederacy, no easing of the occupation of southern cities, and notably, new rights and protections for former slaves. So if Stanton wouldn't ease the way for William A., maybe Johnson would.

But because this request is Stanton's to grant, he must ask his permission.

The president's short notation on the letter is this: "Respectfully referred to the Honorable, the Secretary of War [sic], who will grant the petition if it can consistently be done. Andrew Johnson, President." But on the same document, Assistant Adjutant General Kelton added a "report," or a retort, that is, a tutorial on army rules to a president who clearly didn't understand this ironclad system. "The resignation of Capt. W. A. Winder 3rd Arty was successful," Kelton wrote, and it "took effect October 10, 1866. The vacancy has been filled by the promotion of the senior 1st Lieutenant of the regiment. Very Respectfully, J. C. Kelton."[26]

The door was closed, or so it seemed. But no one could or would anticipate the persistence of William A., the former captain—abruptly-turned civilian. Since 1846, when he was a civilian paymaster in the U.S.-Mexico War, and when he eventually donned a uniform and got his first rank, the army life was his life, however unwanted, however turbulent it was. Early on William A. had bowed to the will of his father and done what was expected of him. His father's final communication to him had ordered him to commit suicide rather than remain with the Union. William A. had turned away from his father and, however haunted, was his own man now. But hardship accompanied his independence. He faced setbacks in his family life, his military career, and his business. Something had to change.

• • •

He was on the move with Rosecrans by his side, far from San Francisco, far from Kelton's stinging rejection that he cannot get back into the army, far from the urgent dunning by Breed & Chase.

"When you see him [Winder] urge the necessity of getting some money," they plead. "We feel the want of it every day and all the time. It is a severe strain on us."[27]

They are unrelenting. If Winder could have paid, he would have. Morse couldn't not help either.

Friend Morse,

... Nothing yet from Capt Winder ... And now the old story. Send us all the money you can by return steamer, as we are in pressing need of it.

Breed & Chase[28]

Chasing copper and trains, William A. and Rosecrans go to Fort Yuma, then on to San Bernardino, California, a rough two-hundred-mile ride on the Butterfield Overland Mail stagecoach. During the war, San Bernardino was roiling with secret and not-so-secret rebel sympathizing bands formed to agitate and fight for the Confederacy if need be. By 1867 "the white males in the San Bernardino Valley formed a militia to eliminate the Indians from the mountains." Hundreds of members of the Serrano tribe were killed over a thirty-two-day period, "driven from their ancient homeland."[29] Into a city of strangers came William A., a man who abhorred the massacres and mayhem and ill treatment of Indians from the time he first served in Florida as a very young man.

Rosecrans and William A. are honored guests of a city that condoned genocide. So what might the Yankee general and the man not any longer entitled to wear his captain's epaulets do for the San Bernardians?

According to a news item, at "about 11 p.m. on May 13, the San Bernardino brass band serenaded the General at Pine's Hotel, where he was staying. In response, he made a short speech, endorsing the beautiful local valley and predicting the time when a railroad would come through and augment the local population and turn the area from waste lands to blossom like a rose."[30]

Talk of roses and railroads aside, while in San Bernardino William A. learned that "gold was found in the placers of Lytle Creek" nine miles from the city, "mainly in river terraces which rise 150 feet or more above the valley bottom."[31]

• • •

Here began another desperate quest for William A., and an uncomfortable, odd pairing arising from the lure of gold. William A. has partnered with Asbury Harpending, the former prisoner he had put in solitary confinement at Alcatraz, the leader of the rebel cell that had commandeered the privateer *J. M. Chapman* in 1863 in an ambitious but aborted piratical scheme to commandeer schooners and seize San Francisco's gold stores for the Confederacy. In 1865, unscathed and unrepentant, Harpending oozed north and made a fortune in northern California's "Havilah and the Clear Creek mining district . . . and laid out a townsite." He wound up with $800,000, and with these riches, Harpending became a mover and shaker in San Francisco, all before he was twenty-five years old.[32]

As a San Francisco real estate developer, mine owner, and railroad speculator who "employed General W. S. Rosecrans and a corps of engineers and began a railroad survey of his property in Sonoma," Harpending owned businesses that cartwheeled from west to east.[33]

With old hatreds temporarily tamped down, in 1867 the "Harpending Co., of New York, started a hydraulic mining operation . . . the first hydraulic mining site in Southern California and San Bernardino's most productive mine at the time." The operation used hoses and a nozzle to direct "high pressure water . . . pummeling the hillsides . . . and sifting the debris for gold." As an agent for Harpending's company (according to a vague contact signed on June 10, 1867), William A., along with "forty men, mostly Native Americans, raked the hillsides and unintentionally created an ecological disaster as the filthy water spurted through the flumes and flooded the farms below, contaminating the ground water and polluting streams." But there was a bit of glory if one ignored the ruined ground and horrified farmers, because for a short time hydraulic mining "produced as much as $2,000 a week in gold." Then torrential rains came and, with them, the end of the venture for William A.[34]

After the Lytle Creek failure, William A. settled briefly in Los Angeles, a city cradled by mountains and rapidly growing. The city beckoned to visitors, and people stayed, building homes and buying up the old ranchos. It was emerging as a regional metropolis rivaling San Diego. "Business, 'which used to come to San Diego, goes to the railroad & then to Los Angeles,'" was the smug retort.

How could a little burgh accessed by the occasional schooner or steamer with no proper harbor rival Los Angeles?[35]

The Central Pacific's "Big Four" financiers—Leland Stanford, Charles Crocker, Collis P. Huntington, and Mark Hopkins—made it happen. Having sewn up the railroad market in the northern part of the state, they then turned their attention south. Forming the Southern Pacific Railroad, they set their sights on Los Angeles, and its tracks reached that city in 1876, "thus creating a stranglehold on railroading in California."[36]

However, while bankers, magnates, and financiers are fighting for primacy in the railroad business, there are still no tracks laid straight to San Diego, in spite of the efforts of Morse's San Diego & Gila Railroad.

With his debt to Morse still unpaid, William A. writes with his usual optimism about an unnamed contact in Boston who has seen the copper ores from the Delphina Mine. "We must be certain to hold on. . . . I think the mine will yet sell for a good price. . . . I will leave no stone unturned to bring us safely out of our troubles," he writes in a faint, hasty scrawl. It was always about holding on.[37]

• • •

In Portsmouth, New Hampshire, amid a bulging household of motherless children and absent fathers, there was a wedding. After a long romance, Susan Boardman Goodwin married a navy lieutenant, George Dewey, on October 24, 1867. On December 20 of that year Sarah "Sadie" Parker Rice Goodwin Storer died of consumption. Sam Storer had left California and gone to Sitka, Alaska, inspired by Secretary of State Seward's purchase of Alaska from the Russians. There he hoped to make a political future and permanent home for his family. After Sadie's death, Sam Storer returned to San Diego, leaving the Goodwins to raise his six-year-old daughter, Mabel. Abby Winder was thus critical to her Portsmouth family, for she was chief caregiver not only to her son Willie but also to the other young children living in her father's house. Resuming her life with William A. seemed impossible.

• • •

In 1868, floundering and alone, William A. must make his way. He could not bring himself to go back east, however. Perhaps pride stopped him. Or was it something else? He may have felt unable to face Abby in defeat or to face Ichabod, whose faith in him was no doubt shaken, whose constant correspondence to help him seemed not to matter to government authorities. Perhaps he was simply too broken and haunted ever to return to the East? Had he done so, he might well have been sucked into a defense of his late father and his half brother that his Uncle William H. was busy arranging.

With his nephew Sidney still hiding in Canada, William H. proposed to Ulysses S. Grant that, if his nephew returned to the United States, it would have to be with the guarantee that he would not be harassed by military authorities. William H.'s long, rambling letter to the president was followed by yet another fervent defense of John H. Winder as being incapable of "inflicting wanton suffering on anyone." Grant forwarded William H.'s communication to Secretary of State William H. Seward, who did nothing about it.[38]

Despite his uncle's pleas, Sidney Winder remained in Canada until Pres. Andrew Johnson's blanket pardon on Christmas Day of 1868 "to all and to every person who, directly or indirectly, participated in the late insurrection or rebellion." Such persons would receive "a full pardon and amnesty for the offense of treason against the United States or of adhering to their enemies during the late civil war, with restoration of all rights, privileges, and immunities under the Constitution and the laws which have been made in pursuance thereof."[39]

• • •

William A. remained in Los Angeles. He formed a new partnership with yet another prominent figure, Col. Charles H. Larrabee, a Union veteran, lawyer, and politician from Wisconsin. Bad health had driven him to move west to California. Good land prospects helped as well. The *Daily Alta California* reported the particulars after the partners had been advertising for a few months: "Col. Larrabee and Captain Winder have established an agency at Los Angeles, for the purchase and sale of lands in the southern part of the state. Colonel Larrabee has served his country actively in the field in the late war and Captain Winder is most favorably known to our citizens for his faithful services."[40]

Their mission was to woo settlers south to San Diego, where land was plentiful, especially since a new community, known as New Town, had sprung from the dirt. Its founder, Alonzo Erastus Horton, a self-proclaimed "Black Republican" and antislavery defender whose religion was "Republicanism," was a determined visionary originally from Connecticut.[41]

Self-made, of varied and various occupations in colder climes such as the shores of Lake Ontario in New York State and the area of Lake Winnebago, in Wisconsin, Horton was a "basket maker . . . lumberjack and grocer . . . cooper [and] . . . a saw mill owner" who had eschewed "land rich in water and woods, but locked up in snow in winter." Now at the age of fifty-three, he'd come to San Diego on April 15, 1867, bedeviled with bad eyesight. When younger, he had been "warned that he had developed consumption and was advised to go West." Arriving in California, at La Playa, he saw the ruins of the original concept of a new town, "walked through a bush covered area," climbed a hill, and had a vision of a place where he "could look back on the long, curving bay, one of the world's finest harbors," idling and ready for a boom. Ephraim Morse agreed that this new city "must be situated in the same area where so many had failed."[42]

Horton asked the county clerk, George Pendleton, to see about "electing a board of trustees who could sell pueblo lands." Once arrangements had been made for such sales, "Horton purchased 960 acres for $265."[43]

William A. found his real estate business faltering in the face of Horton's monopolizing New Town enterprise. With not enough land buys to bring success to Winder and Larrabee's firm, his partner Larrabee moved on. Winder turned again to the mines. But a blurb in the *San Francisco Daily Bulletin* of April 14, 1869, stated that at Rosecrans and Winder's Delphina mine "there was not much copper to be had," just "a little copper stain in the rocks." The business of mining was no longer viable for Winder. He must move on.[44]

• • •

William A. decided to settle in Old Town. He had a plan. To ease the way with Morse and try to make him understand he could not pay him (though Morse too is crushed by debt), he wrote to Morse, saying, "I am going to tell you something which you will under no circumstances mention to a living soul for the present." He continued, "The whole delegation from this coast are pledged to get the Southern Atlantic and Pacific road through this winter . . . it is to run from here [Los Angeles] to San Diego. I am to have a good deal of say on the matter."[45]

Despite Winder's admonition to Morse not to tell a living soul about the railroad delegation and his bona fide promise that he would have a good deal of say on the matter, perhaps William A. was unaware that his secret was hardly that. The year before, many "living souls" would no doubt have been heartened and hopeful at the news of a "railroad meeting of the stockholders of the San Diego and Gila Southern Pacific and Atlantic Railroad Company," with Morse submitting the names of "thirteen stockholders for election as directors of said company."[46] This item appeared on October 10, 1868, in the very first edition of the *San Diego Union* newspaper. From 1860 to 1868 residents throughout San Diego had had to rely on the steamers or the overland mail to bring them newspapers, as there was no telegraph line to San Diego. It would be old news, yet new to the residents living in near isolation.

The *San Diego Union* was the creation of William Jeff Gatewood, a recent arrival in Old Town from Calaveras County, where he'd helmed the *San Andreas Register*. Urged by his brother-in-law Philip Crosthwaite to come south to be with family and with a desire to "do something for Old Town"—New Town's rapid growth was drawing Old Towners to Horton's bold enterprise—Gatewood found "quarters [on the Plaza] in a frame building belonging to Jose Altamirano. With an old Washington hand press and a very good assortment of type," he was in business.[47]

The "Editor and Proprietor" of the new *San Diego Union*, the first newspaper in San Diego since before the Civil War, was welcomed. Imagine the excitement that greeted the four-page Saturday weekly, costing "twelve and a half cents a copy, fifty cents a month, three dollars for six months, or five dollars a year." It was a

banner event, led by an editor of conscience whose mission statement to his readers promised that his editorials would always
remain neutral. "Neither political tirades, nor personal abuse will
find place in the columns of the *Union*," he wrote. He also assured
readers that his "influence shall be used in urging the people to
lay aside the animosities engendered within the last few years."[48]

The *Union* carried a mix of information on local events, such as
an announcement that there was a "meeting of the stockholders
of the San Diego and Southern Pacific and Atlantic Railroad Company."[49] (Morse was a stockholder.) William A.'s demand that he
keep the railroad business a secret was outed in this marvel of a
newspaper that advertised wares and services from San Francisco
but especially those available at Old Town. Need an attorney? See
William A.'s friend "Benjamin Hayes, Attorney and Counselor at
Law" at his "office on the Plaza." How about "all kinds of jobbing
and repairing done on short notice"? See "E. W. Nottage, a Tin
and Sheet-Iron and Copper Worker." A notary, a blacksmith, land
agents, notices of births and deaths, a bathetic short tale of a fish-
erman whose adopted child vanished into the sea and miraculously
returned, poetry, and advertisements for cure-all nostrums, such
as "Helmbold's Fluid extract Buchu . . . for the enfeebled, inconti-
nent and delicate," could all be found in the pages of the first edition of the *Union*. For those seekers of proper medical help, there
were two physicians in Old Town: D. B. Hoffman, "Office and
Residence on the Plaza," and Edward Burr, a graduate of Jefferson College, a "physician and surgeon to the County Hospital."[50]

Dr. David B. Hoffman, already a town icon, known for his
humanity and interest in mentoring other physicians new to the
profession, will play a large part in allowing William A. to realize
a lifelong dream that would spring to life in San Diego. With Los
Angeles and land sales failed and fading, he came back to the small
hamlet of Old Town. He cannot, he will not any longer endure the
dips and stutters of a life lived atilt—the suspicions, the failures,
the shame of his cursed kin.

1. Dr. William A. Winder.
Lithograph, 1886.
Courtesy San Diego
History Center.

2. Abigail Goodwin Winder, 1870. Courtesy Strawbery Banke Museum, Portsmouth, New Hampshire.

3. Former New Hampshire governor Ichabod Goodwin, 1880. Courtesy Strawbery Banke Museum, Portsmouth, New Hampshire.

4. Gen. John H. Winder, CSA.
Library of Congress.

THE NEW AMERICAN IRON STEAMSHIP "CHAMPION," OF THE VANDERBILT LINE.

5. The new American steamship *Champion.* Library of Congress.

6. Mission San Diego, 1856. Courtesy Pentacle Press.

7. Judge Oliver Witherby.
Oil portrait by William A.
Winder, 1884. Courtesy First
San Diego Courthouse.

8. Capt. William A. Winder (*center, left hand on cannon*) at Alcatraz, 1864. Courtesy Bancroft Library, University of California, Berkeley.

9. Alcatraz Island, with the old Citadel. Photo by Carleton Watkins. Courtesy Metropolitan Museum of Art.

10. Government-suppressed photo of Alcatraz, 1864. Courtesy Center for Sacramento History, Florence Markofer Collection.

11. The old Winder Building, Washington DC, built by W. H. Winder, 1860–80. Library of Congress.

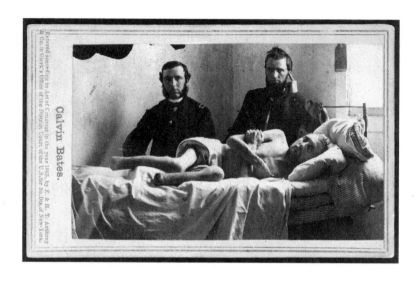

12. Andersonville prisoner Calvin Bates, late 1864 or early 1865. Library of Congress.

13. Andersonville prisoners receiving rations, August 17, 1864. Library of Congress.

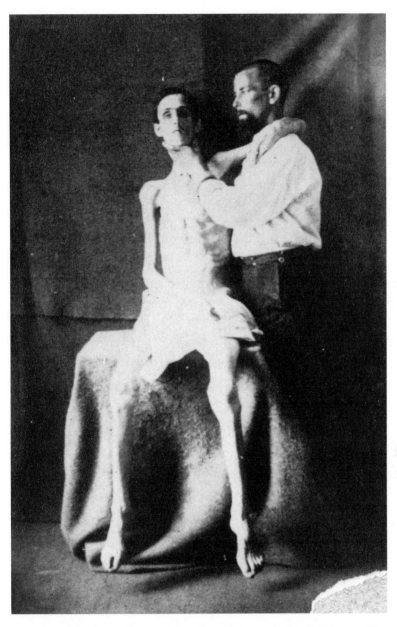

14. Belle Isle (Richmond) prisoner at the U.S. General Hospital, Annapolis, 1864. Library of Congress.

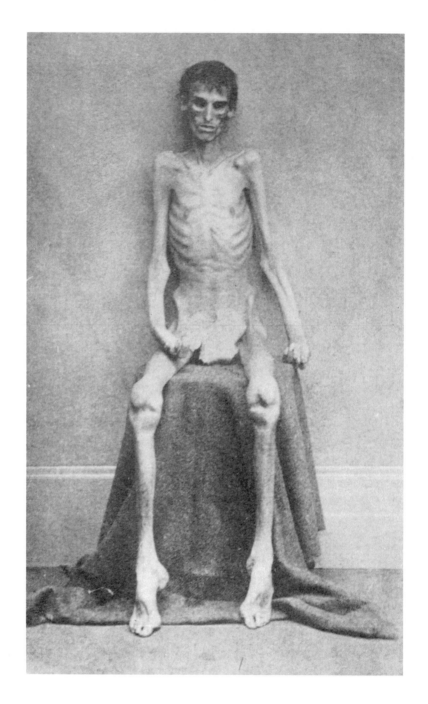

15. Belle Isle (Richmond) prisoner, 1864. Library of Congress.

16. Trial of Capt. Henry Wirz, the Andersonville jailer, 1865, Washington DC. Published in *Harper's Weekly: A Journal of Civilization* 9, no. 460 (October 21, 1865). Author's collection.

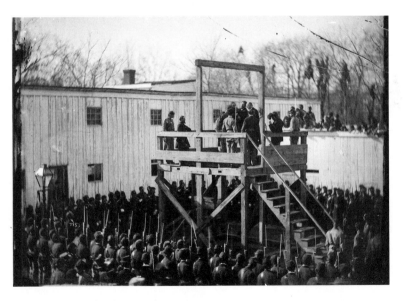

17. Capt. Henry Wirz's hanging, Washington DC, November 10, 1865. Library of Congress.

18. Crow Dog, slayer of Spotted Tail, Rosebud Reservation, 1894. Courtesy South Dakota State Historical Society, John A. Anderson Collection.

19. Gathering for the Fourth of July parade at the Rosebud Reservation, 1897. Courtesy South Dakota State Historical Society, John A. Anderson Collection.

20. Reading the Declaration of Independence at the Rosebud Reservation, 1897. Courtesy South Dakota State Historical Society, John A. Anderson Collection.

21. Men of the Brulé Sioux, Rosebud Reservation, 1894. Courtesy South Dakota State Historical Society, John A. Anderson Collection.

22. Old Town San Diego, 1869. Courtesy San Diego History Center.

23. Panorama of Rosebud Agency, 1889. Courtesy South Dakota State Historical Society, John A. Anderson Collection.

24. Panorama of Rosebud Agency, 1891. Courtesy South Dakota State Historical Society, John A. Anderson Collection.

25. Gravestone of William A. Winder, Proprietors Burying Ground, Portsmouth, New Hampshire. Courtesy Strawbery Banke Museum, Portsmouth, New Hampshire.

12

Heal Thyself

If one could blink through a stereoscope at an image of William A. Winder in the late 1860s, there would be no soldier there. Long gone is his captain's uniform. Gone were the epaulets, stored away in a tin box. He is a full-bearded gentleman in gentlemen's dress—a velvet-collared frock coat, a gleaming white shirt, a thin black tie. Blink again, and if he blurs, wait. You might see him in Old Town. Do not think the place is any less raucous than it was before the war. Picture it in daylight, a swirl of skirts with dirt spattering ladies' hems, for it is usually muddy or dusty in Old Town. Perhaps William A. boards for a night or a longer stay at the American Hotel, "on the South side of the Plaza," where there is a "bar stocked with the choicest wines liquors and cigars . . . a fine billiard table, where the Knights of the Cue can be accommodated at all hours of the day."[1]

There are still dog fights, bloody tethered bears torn by mastiffs, bulls gored for show, gunshots by night, and drunks, among them Judge Oliver S. Witherby. Ephraim Morse, a diligent diarist, witnessed the half-dressed judge stumbling along the plaza, past the courthouse, and then carried home semi-conscious, to preside the next day over the sentencing of a man whose name he'd likely forgotten.

"I never saw a man suffer from drink more after a spree than Judge Witherby," Morse had once written about the judge, "yet he starts in to get drunk just as deliberately and makes his preparations as quietly as though he was going on a journey. He had at one time a contract with Dr. Hoffman to attend him after his sprees for a certain sum each time, which he paid with perfect satisfaction."[2]

Despite his disapproval of such behaviors, the uncommonly fair

Morse rarely had an unkind word to say about any of his neighbors, reserving his occasional vitriol for the bigoted southerners, the so-called Copperheads who had caused his wife, Mary, to be driven from her post as a schoolteacher. Even William A., who has so disappointed him, does not come under withering personal fire. They are old friends. This is Old Town, where forgiveness is not an illusion.

On one of his trips to Los Angeles from Old Town—to close out his land business and be done with it—an observer could have followed William A. along the plaza and heard Alfred Seeley inducing travelers to take his stagecoaches to Los Angeles. Like a town crier he proclaimed, "Old Town is *the* town, the real San Diego!" One could walk a few steps to the point of departure for his "San Diego–Los Angeles line." Mind the mules and the mud, the drunks and the stray dogs, and step into the ticket office at the jewel of the plaza, Seeley's Cosmopolitan Hotel.[3]

Before Seeley purchased the building, it had been a crumbling adobe structure that was "once the finest residence in Old Town and host to all the famed personalities" who had been guests of the owner, Juan Bandini. Seeley saw profit in the ruin, bought the place, and added a wooden second floor of guest rooms. From the ticket office in the hotel, a traveler could buy a one-way fare for ten dollars and depart by stage from the Cosmopolitan any Monday, Wednesday, or Friday at 5:00 a.m., arriving in San Juan Capistrano at 7:00 p.m. for an overnight stay. At the tip of dawn, with the horse team refreshed and hitched, the travelers would make for Los Angeles, where the stage pulled in at 4:00 p.m. It was a rough trip in all weathers, with winter rains pelting passengers atop the stage or summer wind and choking dust blowing through the heavy canvas curtains. Before the railroad came, the steamer *Orizaba* was the only other way to get to Los Angeles. Grab a buckboard or, if lucky, a carriage and bump along seven miles to the wharf at New Town. If the sea was calm, the *Orizaba* could make it to Los Angeles in three days. As one local historian has noted, "Passengers paid from thirty to sixty dollars for a round-trip."[4]

Whatever his mode of travel, William A. would come back to Old Town, which was no longer just a stopping place for him. It would be home, or something like it. There he would try to heal and hope he would not be judged for his infamous kin, his failures, and his aloneness. And if the townspeople speak of the war to William A., their divided loyalties are now tamped down by a desire to make a life far from their pasts; he is among them now. Even the proud Yankee Ephraim Morse is forced to pay William A.'s debts of nearly $16,000 by selling some land and making up the rest in cash. Although Morse railed at William A. for the money he owed and told him of the betrayal he felt for having a fellow Mason break his trust, Morse knew Winder's failures were not his fault, knew he was at heart a decent man, one simply done in by desperation, gone to ruin in the tortured game of the mines. But they would not be neighbors, not at this time. After falling under the spell of Horton's New Town, Morse would soon sell his general store and move to New Town. Horton's mushrooming vision was drawing people away from Old Town. The merchants, saloonkeeper, and innkeepers were ready to do battle if their businesses were threatened. After all, the county seat was there and thus the property deeds; important documents were kept at the Whaley House. As long as Old Town had the *San Diego Union* and the everything-for-everyone hometown pride newspaper rooted on the plaza, perhaps there might not be a great desertion to New Town. That dream was soon dashed, but William A. had faith and stayed in Old Town. With no telegraph from San Diego to anywhere until 1870, William A. would have to be informed by a personal letter or newspaper item of an important event in the life of his eighteen-year old son, Willie. The *Farmer's Cabinet* in Amherst, New Hampshire, announced, "Hon. J. H. Ella, M.C., has appointed Wm. Winder, of Portsmouth, a grandson of ex-Governor Goodwin, to a cadetship at the Annapolis Naval Academy."[5]

Willie's uncle, Lt. Cmdr. George Dewey, was a U.S. Naval Academy instructor at the time of Willie's admission. With no wars on the horizon, would his father be proud? Was William A., whose own father had unsuccessfully tried to get him into West Point? Young Willie, the son William A. had not seen since 1865, had apparently chosen a life at sea. Would he too face ferocious storms, the perils of which haunted his father? With no correspondence extant between them, Willie's wishes are unrecorded. At least, should he graduate, he would automatically be an officer, a captain, unlike his father, who as a civilian rewarded for an act of bravery during the Mexican War was only afterward made an army man, a second lieutenant. Would young Willie bring a measure of lost honor to his family?

• • •

William A., whatever honor remained to him, was determined to find a calling, to find his place. In 1869 "everything was booming in Old Town," the California historian Theodore Strong Van Dyke wrote many years later, as he looked back nostalgically at the tattered little enclave. With "twelve stores . . . some of them carrying large stocks[,] . . . fifteen saloons, four hotels, two express offices . . . besides being the county seat," there were also two "express offices," a courthouse and a Masonic lodge, which was as much a social center as a fraternal organization., In 1868 William A. had joined the Masonic Order of the San Diego Grand Lodge, Number 35, located at Louis Rose's home on the plaza. There among the leading citizens of the town was ritual bonding, fellowship, and, for William A., the future.[6]

With William A.'s year of cobbling together new life came news of Ulysses S. Grant's uneasy ascendance to the presidency. And news of a life ended. Winder's perceived nemesis, Secretary of War Edwin Stanton, died on December 24, 1869, serving as a reminder of a time when William A. was guilty only of being a Winder, of his premature resignation from the army, and of his self-imposed exile.

• • •

With past agonies suppressed or settled and with a new decade beginning, William A. was looking forward and was soon rewarded. Success in Old Town didn't require a long résumé or a command structure to defame, promote, or defend him. He is officially and firmly in place. He is home. William A. Winder is indelibly recorded in the 1870 San Diego census, in Old Town, which was designated "City of San Diego" while New Town was "South San Diego." When visited by the census taker—in this case, Assistant Marshal Ben

Truman—the occupants of each dwelling were asked to state their name and age as of their last birthday, as well as their occupation, place of birth, and value of real and personal estate. Winder lived alone, and his birthdate was given as "1829," curiously not his actual birth year, which was 1823. His occupation was "surveyor," with a value of real estate a surprising "four thousand dollars." This amount may well be wrong, as figures were often muddled. Census data were frequently and famously inaccurate. His "personal estate" was marked as zero. His place of birth was "Maryland" and a check in the box designating American citizenship, reserved for males only, affirmed his status. Perhaps Winder, at age forty-seven—and thus well into middle age—made himself younger. Or census taker Ben Truman misheard him.[7]

At the same time that Winder the surveyor was flailing and failing at land purchases in Los Angeles, the *San Diego Union* reported that he was going to be "appointed a Justice of the Peace" for the Township of San Diego. The job, unpaid and requiring no prior legal experience, was an appointment by the San Diego County Board of Supervisors. At the small Old Town courthouse, or other plaza sites so designated, petty criminals would be judged and sentenced, land disputes settled, and anything that might be arbitrated without a lengthy jury deliberation was usually handled by the justice of the peace.[8]

His appointment would become official by 1872, but for now, the *Sacramento Daily Union* noted, William A. and Old Town leaders envision tracks—railroad tracks—not across the country but between opposing camps: "The San Diego Bay Shore Railroad Company . . . proposed to build a railroad from a point in Old Town to a point in Horton's Addition, a distance of four miles. Capital: $100,000, in shares of $100 each. Directors: Levi Chase, S. S. Culverwell, E. M. [sic] Morse, Wm A. Winder, W. Jeff Gatewood, J. S. Manassee [sic], and George A. Johnson."[9]

There were obvious reasons to connect Old and New Town, though not to bond them irrevocably. Horton's Addition, the bold and increasingly successful brainchild of Alonzo Horton, was well under way. He'd opened the San Diego Bank, a theater, a building called Horton Hall, and the glorious "one hundred room Horton House Hotel . . . that held its gala opening on October 10, 1870." Rooms were "richly carpeted . . . with marble-top tables and washstands." From the rooftop cupola, a "360-degree view was breathtaking." Despite all the splendor and all the sweeping views, the community was still without a railroad and thus in relative isolation.[10]

And in that isolation the two towns go to war. When the "Board of Supervisors, upon petition of residents of New San Diego, ordered the removal of all county records" from the Whaley House and demanded they be sent to New Town, furious townspeople formed a posse, stationed armed guards to protect the records, thrust a large cannon into view, and refused to stand down.[11]

"Old Town has seceded . . . the watchword is 'Old Town Now and Forever,'" the *Daily Union* reported, joining in the fray.[12]

The battle was lost when after a long fight some members of the county's board of supervisors, the holdouts for Old Town, were replaced. "Old Town's Day was done," writes local historian Richard Pourade. Old Town was not in a state of total collapse, but in reality the primacy of the little pueblo, with its ruckuses, bold and brazen roustabouts, and uneasy loyalists, was diminished and, as a last slap, deemed unhealthy. New Town beckoned to consumptives and asthma sufferers, and lots in New Town sold, and sold for a song, as Horton's golden child offered hope and a sunshine cure in the open air, mild climate, and temperate ocean breezes, considered far healthier than the inland heat, sand, and dust of the musty and defeated old neighbor.[13]

Holding firm with his innate loyalty, William A. burrowed into Old Town in spite of the baleful forecast for the future of the place and began a new business on the plaza just before Christmas of 1870.

"Captain Winder, Agent of the Lower California Colonization Company, has issued 150 certificates to colonists who have located in different sections of the company's lands," the *Daily Alta California* reported.[14]

Soon William A. was appointed "Old Town agent for the Lower California Company."[15]

Another struggle against failure loomed with this colonization enterprise, but over the next few years William A. would define himself as never before and in a way that would not have been possible except in his dreams. At the age of sixteen he'd "shown a fondness for medicine . . . and began to study it, and fit himself for practice, . . . attending lectures with Dr. Charles Kraitzer in Philadelphia." He was now eager and ready to truly pursue a career in medicine.[16]

It was likely that William A.'s father had forbidden his teenage son further study and insisted he must keep banging on the gates of West Point, albeit with the tools of patronage and pleas, but admission did not result. And so it was that John H. Winder's aimless yet obedient boy drifted into the Mexican War and into a reluctant peacetime army career. So why then could not this son march straight to Richmond? As John H. Winder brooded and faded, the sights he'd seen weakened him; the piles of corpses at Andersonville, Blackshear, and Millen, the unremitting excoriations of the press and his own government's failure to ameliorate his overburdened state finally drove him into an apoplectic fit resulting in his death in a tent at the prison in Florence, South Carolina. If, consciously or unconsciously, William A. is defying that father whose molten rage at his son's allegiance to the Union pulsed even from the grave, whose alleged inhumanity caused such suffering and death, and though the many thousands of lost Union prisoners are beyond help, here is a chance; here will be many chances over the next decade or more for William A. to heal himself and others, one patient at a time.

Would William A. present himself as a well-prepared physician when in fact he possessed, at best, rudimentary medical knowledge? In his small chosen hometown would it matter to the ailing and indigent ready to welcome and seek treatment from a gentleman who hardly seemed to be a snake oil salesman like so many so-called medical men who roamed the West?

"This city is getting to be the paradise of quacks and imposters," raged the *San Francisco Daily Evening Bulletin.* "The distinctions in the public mind between educated physicians and pretenders appear to be well nigh broken down."[17]

Those real concerns were voiced in San Francisco, but what did it take to be a doctor—a real doctor—in San Diego? The San

Diego County Medical Society was formed in July 1870 to oversee professional conduct and treatments and to defame the many peddlers of nostrums, toxic herbs, and bogus bottled cures. And with "no national laws which regulated the medicine or training of physicians in early America," they strutted along the plaza brandishing murky liquids, sugar pills, bags of odiferous, often deadly potions promising restored manhood and eternal health, unlike those who were serious about trying to understand afflictions of the limbs, organs, and brains as best they could. But not all standards were high in an infant science that often defeated the most credentialed practitioners. Some of these practitioners were the product of "two-year diploma mills whose standard for admission was the student's ability to pay rather than his previous academic achievement." Such institutions offered only a limited curriculum of "anatomy, pharmacology and medicine," as well as surgery and "a minimal course in obstetrics . . . though [students] never performed a delivery . . . [and] many did not have the opportunity to observe one." Cadavers chilled by winter cold rotted in warm weather for lack of refrigeration and were usually plucked from a potter's field for a few coins and dissected during anatomy lessons. Summer dissections? Never. While some medical students would find a hospital where they could "continue their studies . . . the average western physician hung up his shingle" and presented himself to the town. Often the doctor boarded patients in his home or used local hotels, tents, and sheds until they could open a proper office. And there were horse-and-buggy house calls over rutted roads and thorny, impassable scrub. The doctor's medical bag was packed with "a stethoscope, some clamps and hemostats, obstetrical forceps, and a variety of bullet probing instruments" for prying shattered metal bits from a man or woman caught in a feud, a duel, a raid, a fracas, or target practice gone awry. They also carried poisons and poultices—"morphine, strychnine, caffeine, belladonna . . . and digitalis." For skin cancer, the doctor would "dip a gold wire into nitric acid," gouge out the wound, and wait. If it healed, the patient survived. If no healing occurred, "the cancer cannot be cured." Amputations for gangrenous limbs and compound fractures were common.[18]

Sundays were busy, nights were long, and kindness was a necessity. Unless the doctor was also one of the town drunks or wore too many hats (patients often couldn't pay, so doctors had to have other income), those lost and overwhelmed by illnesses they didn't understand and cures they could not uncork from a bottle saved some and lost others. In San Diego physicians would often rely on the timeless remedies employed by the gentle, abused, and randomly dislocated Kumeyaay and Cahuilla, the indigenous inhabitants of what became San Diego County. Native plants used by these tribes contained curative substances that could be extracted and used after boiling, grinding, or liquefying them and then ingesting the product or applying it topically. For example, the pulp of aloe vera was good for sores, sunburns, and insect bites. "Angel Hair (growing on buckwheat)" treated spider bites. A small piece of "oak apple" could be chewed to treat sore throats, black walnut tea was for stomach ailments, dandelion greens and horsetail stem tea were good for blood purification, rose petal tea could bring down a fever, and sage vapors and Yerba Santa could be used for asthma and to relieve congestion.[19]

There were other medical practitioners who eschewed the remedies that grew all around them. Dr. Edward Burr "came to San Diego from Oakland soon after the Civil War" and was coroner and county physician. He was a "doctor of the old school," a compliment it seemed, for when a smallpox epidemic threatened Old Town he sprayed travelers alighting from Seeley's stage with "some liquid from a small perfumery spray," the contents being unknown. There was Dr. George McKinstry Jr., a sheriff, dentist, surgeon, and former San Francisco businessman, as well as Dr. David B. Hoffman.[20]

The first request for Old Town resident William A.'s medical advice was noted in the San Diego Union when he was asked to "give an opinion on George A. Pendleton's health."[21]

It is not known what befell Pendleton, but William A. would have hurried to his side, as he was nearby. Whatever the ailment, Pendleton died in March 1871, one of the last holdouts for Old Town's rule among those who resisted the shift of economic and political activity to New Town. Seeking William A.'s opinion but not treatment indicates that some in the town knew this smart, gentle man had become not just a justice of the peace trying cases or a railroad dreamer (his Bayshore Railroad Company, begun in June 1872, was still in business) but someone with at least some medical knowledge. But until William A. was fully formed in this much-desired new incarnation, he retained his position as a justice of the peace. Further cementing him to Old Town, his appointment to that position becomes official and a point of pride as he waits for a chance to minister to patients and fights a legal battle with an old enemy and former partner—and wins.

The ever-zealous Asbury Harpending, late of the Lytle Creek hydraulic mining debacle and formerly William A.'s prisoner at Alcatraz, owes him back pay according to an agreement signed between the two men on June 10, 1867. Although Harpending found "the enterprise disastrous and unprofitable," for which he blamed William A., he still owed William A. more than $1,000. Suing the wily Harpending was a challenge. Ultimately William A., now working at an unpaid honorary position, is awarded a much-needed $1,500. Harpending, still a raging rebel and now also a swindler and rich San Franciscan, was once again defeated by his old jailer.[22]

• • •

Freedom, unconstrained freedom, is William A's to find and never lose again. He is a pioneer, a man who was sent west, eagerly returned east, and headed west again. Now he has stayed, finding prominence yet not prosperity, but that may come. It must come. He forms a society of hardy souls, men like him who had come to San Diego by 1853. Never mind that he did not arrive in California until 1854. He needed to plant himself, unconstrained as a charter member and founder of the proud Pioneers of San Diego Society right there in Old Town.[23]

In defiance of New Town, which promises prosperity for all, "Justice W. A. Winder and T. P. [Thomas P.] Slade, Esq., have removed their offices to Whaley's brick building [in Old Town]. They now occupy the rooms formerly used for Court purposes. No better offices in either Old Town or New San Diego than these!" The *San Diego Union* printed this boast before the newspaper is sold to

Douglas Gunn, an ardent Republican politician and literary pioneer, and relocates to New San Diego in a shocking defection but a good-for-business move.[24]

By mid-February in New San Diego the volatile, occasionally murderous Col. Cave Johnson Couts has summoned his friend William A. to New Town to treat his Indian servant, Juan, who is suffering from syphilis, or "syphilides . . . second stage," as William A. records in the first entries of a bill he will eventually send to the Couts estate. Whether poured from a bottle of bogus swill, swallowed as a pill, placed under the tongue, or rubbed on pustules that erupted all over the body, "miracle cures" abounded for the wasting venereal disease. Syphilis was a scourge, and treatments such as a tincture of mercury/quicksilver sometimes produced results, depending on how far the disease had progressed. Juan's fate is unknown. William A.'s bill for his care was sixty dollars, a hefty sum for what one would hope was decent care.[25]

On April 20, 1872, anyone in New Town, whether ailing, inebriated, or hale, who ventured to the top of the Horton House Hotel would have seen a "dense column of smoke rolling upward from Old Town," where fire left "the Business Portion of the Place in Ruins." The south side of the plaza was ablaze, the fire having been ignited by a defective or clogged stovepipe in the courthouse. As the inferno burned for hours, merchants dragged their wares, papers, and personal possessions away from the flames and into the middle of the plaza. In spite of the uncommon valor, pluck, brawn, and prayer of residents, noted the *Daily Union* reporter who'd rushed to the scene, "the flames had done their work when the Hook and Ladder Company, their sturdy dray horses dragging hoses and water barrels, reached the ground." Although thousands of dollars in damage was done to the wooden structures, and the thick-walled Estudillo adobe stopped the flames from spreading across the walkways to the north side of the plaza, no one was killed or even injured. What now of Old Town, half gone? It would be rebuilt, yes, but the last smoldering embers drove some stalwarts out of the place to settle in New Town once and for all. William A. Winder's office—away from the conflagration—was intact. And so was his fixed devotion to what remained.[26]

The year of the fire, 1872, was also an election year, and William A. has ventured into politics now that he holds a position as justice of the peace. On the national scene the Radical Republican incumbent president, Ulysses S. Grant, who is bent on securing the rights of the freed slaves, will be opposed by Horace Greeley, the curious, contradictory founder and powerful editor of the *New York Tribune*. Although always registered as a Republican, Greeley was at first supported by the Democratic Party in his presidential bid. Greeley favored Confederate amnesty and rejected the punitive efforts of the Radical Republicans. He had even posted part of Jefferson Davis's bond after efforts to try him for treason had faded. Greeley was the nominee of the split faction of the Republican Party, the Liberal Republicans. At the Republican convention in Cincinnati from May 1 to May 3, the Liberal Republicans put forward Horace Greeley as the candidate who best represented one of their most controversial tenets, that "universal amnesty will result in complete pacification in all sections of the country," as well as an excoriation of Grant as "deplorably unequal to the tasks imposed upon him by the necessities of the country, and culpably careless of the responsibilities of his high office."[27]

William A. stood with the Greeley supporters, at least temporarily. It was a conflicted ticket. Greeley's running mate was Benjamin Gratz Brown, a former governor and senator from Missouri. He was an ardent abolitionist who also believed in amnesty for former Confederates. If ever there was a Union man, it was Gratz, and he was credited with keeping Missouri from seceding during the war.

So what was behind William A.'s support for the Greeley/Brown ticket? "Judge William A. Winder," the *San Diego Union* reported, held a meeting at his "office in Old San Diego . . . to elect delegates to the State Convention . . . pursuant to a call of the Democratic County Central Committee."[28]

Might William A. have believed in forgiveness, in universal amnesty? For his family perhaps? Or was it a lingering resentment of Grant, who had stymied his attempt to obtain a twelve-month leave, thus resulting in his premature resignation from the army becoming permanent? Had William A. been given the leave he requested, it is likely that he would not have resigned at all. William A.'s anger at his treatment while serving the Union and his stymied attempts to fight at the front are matters of record. But because he left no communications that would have illuminated why he threw his support behind Greeley, what can be stated is this: William A. was not elected as one of the delegates who would attend the Democrat Convention in Baltimore July 9–10 (he did serve as secretary for the local Democratic committee). The Confederate Winders—uncles, half brother, grandmother, and aunts—all remained alive and embittered in Baltimore, so it would have been extremely awkward for William A. to have traveled there.

With his empathy toward Native Americans being a matter of record, it is tempting to speculate that William A. opposed Grant because of the president's well-known ill treatment of indigenous peoples—his demand that they be "civilized" and his order that their lands be commandeered by the federal government in the name of western expansion, which prompted mass slaughters of the warriors and the buffalo that sustained them. What is of record is the *Weekly World*—subsequently the *Daily World*—and its frequent coverage of William A. The *World* was a Democratic organ rivaling the Republican *Daily Union*. Its offices were in New Town. The newspaper began printing profiles and features about him in a series of lengthy, mildly gossipy articles about his adventure-filled life and his habits, with nary a mention of the Confederate family living and dead that still made news. For many years it was as though William A. existed apart from any painful associations. Clearly he wanted it to be so.

The *Weekly World*'s first article of note—an interview, one of several he gives an eager journalist—reports on a trip he has taken and expresses his concerns about the growth and prosperity of his adopted city. Under the headline "Wilmington Breakwater," the article reports that "Capt. Winder" has "arrived from Wilmington [San Pedro Bay] on the steamer *Pacific*. He says to us the breakwater does not seem to be 'nearly repaired.' Hundreds of feet, more or less, of ugly gaps, are visible to the passer-by. He fears our neighbors will find great difficulty in making a substantial and commodious harbor in the roadstead of San Pedro." If they could not get a railroad, he reasoned, then they should at least have a good harbor for anchor. Then it was on to San Diego and home.[29]

Oddly, this article refers to him as "Captain Winder," a title he no longer held and one he'd precipitously discarded, hurt and angered as he was by the unfair accusations that smeared his loyal tenure in the war. The press did that on occasion. It is odd, but it happened more than once.

Of William A.'s wry humor the same newspaper reported, "Dr. Winder, the other day, being on the witness stand, and hard pressed by attorneys to describe with great particularity the effect of a gunshot wound suggested that two lawyers might be taken out into the Court-yard and experimented with, that being a practical test and no loss to the community."[30]

The newspaper seems near to eavesdropping as it reports that Winder is buying and giving away land: "A beautiful young lady yesterday presented Dr. Winder with a lot, off hand, free, gratis, and for nothing. 'Can such things be and overcome us like a summer cloud'? We remind that young lady that this is leap year, and if she proposes to endow us with all her remaining lots, including herself, which we know is a 'good lot,' Barkis is willin'." The besotted reporter, clearly entranced with the young lady in William A.'s offices, likens her to a character in Charles Dickens's *David Copperfield* who is ready, eager, and "willin' " to marry.[31]

San Diego was willing, too—literally willing a railroad into being, with hope afresh for Winder and all residents of Old and New Town. In 1871 "Congress chartered the Texas and Pacific Railroad Company with former Senator John S. Harris of Louisiana and Thomas A. Scott as President . . . backed with the power and resources of the Pennsylvania Railroad, of which Scott was president."[32]

The towns celebrated, imagining "the screams of steam whistles," passengers arriving and departing; a new day—new life and energy—was coming. There would be prosperity and tourism— and a long wait.[33]

The months melted into the next year when, despite opposition from stakeholders in the northern part of the state, Congress authorized the Texas and Pacific Railroad Company to "build and equip a railroad from the Mississippi River to the Pacific Coast."[34]

Tom Scott himself was to come and bestow the town with a railroad once and for all. By August the place was in a frenzy as the steamer *California* slid into Horton's wharf, delivering "King" Scott himself "and his party of seventeen officials and aides" to a raucous reception.[35]

With promises, collections of bonds (from the sale of pueblo lands) thrust into his hands by eager San Diegans, as well as his own store of funds, why did Scott not finalize the venture and build the railroad? A few weeks later the *California* brought more of the railroad survey party. Another passenger aboard the steamer to San Diego was one most dear to William A.: his friend María Ruiz Amparo de Burton, the widow of Henry S. Burton. She had recently written a novel and wished to remain anonymous, but her relative anonymity would not last long. On September 21, 1872, the *Weekly Alta California* reported J. B. Lippincott's publication of *Who Would Have Thought It?*, calling it "a new sensation for the Public."[36] María Amparo Ruiz de Burton had not identified herself as the author for fear she would not be taken seriously, as English was not her native language, and "because everyone would then criticize the work."[37]

Also onboard the steamer *California* was a correspondent for the *Weekly Alta California* who was covering the much-heralded visit of a group of the Texas and Pacific Railroad party. He met María, whom he described as a "native Californian," and was taken by her beauty, which was of the "pure Castillian type, graceful nonchalant," and her form, features, and the "bright glance of her eyes." Smitten and tired of railroad chatter, he asked if she'd read the new book *Who Would Have Thought It?* After much prodding, Maria assured him that she'd read it. Finally she admitted she'd written the book but begged him to keep her identity a secret. Perhaps he would, but first he asked her to tell him her story, that of her life as the daughter of proud landed Spaniards, her marriage to Henry Burton, their time in the East during the war, when she met President Lincoln, "her associations . . . with the best society and with cultivated and intelligent people . . . and her claim to the Jamul Rancho in San Diego County . . . the recent recognition of her rights to the land," and the early death of her beloved husband. Still she demanded anonymity-as-authoress, but the correspondent told all and praised the work: "The book will be read with pleasure on this Coast at least, even though the sentiments contained herein may be considered contrary to received opinion."[38]

The novel featured the hypocrisy and latent racism of a New England abolitionist family when a dark-skinned girl was brought into their household. It also lambasted corrupt politicians and war profiteers. Satire and sadness over the wretched state of war and accusations of disloyalty roam the pages and echo William A.'s own difficulties. He was her dear friend, frequent visitor to Rancho Jamul, confidant, and ultimately a great help to her ailing son-in-law, Miguel Pedrorena, married to her daughter Nellie. She would write again. And William A. would be there.

• • •

Winder was very much present in Old Town with his medical practice, as was frequently reported in the local press. In September 1872 a barber employed in Old Town, "while riding a horse though the plaza[,] . . . was thrown violently to the ground striking on his head. Doctor Winder was called in and found that he was suffering from a severe concussion of the brain. The injured man had not recovered consciousness at noon yesterday and it is feared that his fall will prove fatal."[39]

The newspaper then reported that, with William A. at his side, "Antonio Ayon"— the injured barber—"was sufficiently recovered yesterday to speak. . . . His physician thinks that his chances for recovery are very good at present, although his condition is critical."[40]

Within the week after the accident the *Union* proclaimed the patient "Out of Danger."[41]

The *Weekly World* was also following the case and reported that "Dr. Winder, who attends Ayon, says his patient is convalescing."[42]

Although concussive injuries were often difficult to treat and required stabilization of the head and neck, as well as constant observation, most likely at William A.'s home in Old Town, his diligence is noted in the press. His patient recovers.

And Winder is also drawing, painting, and fascinating his

patients and a reporter from the *Weekly World*: "Dr. Winder declines to shake hands with us anymore. His lady patients all want to know how he gets his hands so black. The Doctor rushes into our office impulsively, extends his hand, and presto, our lead pencil dust is all over it. We are seriously thinking of hiring a boy to sharpen our lead pencils."[43]

Sometimes Winder's appearance in the local press was more of a gossipy squib: "Dr. Winder says that brandy and soda water are good for any ailment. He knows by experience."[44]

The local press continued to fan the hope that trains, courtesy of the railroad magnate Thomas Scott, would soon be rumbling down the tracks to San Diego, but it was reported that Dr. Winder might bring something even more precious to this arid land.

"San Diego has but two capital needs—a railroad and a liberal supply of water," the *Weekly World* reported. "To Dr. Winder, in large measure, it is owing that we have at length a certain prospect of a beautiful supply of water. That gentleman has not waited to the other day to inform himself of the needs of our city." The article then praised William A.'s "steady belief in the future" of San Diego. It seems that "Dr. Winder has been working for some weeks on his project and it is now a fact accomplished." He has formed a company whose "stock is divided into a hundred shares," all subscribed. The *Weekly World* offers this bit of background: "Some time ago the city granted the right of way to parties who projected a City Water Works," but they "neglected to avail themselves of the franchise." William A. and others have allied themselves to a new corporation." It was to "put down eleven inch mains. . . . They propose to draw their water from the bed of the San Diego River, and to carry it up from Mission Valley over the Mesa. Water in the needed amount may easily be obtained at a slight depth. . . . Proper machinery will of course be secured to pump it into the mains." A grateful *Weekly World* "hails the formation of this company, . . . the San Diego Water Works. . . . Its organization will be a monument in great part to the zeal and activity of an old friend of San Diego, Dr. Winder."[45]

And it was a monument, though the city struggled with systems of pipes, which saltwater sometimes infiltrated, and reservoirs.

Water had finally come, but still the railroad did not. And "the old friend of San Diego," the steadfast supporter of the city, the doctor of diligence, was elevated and written about; he had become a celebrated, admired fixture in the land of his chosen exile.

The *Weekly World* delivers a paean of sorts in the embellished, swirling language of the newspaper. It is simply intended as a portrait of William A., but as will be seen, even with allusions to intemperance, it is a paean nonetheless.

"Everyone in San Diego knows Dr. Winder," the article states. He is "a fine type of the old English gentleman. He belongs to an aristocratic Maryland family, but he is evidently descended from one of the thoroughbred English aristocratic families."[46] Note there are no mentions of his Confederate family. His history was well known, but the *World* kindly omitted any mention of it here, clearly not wishing to raise the specters of the dead or excoriate the living.

"Dr. Winder is a blonde," the reporter wrote as he marveled at William A. with a good bit of hyperbole. "He is just verging in the sere and yellow, but his shapely trunk has all the symmetry which shows that he must have been an Adonis in his younger days. A tradition of centuries of the Saxon race beams from an eye whose blue has been tempered, but not dimmed, by the progress of years and things. Just an occasional crow foot or two about the corner of the eye, indicates that the Doctor is not superior to the lot of man."

The reporter offers some of Winder's history:

> When the Doctor, many years ago, was stationed in Florida, he was a model of manly beauty. He was a soldier and bore the Commission of the United States. His eye was then a mass of liquid cerulean whose glance was potent with the impressible fair. A form which has now received from nature just a trifle of embonpoint, was then a miracle of lithe grace. The young army officer was in his element. The swamps gave him license to imbibe . . . and Word was sent along the line that the detachment commanded by Captain Winder had to advance towards Billy Bowlegs.

Chief Billy Bowlegs had refused to leave Florida, and he had survived massacres until his tribe was provoked by the army to rise up again in 1855. In addition, Chief Bowlegs was made to serve as an example of a subdued chief and brought to Washington DC.

The *Weekly World* continues William A.'s colorful story, much but not all of which is of record: "The commandant heard the proclamation with dismay. A swamp, nine miles in length, of unknown depth, lay on [the] way to the next post. . . . He says that for nine miles he waded through that water and that at no time was it lower than his mouth. It very frequently exceeded that height but never went below it. The water transit was bad enough, but the Doctor says the most aggravating feature about it was the alligators; they were continually darting between his legs and tripping him up." Despite the reptiles "he stomached his chagrin and worried through it. When the Doctor and his command emerged on the other side they felt very damp. . . . He tells us that his first command, in emerging from the water, was addressed to the Sergeant Major to detail two men to hold his legs. [His legs'] natural impulse, after being released from the weight of water[,] was to locomote on their own accord. An hour or two's firm exertion of the Doctor's will, assisted by the occasional friction of the orderlies, brought them to a proper temper."

The next creatures encountered were of the eight-legged variety:

The Captain now says that the leaves began to move. The luxuriance of the foliage in Florida, now that it was fallen, piled the leaves a foot thick, nearly. A universal rustling was observable all through the forest. The murmur of gently shaking dry leaves sent a lullaby through the air. It was a unique spectacle, and Dr. Winder was interested to the center of his sensibilities. He focused his gaze on the phenomenon and assures us that that wood was one collection of squirming scorpions, who, in flopping their tails, threw the leaves up into the air. This was too much for us. Everybody who knows the Doctor knows that he can't even go out nowadays to hunt without meeting any number of rattlesnakes.

The man who marched through dismal swamps in the East and faces rattlesnakes in the West is now about the business of bringing a sanitarium to San Diego, a much-needed place of healing, rest, and cure for those afflicted with all manner of lung ailments.

With tuberculosis wasting and killing huge numbers of patients, and because the actual cause of the disease was not known, it could only be observed that sick patients appeared to get better with good care in bright, clean places, in bright, clean air, which amounted to taking the "climate cure."[47]

Where better to bring consumption patients than San Diego? It seems, says the *Weekly World*, that "our fellow citizen [Dr. Winder] has enlisted the help of Dr. John Jay Smith" of Philadelphia, given him "authoritative information," and touted the benefits of the "climate, soil and temperature . . . as no place in the United States or Europe is better adapted for the establishment of such an institution." Prosperity would come with the sufferers: "within the next three years we have no doubt but that we shall have quite a number of those beneficial institutions." In another three years there would surely be a railroad to bring them by the carload. Surely.[48]

The year 1872 has been good to William A. But tragedy again enveloped his wife's family. Five days after Cmdr. George Dewey's wife, Susan Boardman Goodwin Dewey, gave birth to a son, George Goodwin Dewey, at Newport, Rhode Island, on December 23, Susan died suddenly of possible "complications of childbirth, or typhoid fever." She was twenty-eight years old. Abby's family took baby George to live in Portsmouth, and with few visits from his father, the boy grew to manhood in the Goodwin home. Abby, now even more precious and relied upon, remained in place, far from her husband. Her mother, Sarah, lamented over the death of yet another daughter, saying "I would have thankfully given my life to save her."[49]

• • •

Panic beset San Diego in 1873. The big banks were floundering, and it was "impossible to finance construction with private capital." The railroad monopolists were shrugging off San Diego as a terminus. William A., consumed in his profession as a physician, must focus on his patients.[50]

The *Daily* and *Weekly World* pay close attention to his movements.[51]

Intrepid as he is, William A.'s health is a matter of concern, however. "We are glad to announce that our friend Dr. Winder is rapidly recovering from his late severe illness," the *Daily World* reports. "We long to see his bonnie face once more in our sanctum." His illness is unknown, but over the next few years old ailments, rheumatism, and general debility become more apparent even as he paints for pleasure and peace.[52]

An out-of-town correspondent wrote, "I had the pleasure, in Mr. Franklin's store, of looking at an exquisite portrait of a lady painted by Dr. W. A. Winder, of your city. That man, in choosing to play military man and physician, has sacrificed gifts, which would have made him famous. The portrait is an interesting study and we never remember to have seen a more artistic realization of the hazel eye on canvass [*sic*]. The manipulation of mouth, throat and [illegible] would do honor to any portrait painter."[53]

The enterprising William A., still serving as a justice of the peace and of course as a doctor too, is now also announced to be "a real estate dealer," with an office in the "Hiscock's Building" at New Town.[54]

With New Town being promoted regularly and many new homes and new residents in place, all seemed promising. San Diego is "today the most active, enterprising, 'go ahead' town in Southern California," the *San Diego Union* raved.[55]

• • •

Raves, plaudits, and family pride surely accompanied Willie Winder as he graduated from the U.S. Naval Academy at Annapolis.[56] Abby and Willie's relationship was exceptionally close. She raised him well but coddled and adored him, this son of an absent father. According to Margaret Whyte Kelly, family matriarch Sarah Goodwin's biographer, "Abby traveled to Washington, D.C. and New York City on many occasions. Often Willie accompanied her on these trips. . . . Willie was a naval career officer, eventually attaining the rank of Captain."[57]

Willie Winder would indeed pursue his military career at sea.

Meanwhile his father would try to heal one of the richest men in Southern California: the irascible Col. Cave Johnson Couts. Forty miles from Old Town San Diego, the Couts family's Rancho Guajome is a vast property where Couts settled with his wife, Isadora

Bandini, and many children. Couts's heart was diseased, and as he weakened Winder attended him sporadically over a three-year period until he died of an aortic aneurysm on June 17, 1874. After treating Juan, the syphilitic Indian ranch worker, in 1872, Winder goes back to New Town to care for Couts. A house call by buggy over rugged terrain did not deter Winder as he traveled from New Town to the Couts rancho, tending to him as best he could with steady solace, hovering over his irregular pulse, and giving stimulants to quicken the pulse and doses of laudanum to dull the pain. A failing heart was not curable.

An accounting of Winder's treatment for Couts has been preserved. The original bill totaled $627.50, with a credit paid by the family or a discount given by William A. of $70.00, bringing the final amount due to $557.50:

July 21, 1873, one night visit & treatment of Colonel Couts—New Town, [$] 2.50.

August 6, 1873, visit and attendance on Mrs. Couts [ailment unknown] at Rancho for six days: [$] 60.00, mileage [$] 40.00.

November 19, 1873, Visit and attendance on Colonel Couts at Rancho—$80.00, eight days. Mileage, [$] 40.00.

March 22, 1874, Visit and attendance of Colonel Couts at Rancho, Six days, $60.00. Mileage, [$] 40.00.

April 25, 1874, Visit and attendance of Couts at Rancho, six days, [$] 60.00, mileage, [$] 40.00.

May 10, 1874, Visit and attendance on Colonel Couts in New Town, [$] 5.00.

June 11, 1874, Attendance day and night for ten days on Colonel Couts in Newtown, [$] 200.00.[58]

Because the Couts case went well into 1874 and the itemized bills are the only extant record of what William A. charged for his services, we must step back to 1873 and see that, although his physician's bag is always at the ready, filled with poultices, instruments, salves, and nostrums, William A. has found a new cause to pursue.

• • •

Although he has led a varied life to date, Winder will now heed the shrill call of Newton Booth, a former California state senator of California and now Republican governor of the state. Booth has formed the People's Independent Party, or the Dolly Vardens. During his time as governor "his administration advocated sufficient protection for the Chinese already living in California, but stressed restrictions on further Chinese immigration." Booth's Dolly Vardens consisted of what one observer called a mix of "soreheads from any party or by any name," and their name allegedly derived from a "calico pattern of the time composed of many different colors and figures" or, as some said, from the name of a character in Charles Dickens's *Barnaby Rudge*. "With their support Booth was elected to the U.S. Senate."[59]

This was certainly a reform movement. Its platform included things like antimonopolies, a limit of one presidential term, and, as Booth decreed, opposition to Chinese migration to California. The number of delegates from each California county depended on the number of voters registered in that county. San Francisco had forty-six delegates, for example, and Sacramento had ten. They were the two largest counties. San Diego (the Eighteenth Judicial District) had two delegates: William A. Winder and David Hoffman. Thus began the organization of the People's Independent Party of San Diego on September 25, 1873, in Sacramento.

As this broth of dissatisfied breakaways vied for attention, panic beset San Diego. As one local historian notes, "on September 13, 1873, the bottom fell out of the stock market in New York. It was 'black Friday.'"[60]

With the crash, Tom Scott, the Texas and Pacific Railroad president, also crashed. Scott had promises from Paris bankers to market $54 million in railroad bonds. He was vacationing in London when the "French brokers tried in vain to reach him to complete the deal." It was too late. With the "American economy on the eastern seaboard in wild disorder," the French financiers abandoned the effort. Scott was ruined. Then flooding rains came to San Diego, and what tracks had been laid were washed out, as was the promised railroad. Soon "the population of San Diego began to decline." Even Alonzo Horton lost heart and sold off parts of New Town, his pride and joy.[61]

Hopes were fading and the city drowning as the holidays approached. But it was not so glum a time for William A. He receives a great gift around the time of his fiftieth birthday on December 5. His wife and son, now an officer on the *Independence*, will visit, if only for a few days. On December 17 the *San Diego Union* reports that "Mr. Wm. Winder, U.S.N., son of Captain Winder, who has been visiting his father in this city, left for Mare Island station yesterday. We hope to meet him again."[62]

Off they all went to San Francisco to settle Willie at Mare Island. By December 18 William A. and Abby were heading back to San Diego, but she returned to San Francisco before Christmas to begin the long journey home to Portsmouth. The *San Diego Union* edition of December 23 recorded that the "passengers per [disembarking from] the *Orizaba* included W. Winder and wife."[63]

The brief reunion is a fleeting portrait of the Winder family, captured as though through a fractured lens. The fragile photo shimmers in uncertain light, fades, and darkens.

13

The Lone and Goodly Doctor

With Abby at sea on her way back to New Hampshire and Willie at Mare Island in San Francisco Bay, waiting to be sent who knows where, the *San Diego Union* mentioned that "Captain Winder has been unwell for several days." He is alone and sick. Again.[1]

But by March, as was earlier noted, William A. is back on his feet and busy caring for Cave Couts, which he will do until Couts's death.

With patients to attend to in both Old and New Town, "Dr." William A. Winder has taken an office in the Hiscock's Building in a prominent business area around Horton Square. In all, there are nine physicians, a homeopath, a druggist, and two dentists.[2]

One might assume that the number of people getting medical treatment and the number of practicing physicians worked out to a small patient load for each. One case that went to Winder was the result of an accident. According to a news report, "James P. Jones, who keeps a bee ranch[,] . . . was seriously injured by a premature explosion of a blast while engaged in removing some rocks. A portion of one of his hands was carried away and the forearm was fractured." Jones was hurried to New Town, where "Dr. Winder assisted Drs. Remondino, Fenn and Gregg" in the amputation of the forearm.[3]

This is the first known record of William A.'s experience with what was a regular and all-too-common occurrence at his father's prison at Andersonville: any gangrenous, broken, or infected limb was hastily removed by often indifferent surgeons. In San Diego the doctors attending Jones, hardly indifferent, may have had no other choice.

By 1875, when William A. was already practicing medicine, hard times in his city had hardened to desperation. The citizens of San

Diego, steady dreamers who had been intoxicated by the promise of the railroad, felt their ardor dampened as "the depression
rolled across the country and slowly settled on California. With
many banks in trouble . . . a run started on the Bank of California. . . . Waves of frenzied people pounded on the closed doors . . .
and demanded their money" as bank president William Ralston
"waded into the ocean, and died." Half the population of New
Town—grown in seven years to "4,000 . . . dwindled to two thousand." Their departure left developer Alonzo Horton deeply in
debt. "He had built a town, but not a city," and if the railroad ever
came, he might not be alive to see it.[4]

The men and women who remained looked elsewhere for income:
to bees and beekeeping, to sheep raising, to mining mirages, anything. There was the Minerva Gold Mining Company, "to operate at
San Rafael in lower California." Minerva stock went for fifty dollars
a share, and Winder was a director of the company, whose "place of
business would be in the city of San Diego."[5] It was another failure
in a failing year, one in which gold values were steeply declining.
According to a government report on mineral resources, "none
of the mining operations have proven permanently profitable."[6]

Also not permanently profitable was Winder's medical practice.
Likely experiencing a dearth of patients in this time of economic
drought, he had been one of the few respected doctors practicing
in San Diego without an official license. In 1875, however, he seems
to have received a diploma from the Keokuk College of Physicians
and Surgeons, located in Iowa.[7]

This diploma is something of a mystery. A close look at the
Keokuk Daily Gate newspaper from the time William A. might
have been there does not have a record of him in any of the numerous lists of graduates. Was it favor, a connection to someone who
must have made possible this important event? But there it was,
in his hands, a medical degree and not a moment too soon, for
in 1876 "the legislature passed 'An Act to Regulate the practice of
medicine in California,'" as a way to weed out the pretenders, the
charlatans, quacks, quick-cure hawkers, and their like. "Holders
of diplomas from recognized medical schools were admitted automatically; other applicants were given an examination." Winder

would present his Keokuk diploma to the medical inspectors, so no examination was necessary.[8]

There is further press coverage of another of William A.'s cases, one that came about when "a serious accident befell Mrs. S. W. Craige" [sic], the wife of the Horton House proprietor, when she ventured out onto the roof, fell through an "open skylight," and tumbled "a distance of sixteen feet" to the ground, "being rendered insensible from the fall.... Dr. Winder who was summoned, raced to her side from the Chollas Valley, a distance of four miles, in the extraordinary time of eight minutes." The *San Diego Union*, knowing that the patient was in critical condition during the day, "was glad to learn her condition was better by the evening."[9]

Another fall brought out Winder again. The ailing wife of *San Diego Union* publisher W. Jeff Gatewood had fallen from a fishing boat at "the end of Culverwell's wharf" and nearly drowned before she was finally pulled from the water. "Notice was sent to Dr. Winder, who, with Dr. Stockton, attended to the case. At last accounts, Mrs. Gatewood was doing well."[10]

Also doing well was a fast sloop named the *W. A. Winder*, which was reported to be taking part in a multiday celebration of the Fourth of July in San Francisco. According to the *Daily Alta California*, at "the annual Regatta of the master Mariners Benevolent Association" the race began on "a fine day," with "a good breeze and good sport." At one o'clock the piers and shipping were alive with spectators to witness the event. The decks of the steamers were crowded with excursionists, all eager to herald the anniversary of "our glorious republic ... dedicated to humanity forever ... and a lasting peace" after "the fiery serpent crept down the trail of the ages ... swift and awful war was the result." Racing along to cheers with "forty-one other entries" was the *W. A. Winder*, skippered by Nels Anderson. At half past one the gun was fired from the Pacific Street wharf, and they were away. It was a twenty-eight-mile course, with the *W. A. Winder* making it in a little more than three hours.[11]

Racing sloops aside, in September William A. departed for Los Angeles to receive a "contract from the War Department to attend the Military personnel [in San Diego] ... who may require treatment."[12]

This contract, ultimately unrecorded, was not given to William A. Worse still was news that the Southern Pacific Railroad, now permanently linking San Francisco to Los Angeles but not San Diego, had dampened hopes for a flow of new arrivals to William A.'s adopted hometown. "Her only rival [Los Angeles's] is, or was San Diego," the *San Bernardino Guardian* sneered, "and the fates seemed 'down on' that ambitious little burgh."[13]

But there in that once-ambitious little burgh is Dr. Winder, now licensed yet facing financial instability. Putting pride aside once again, he writes to Alexander McConnell Kenaday, secretary of the Association of the Veterans of the Mexican War, in Washington. In doing so, he was reaching back into his own history, to the war that had made him an army officer, a war whose spoils included California, the land of his self-imposed exile. Couched in his request for a badge awarded to those who'd served in that war was a plea.

"Dear Sir, I served in the Mexican War, first as a paymaster's clerk, and was appointed a 2nd Lieutenant in the 3rd Artillery before the war closed," he wrote. This was not entirely true, as William A.'s appointment came shortly after the war, but it made for a good argument. "Now I wish to obtain one of the badges given for that war, and any other advantages growing out of it." What advantages would be gained and how could they help him out of his financial straits? Here then is the true request:

> Will you do me favor to tell me how to proceed, and whether I am entitled to any of the privileges to be conferred upon those who served? I resigned as a Captain of Artillery at the close of the late war, is there any [illegible] by which I could get back in the army, and then go on the retired list. My military history can be had at the War Dept, and I am suffering from bad health induced by exposure while in the service, of course I will pay all necessary expenses.
>
> Respectfully, yr obdt sevt,
> Wm A. Winder[14]

William A. hoped his request would appeal to Kenaday, a Mexican War veteran. Like William A., Kenaday had performed on impulse and with heroism. At the Battle of Churubusco he particularly distinguished himself by unloading gunpowder from a burning weapon.

Kenaday forwarded William A.'s letter to the War Department. By May 13 the request had been received. On May 27 Adj. Gen. Edward D. Townsend, who was well acquainted with William A.'s history, responded to Kenaday.

"Sir: In reply to your note . . . calling attention to an inquiry of Captain Wm. Winder late of the 3rd US. Artillery as to whether there is any way by which he can be restored to the army . . . , I have to inform you that he could only get back by a special act of Congress, or by appointment as 2nd. Lieutenant by the President and that even then his retirement would depend on the result of an examination in accordance with the law by an Army Retiring Board," Townsend wrote. As an afterthought and to further stymie this request, Townsend scrawls in dark ink across the page, "I may add that . . . it is not customary to restore officers or to appoint persons physically disqualified." The bad health Winder has disclosed closes the door. But a crack remains (a presidential okay or an act of Congress), one he will attempt to open again and again.[15]

• • •

With the election of a Republican, Rutherford B. Hayes, to the presidency—a then-noteworthy contest, as Democrat Samuel Tilden won the popular but not the electoral vote, the occupation of the former Confederacy by Union troops ended and Grant's sway over the country and over army matters also ended. In the year to come Old Town will host the Democratic county convention with "seventy-four delegates present."[16]

William A. will be nominated for the office of county coroner as a Democrat and ultimately lose to the Republican opponent, Dr. Charles Fenn. This defeat meant the loss of a salaried position. Nothing in the record indicates that William A. was ever anything but a Republican, a Lincoln Republican at that, though voter rolls for the years he dutifully registered gave no party affiliation. This brief Democratic turn was a run at opportunity.

Although the coroner's post was lost to him, there are still patients who need him. William A. rushes to an emergency in which a young child suffered a serious injury from either a rock thrown or a shot from a pellet gun aimed at her. "Dr. Winder was called to attend the little sufferer, and found a deep jagged wound two inches long extending across the knee," the Weekly Union noted, damning the dangerous so-called "nigger shooter," a contemporaneous term for the pellet gun that had presumably caused the injury. The child, though scarred and in shock, had her bleeding stanched and her knee wound closed with silk thread, and she recovered. So must William A., reeling from disappointments, but at the ready with his doctor bag and his devotion. As the summer slumps into autumn and then winter, his rheumatism worsens but not his will. Never his will.[17]

• • •

Barely has the year 1878 begun when a small but determined band of California notables acts in support of a highly regarded and unimpeachably loyal former army officer's desire to be reinstated in the army. From Sacramento comes California state senator John W. Satterwhite asking on William A.'s behalf for former California governor Frederick Ferdinand Low's help.

"I understand that Capt. W. A. Winder is desirous of being reinstated in the army," Satterwhite writes, "and that you [Low] are making an effort in his behalf to that end. It affords me great pleasure to endorse any application you may make on behalf of Capt. Winder." Low knows "somewhat intimately Capt. W. when an officer of the army"—Low was the collector of the port at San Francisco during the Civil War—"and I hazard little in saying that the army never had a more accomplished, competent and brave officer."[18]

Upon the heels of this correspondence came a signed petition sent from Sacramento to Pres. Rutherford B. Hayes: "The Undersigned, members of the Legislature and citizens of California, respectfully request the reinstatement of Wm A. Winder, late a captain in the 3rd Regiment Artillery. Captain Winder served some eighteen years in the army, having received his original appointment for services during the Mexican War, and during the late war . . . he held the command of the most important post (Alcatraz) on the Pacific coast, giving entire satisfaction to his superior officers as well as the citizens of the State." Surely the petitioners well knew of the accusations of disloyalty Winder had suffered, but it seemed to Sen. John W. Satterwhite and several others that the war and its agonies were past.[19]

The letter expressed pride for what had been an exhausting test of endurance for William A. during his command at Alcatraz. Now he was filled with regret at his hasty, emotional resignation from the army. William A. is clearly in financial distress, as evidenced by a letter sent to him by Ephraim Morse. William A. was once deeply in debt to Morse and has apparently appealed to him again for a loan. Time has passed, and Winder has had to swallow his pride and beg for funds. How Morse responded to this request is at once startling and moving.

"Dr. Winder," Morse writes, "I would accommodate you with pleasure if I could do so, but I have not the money." This should have been enough, but Morse goes on. "Four or five years ago, I b[r]ought a large amount of money from the East—left me by my father—and today it hardly yields me income enough to pay my expenses. . . . I hope better times are in store for us." He regrets not being able to lend William A. any money. They are two men who have weathered distrust, disappointments, fire, the demise of their beloved Old Town, and a depression.[20]

The parade of petitioners continues.

Senator Satterwhite has written to Peter Dinwiddie Wigginton, a member of Congress from California: "Dear Sir, Dr. W. A. Winder wishes to be reinstated in the army and at his request I have procured the written recommendations. Winder is a resident of San Diego and wishes me to forward the papers to you and request that you present them personally to the President."[21]

Immediately, Wigginton wrote to President Hayes: "I enclose applications of Dr. Winder for reinstatement or appointment to [a] position in the Army together with recommendations of Ex Gov. Low of California and Senator Satterwhite of that state. Asking your attention to the matter and such reply as you may deem proper in the business. Very respectfully yours. P. D. Wigginton."[22]

Perhaps these communications are crossing in the mail, as William A. doubles down in his efforts to gain reinstatement in the army so that he could retire with a military pension. He writes to Wigginton, reminding him that he has "forwarded some papers requesting the President to reinstate me in the army. . . . I request that you give me your personal assistance in this matter." William A. details his service yet again, saying, "Before leaving Washington I called on the President [Lincoln] and stated my case that being of Southern birth my loyalty might be suspected." Lincoln, he said, "fully appreciated my position and considered my allegiance to the government" and the Union. When William A. assured the president that he would "perform my whole duty to the best of my ability . . . he [Lincoln] expressed himself perfectly satisfied and I did do my whole duty although I did find that I was an object of suspicion to the radical so called loyal citizens of San Francisco, who applied to General Wright to remove me from the command of Alcatraz, for no other reason than that of my Southern birth." Wright asked these unnamed citizens "for charges, but as they had none to make," William A. wrote, "he declined to make the charges." Winder wrote all this to explain why he had resigned. "My pride compelled me to resign, since which time I have been unfortunate in business . . . and would like now to be reinstated, or get some other appointment of equal grade. . . . I trust that you will pardon the liberty I have taken."[23]

As he waits for answers over the hot, dry summer, the *Los Angeles Herald* reports, "The friends of Dr. W. A. Winder in this city will regret to learn that he is lying very ill at his home in San Diego."[24]

• • •

The year 1879 finds William A. at his easel, engrossed in his oils and brushes, pots of watercolors and graphite. It is an avocation that began when he was a young man, and now, as an older man with stiffening hands, he is making art again, and doing so with singular determination. He is painting a group portrait and gratefully acknowledges his friend Alfred Henry Wilcox's gift of a canvas, something he could not otherwise afford. William A. is painting a "camp scene" and needs a "small photograph" of Wilcox to complete the painting. They are two men of the same age.

One is a struggling doctor, a man who paints for personal peace, while the other is a former sea captain, Colorado River explorer and pioneer, the owner of a steamship line, and a wealthy man whose image William A. will fix forever on this gift of a canvas. "How am I ever to repay your acts of thoughtful kindness I cannot now see," he writes, but he also assures Wilcox that he will somehow "manifest his gratitude."[25]

In a postscript to the letter that suggests perhaps Wilcox has suffered with a common and painful condition, William A. writes that he is seeking a device with "Galvanic Faradic batteries. . . . I wanted one with which I can remove piles." For those patients willing to endure electrical current sent through a two-celled battery through a wire to an inner or outer hemorrhoid with the hope that the offending mass might be excised, this practice promised relief.[26]

William A.'s lingering ailment was not medical but financial and sent him back to what has become a tireless pursuit: yet another request for an army reinstatement. This time he sent his request directly to Pres. Rutherford Hayes.

"Sir," he writes, "sometime since I made an application to be reinstated in the army, that application failed, I now enclose a slip cut from a paper by which you will see how officers born in the South whose idea of loyalty induced them to sacrifice all personal feelings and remain in the service of the government, were looked upon by people generally, and how the lamented Lincoln looked upon them." He notes that he served eighteen years and "until the close of the war, I experienced the same treatment but had no General Steedman to speak for me." William A. then refers to an officer, a Major Wyse, "formerly of my regiment [who] has been restored as Lieutenant Colonel and placed upon the retired list. The Major resigned about the commencement of the war, am I then not entitled to be restored with the rank of Major, and am I asking too much when I ask your kind consideration." William A. "trusts, sir[,] that you will pardon this direct application, but I have no political friends, and therefore determined to apply directly to you." He reminds President Hayes that "my case has, I believe[,] been laid before you, therefore any long statement is unnecessary." William A. asks that the president might "consider this application as confidential, in case that you cannot comply with the request."[27]

William A.'s mention of Gen. James B. Steedman is likely a reference to "How Lincoln Relieved Rosecrans," an article that relates the story of how President Lincoln summoned Gen. James Blair Steedman to the White House. The president, disappointed and troubled by General Rosecrans's performance in the field, asked Steedman, "Who beside yourself . . . is there in that army who would make a better commander?" Steedman had just defended Rosecrans, and though momentarily stunned by the president's question, he "promptly" answered "Gen. George H. Thomas." The president agreed that Thomas would indeed make a better commander but added, "Mr. Stanton is against him, and it was only yesterday that a powerful New York delegation was here to protest his appointment because he is from a rebel state, and cannot be trusted." Steedman replied, "A man who will leave his own state [Thomas was a Virginian], his friends, all his associations, to follow the flag of his country can be trusted in any position to which he may be called . . . that night the order went forth from Washington relieving General Rosecrans of the command of the Army of the Cumberland and appointing Thomas in his place."[28]

With William A.'s pointed reference to this startling article in his rather presumptuous letter to Hayes, the recurring theme of Stanton's distrust of southern-born officers and his ongoing refusals to reinstate William A. in the army fixes direct blame on the war secretary and not on the military rule according to which once one resigned, one was always replaced by an officer next in line.

• • •

If there was ever a thought or hope that William A. would ever see his brazen, zealous uncle William H. Winder, any possibility ended with his death on October 18, 1879, at the age of seventy-one. The lifelong bachelor, embittered by his years of struggle to clear his brother John H. Winder's name, died "at his residence in New York of an affliction of the heart, a sickness of two weeks," and was buried in Baltimore's Green Mount Cemetery, the final resting place of famous and infamous Marylanders, among them John Wilkes

Booth. Noting William H. Winder's arrest, though not mentioning his secessionist adherence and anti-Lincoln stance, of particular irony was that the article announcing his death noted that the Winder Building, his singular building achievement in Washington DC (purchased by Secretary of War Jefferson Davis in 1854 for $200,000), was later occupied by the Union government "for the War Department's use" during the Civil War.[29]

Known at the time as "Winder's Building," the seventy-five-foot tall structure had 130 rooms. "At the time," one source notes, "it was the largest and tallest office building in the nation's capital. Among the government offices it housed were the Navy Bureau of Ordnance and Hydrography and the Navy Bureau of Medicine and Surgery." It also housed the Quartermaster General's Department, which, "under the capable direction of General Montgomery Meigs, led the massive effort to supply the Union Army from the offices in the Winder Building." Toward the end of the war the Bureau of Military Justice, helmed by Judge Advocate General Joseph Holt, the fervent and vengeful prosecutor of the Lincoln assassination conspirators, headquartered there.[30]

• • •

If William A.'s uncle knew that his nephew was a doctor, a highly regarded one at that, might he have had a jot of pride, a jot of forgiveness for the young man who studied medicine and pined to practice?

William A.'s last recorded treatment of a patient, at the end of 1879, was noted as follows. He wrote a letter to a Los Angeles physician, Dr. Henry Worthington, who was visiting San Diego and told him he has been "unexpectedly called to go into the country." He begs Worthington to see "my friend and patient Capt. [Alfred] Wilcox, who has Ballenitis and threatened Paraphymisis." William A. is referring to a swelling of the foreskin—likely caused by an infection—that can lead to gangrene if not treated. Imagine this painful condition as Winder tells Dr. Worthington what he has done so far: "I have touched the parts with a solution of nitrate of silver today & a lotion, also ordered Bismuth sprinkled over glans penis and [prepuce] if no improvement takes place by tomorrow."[31] As

175

for the remedy, in this case the solution of nitrate was both "antiseptic and cauterizing." Bismuth was a powder mixed with carbolic acid that could "prevent putrefaction . . . [and is] also used as a surgical dressing."[32]

William A.'s dedication to his patients—old or young, rich or poor, even after suffering badly from rheumatism and chronic bronchitis—is illuminated in a letter written many years later by Horace Bradt to the San Diego historian Winifred Davidson. "Dr. William A. Winder, who for many years practiced his profession throughout this county, has so impressed me, that I feel having known him quite intimately for many years. . . . I have many times taken him to call on the sick, when none but a thorough humanitarian would dare to face the elements," Bradt wrote. "One time in particular during a heavy rain and wind storm, over rough and muddy roads, even covering himself with a heavy canvas, when sickness really should forbade [sic] him to leave his bed, yet with his regard to an unfortunate calling for his services, he would brave serious inconvenience for himself." Bradt stressed that "no one ever called for his professional services, be he rich or poor, that did not receive his most distinguished services." William A. indeed often saw patients for free. "All glory to his name, which should never, never die," Bradt proclaimed.[33]

14

Pension or Ruination

B y 1880 all glory to William A. Winder's name was more wish than fact. Glory to the Winder surname was past salvation. But in his role as Dr. Winder he endured, though precariously. Three days into 1880, while attending his patient and friend John "Don Juan" Forster at his vast ranch in Santa Margarita, the carriage William A. was traveling in toppled over, spilling him to the ground. He sustained "injuries of a serious character." Broken bones, internal injuries? The record is silent.[1]

While he recovered at the home of his friend Chalmers Scott over four long months, a new attempt to reinstate him in the army begins. Letters of endorsement and tribute arrive at the office of New Hampshire senator Henry William Blair, once a fighter in Ichabod Goodwin's lauded Fifteenth New Hampshire Volunteer Infantry. Senator Blair, perhaps at the behest of the Goodwin family, has put forward a bill (S. 1008) for "the relief of Wm. A. Winder." Relief would be just that, but in spite of Maj. Gen. Irvin McDowell's negative response to William A.'s request for an endorsement (that letter is not extant) and in response to Blair's request, McDowell wrote to Winder, saying, "I never doubted . . . your loyalty to the Government. I had implicit confidence in your zeal and ability as a faithful officer . . . and have on several occasions so stated officially."[2]

How much more could be said about Winder's loyalty during the war? Wasn't that by now an unimpeachable fact? Engineer Robert S. Williamson writes that he has known William A. for eighteen years and "always considered you an efficient officer and never doubted your loyalty to the Government. I understand you wish to be reinstated and placed upon the retired list. I wish you the success you well deserve."[3]

Another letter to Senator Blair came from Major of Engineers George H. Elliot, who knew William A. well while he commanded Alcatraz; he had endorsed the taking of photographs on the island that had caused Captain Winder so much trouble. Elliot wrote, "I now take pleasure in testifying to Captain Winder's abilities, professional pride and sleepless anxiety, that all under his charge should be faithfully administered and guarded." Elliot then refers to the time when "there were plots to seize the fortified places in the harbor of San Francisco and detach California from the Union, and when Alcatraz was made the military prison for the disaffected."[4]

Unfortunately for William A. the rebuke and utter dismissal of Blair's bill by Sen. John Alexander Logan of the Committee on Military Affairs was another rejection in what was becoming an increasingly frustrating and still fruitless effort to regain his former officer's status and be placed on the retired list. Logan, from Illinois, had been a Union general in the Civil War. "Black Jack" Logan's known crusade for African American rights, his hatred of slavery, and his ferocious hatred of all things Confederate may well have prompted the following response to Blair: "Your committee having under consideration the bill (S. 1008) for the relief of W. A. Winder, late a Captain in the Third Artillery, providing for his reinstatement to his former rank in the army find that the said Winder resigned his commission as captain of his own volition"—and here was the blow—"without having in any way distinguished himself during his term of service from 1848 to 1866. Your committee would, therefore, recommend the indefinite postponement of this bill."[5]

With indefinite postponement gnawing at William A., a curious reporter from the *Los Angeles Herald*, clearly unaware of Winder's struggles, asked him about an old comrade from a time long past: the Democratic presidential candidate, Maj. Gen. Winfield Scott Hancock, the opponent of the Republican candidate, James A. Garfield. The *Herald* reporter asked William A.'s opinion of the once-fiery Civil War fighter now looking eagerly to the presidency.

"Knowing that Captain William A. Winder, of San Diego, has been on intimate terms with Gen. Hancock since the days when both were young," wrote the *Herald* reporter, "the other day we addressed the captain a note requesting him to give us his impressions and recollections of his old time friend, with whom he had served in Mexico . . . 'In reply to your note,' says Captain Winder, 'I will say that I have known Gen. Hancock intimately for many years . . . ever since the time when Gen. Hancock and myself were young, and shot quail together at Jefferson Barracks.'" William A. lauds the candidate, saying that he fully believes he will become president. The article also states that "during the war, Capt. William A. Winder, instead of being in command of a Confederate Bastile [sic] at Belle Isle, was commandant at Alcatraz, in the Bay of San Francisco. . . . In addition to having been a Union officer during the late war, Capt. Winder originally received his commission in the regular army for conspicuous gallantry in the Mexican War, on which theater he had a splendid opportunity of observing the soldierly qualities of Hancock in his youth . . . the tribute was well deserved, and comes from a man who always stood by the Union."[6]

General Hancock had served on the front with gallantry during the Civil War, notably at Gettysburg, where "despite sustaining a serious wound from which he never fully recovered, [he] earned . . . official thanks from Congress."[7]

Although this article illuminates William A.'s fond reminiscences of the youthful Hancock and endorsement of his presidential candidacy, it also contains one of the first records noting the similarity in the fact that both father and son commanded prisons during the war. Despite the notable and puzzling omission of John H. Winder's name and infamy at Andersonville, here in print was the glorification of William A.'s army career, a tribute that once again bore no fruit in the effort to get him back in the army.

With no reinstatement forthcoming, William A. believes he is sinking beneath the water, an image calling up the old sea demons that have haunted his life.

"The drowning man catches at a straw," he writes Alfred Wilcox, admitting the "old but true proverb" likening himself to such a desperate sort. And as a "preface to what I am about to say," he again pleads for funds. This time, "there is a chemist here [in San Diego] who proposed to open a drug store . . . and proposed to me to go in with him . . . to do so will require $700 for which I can give security on the goods. . . . Another drug store is needed here," he notes, indicating that such an enterprise would promise large cash profits, and "I being in such bad health . . . am exceedingly anxious to embrace this chance to make a living as it is hard for me to attend sick calls day and night." And yet he continued to do so throughout this time, through inclement weather and his own growing debility. Finally he asks for a loan—"out of dire necessity"—of $500. He promises "good security," with two lots of land he owns, as "desperation gives me the courage to ask it." And he gives Wilcox news of the railroad. This time, after the Texas and Pacific debacle, "the Santa Fe Railroad bested its rivals and got a terminus on the Pacific Coast." With its subsidiary the California Southern Railroad making this invaluable connection, "a load of ties on the way and one of rails, the company have bought the National Ranch . . . and four hundred acres . . . so you see they are in earnest," William A. wrote.[8]

• • •

Jubilations ceased when the "heaviest rainfall on record" washed out roads and destroyed a train. The fits and starts in the project to extend railroad service to San Diego must have been maddening. But finally "ground was broken on December 20, 1880 . . . between National City and San Diego."[9]

With this news, the city rejoiced. "San Diego's waterfront was alive with activity that hadn't been experienced since the Gold Rush," the historian Richard Pourade writes. Ships bulging with railroad ties arrived, and Chinese laborers were brought down from San Francisco. Ships from Antwerp, Belgium, and New York came "with three locomotives and thirty flat cars," all of which elated and enlivened the hopes of the 2,637 San Diegans.[10]

And for William A., news that his son Willie has been promoted to lieutenant meant that, for better or for worse, he would remain at sea. His father would continue to heal the sick, paint and draw, fight illness, and, like a locomotive, a bit worn now with time, keep rumbling toward the future.

• • •

The future was no more for William A.'s uncle, the former lawyer Charles H. Winder, whose unremitting struggle to clear his brother John H. Winder's name finally ended. He died on April 10, 1881, in Baltimore and was buried at Green Mount Cemetery on April 13, near his brother, William H. His nephew Sidney Winder was a pallbearer. The record is silent on any of William A.'s reactions to the fact that the uncles who had waged a civilian war against the Union and by default, against William A., were now gone.[11]

By September 1881 there came a pyrrhic victory for William A., at last. He became president of the Veterans of the Mexican War, the organization he had so desired to be a part of, having lobbied for the badge of honor vets displayed. Because he was admitted in 1879, might he ask to be considered for a pension? The answer would have been "not likely," as he enlisted as a civilian and was not commissioned until after the war.[12] Winder's desire was unrealistic, but in the mind of William A. profit of any kind, from any source, was a necessity.

Art soothed his unquiet spirit, though, so he made art. And more. Exactingly and carefully. At least that is what he was doing when a reporter from the *San Diego Sun* found "Dr. William A. Winder busily engaged in finishing a very pretty lady's work box of quite a new pattern; designed by himself, it is of Gothic architecture handsomely ornamented and made with only a knife and a file. It has a large cushion containing an emery bag, three drawers for needles, buttons, &c. Around the base are fifteen spools of thread and silk so enclosed as to protect them from the dust, a place for scissors and a bay window with a looking glass. . . . The lady who is lucky enough to get it will be pleased."[13]

No matter the unknown recipient, it seemed that "Dr. W. A. Winder has very kindly donated the pretty lady's work box, recently designed by him, to the coming Catholic fair," the *Sun* reported. "A great number of fancy articles are being made by the ladies and subscriptions freely coming in; so that the fair will, undoubtedly, be a success, and a suitable house for Father Ubach will be the result."[14]

Father Antonio Dominic Ubach, a native of the Catalonia region in Spain, was a fervent defender of Native American rights, often and regularly, like William A., protesting their ill-treatment. He was serving in Old Town when residents objected to Indians attending schools with white children. To stem the controversy, he founded a school for Indian children. According to the historian William E. Smythe, Ubach was the "Father Gaspara" of Helen Hunt Jackson's novel *Ramona*, published in 1884, "a circumstance which gave him wide fame and made him an object of extraordinary interest to all strangers."[15]

Ramona was the best-selling story of two lovers, Ramona Ortegna—half Indian, half Scottish, and with a vengeful, bigoted, and arrogant stepmother—and Alessandro Assis, a full-blooded Indian. The couple were "repeatedly driven" into flight by "grasping Euro-American settlers" and by a "government unsympathetic to Indians." Supposedly the couple made their way to San Diego, where they were wed in Old Town by Father Gaspara/Father Ubach. The novel contained much romance, with dollops of imagination, from the pen of Helen Hunt Jackson, an unlikely reformer who exposed bigotry; she and her novel were compared to Harriet Beecher Stowe's *Uncle Tom's Cabin*. The popular novel, with its mix of myth, romance, and racial polemic, made Ramona's supposed wedding place, a chapel in Old Town, a tourist attraction.[16]

Although William A. was not a Catholic—actually a tepid Presbyterian—the presence of Father Ubach in Old Town is a reminder that, unlike so many residents who defamed and denigrated the Indians in their midst, William A.'s tireless kindness to his patients of all origins, tribes, and financial circumstances was as embedded in his being as that of the parish priest.

While Father Ubach would continue to save souls, William A. was in Santa Margarita hovering over his desperately ill friend Don Juan Forster, as he weakened from a disease that has spread throughout his body; the particulars he will communicate to Alfred Wilcox in the coming days. The imminent death of this larger-than-life English don, the once genial comrade William A. has diligently doctored, painted, and praised for his hospitality, is in sharp contrast to the gleeful world beyond Forster's lands and down the road in New Town.

"A happy New Year to All," exclaimed the *San Diego Union* on the first day of 1882. With undisguised glee, the newspaper reported what so many knew: "It is our pleasant duty to announce to the readers of the *Union* that arrangements have been perfected for the extension of the California Southern Railroad to be connected to the Atlantic & Pacific." And business explodes with the news. "Five acres near railroad" were advertised for sale and selling fast. "Homes for all. Come all you shearers of sheep, Gunsmiths and Cutlers, Boards of Supervisors, Real Estate Dealers by the dozens." New Town was prospering, and the Consolidated Bank of San Diego proudly boasts of "$200,000 in Capital." It is 1882, and residents wanted it to bring health and wealth and, of course, trains.[17]

When William A.'s patient Don Juan Forster died at the age of sixty-seven on February 20, 1882, the devoted doctor agonized over whether or not he could have saved him. With an ulcerated leg, weakness, an "extreme[ly] rapid and nervous asthenia . . . the disease had left the outside, or attacked the brain and throat . . . there was a septicemic condition apparent," William A. wrote Alfred Wilcox shortly after Don Juan died. He assured Wilcox that "Dr. Worthington of Los Angeles, who was called in consultation, says, 'it is my opinion that under the circumstances all was done, that could have been done by anyone . . . the treatment was prudent, rational and based on clear clinical evidence.'" If he doubted himself, and if Worthington's assurances were of comfort, William A. still has other patients, other concerns. He notes his need for yet another "Galvanic Battery . . . with sufficient intensity for electrolysis of small tumors, treating the nasal cavity, eye, ear & uterus. . . . I have had three, which work very well at first, but soon prove to be of little use." Perhaps Wilcox will furnish the money for more. Winder also suggests he is lonely and longs for a visit from Wilcox: "There are very few here now for whom I have any feeling in common, or in any way sympathize with."[18]

As in other trying times in William A.'s life, he falls ill. But the *San Diego Sun*, always keeping a close eye on him, reported that "Dr. Winder, who has been indisposed for the last few days, we are happy to state, [is] able to be around again."[19]

Winder was around again, and painting—for wellness, for peace.

"We saw at the office of Dr. Winder yesterday two very strik-

ing paintings—the work of the doctor in his leisure moments,"
wrote a *San Diego Union* observer who'd stepped into the solitary
artist's sanctum. The writer admired "a picture of two Abbes who
have just finished a luxurious repast; one of them is relating an
irresistibly funny anecdote, and the other, laying [*sic*] back in his
chair, his legs stretched out at full length[,] is overcome with mirth.
The details are exceedingly well wrought out. The other painting
represents St. Jerome, and is a life-size bust, wonderfully impres-
sive. These pictures deserve a better notice than we are competent to give them."[20]

Days of painting and praise gave way to news of the sudden summer death on July 4, 1882, of Ichabod Goodwin, William A.'s father-
in-law, supporter, and defender. The death was no doubt a blow to
him and a grievous shock to his family and community. At sixty-
eight, "after suffering for several weeks with an abscessed liver,"
the former governor seemed immune to all measures designed to
restore his health. A few weeks before his death "he appeared in
public for the last time . . . to pay homage to the New Hampshire
men who died in the Civil War," many of whom were in the regiment he funded and fretted over, as the local boys proudly embodied
the "fighting Governor's" will to win. In the mansion on Islington
Street in Portsmouth, New Hampshire, its residents—including
William A.'s fifty-two-year-old wife, Abby—were plunged into
mourning. The couple's son, Willie, the little boy who'd roamed
the rocks of Alcatraz as his father was shamed, accused of disloyalty, praised, and shamed again, was now thirty-one.[21]

Did Willie and his mother, distraught over the loss of the family patriarch, know that a portion of the often sickly William A.'s
pension case was received by the Adjutant General's Office at the
War Department on November 23, 1882? "Claims liver disease in
Fla [Florida] in '49. Chronic Bronchitis & Rheumatism from exposure on wreck [of] *San Francisco*, & exposure in Dec. 1853." The
record of these old ailments was duly noted in an effort, it seemed,
to underscore his later debility.[22]

As the holiday approached, he anticipated spending it at Rancho Jamul, the home of his friend María Amparo Ruiz de Burton,
where he was to be a guest of her daughter Nellie and her husband

Don Miguel de Pedrorena, the young scion of one of the original Castilian families of Old Town.

One last glimpse at the artist before he departs for Christmas.

"Dr. Winder has recently painted a portrait of the infant child of Mr. and Mrs. J. H. Tebbetts, which is one of the finest paintings we have ever seen. The likeness is perfect. It is an artistic gem," wrote a reporter for the *San Diego Union*. Imagine the reporter studying the baby's portrait, the child's image alive and glowing on the canvas.[23]

If only the close of the year had ended on this glad note.

Instead "Don Miguel de Pedrorena died very suddenly at his residence in Jamul Valley Monday night [Christmas Eve] at half past eleven o'clock of acute laryngitis," the *San Diego Union* reported. Having been in New Town in seemingly good health, "he called at the office of Dr. W.A. Winder and asked the Doctor who for thirty years had been an intimate friend of the family to come out to Jamul and spend Christmas." The next morning, ready to go and be with a family he loved, William A. saw that Pedrorena was "suffering from a severe cold . . . Doctor Winder told him he was too ill to take the long drive . . . and prescribed for him." The article does not mention what remedies were attempted. Pedrorena's mother-in-law, María, and his wife, Nellie, were waiting for him, and Pedrorena had promised them he would "return for Christmas, and that promise must be sacred." With William A. by his side they left town, and upon their arrival at the ranch "he seemed to be much better . . . [but] suddenly began to suffocate, and died in less than ten minutes."[24]

Two friends dead on his watch. It was of little comfort that William A. had done all he could. There was in fact no comfort in store for William A. The winter cold makes his bones ache. The presence of a visitor could perhaps warm him somewhat, but the person who does come to him is a stranger who asks him to speak of a long-ago time when storms and disease and courage defined him.

Thirty years after the *San Francisco*, the ship that was to bring William A. and three hundred U.S. artillery troops to California, was destroyed by raging hurricane winds that killed hundreds, the press reported the death of Capt. Robert Crighton, the commander of the *Three Bells*, the rescue ship that finally arrived at the scene of the broken, battered, and sinking *San Francisco* in 1854. His death sparked new interest in the old tragedy. Knowing William A. had been on the stricken ship, a reporter from the *San Diego Union* made a "New Year's call" to him. Before the reporter could poke at William A.'s memory of the event that had forever traumatized him and get him to revisit the time he became an accidental hero, the man marveled at William A., at the mélange of artist and healer he saw before him.

Picture him at a hard-won sixty, long beard, strands of yellow speckled with gray, a full mustache, his inward, unrewarded middle-distance, blue-eyed gaze. The reporter saw him "comfortably seated in his rooms surrounded by a medley of medical works, oil paintings, surgical instruments, and fine engravings which made one doubt whether he was in an artist's studio or a doctor's office." A saber hung on the wall, "and various military books in the book-case were calculated to further puzzle the strange visitor to the inhabitant's presence."[25]

The reporter ladled bits of William A.'s career to his readers, praising the "the gallant officer of the army, of many years service a veteran of the Florida and Mexican wars . . . and commandant of Fort Alcatraz . . . with the rank of Captain of the Artillery [and] . . . for the last eight or ten years an enthusiastic student of medicine." And then more of the reporter's awe at the artist: "Pursuing the work of the pencil and brush as a diversion in his leisure hours, the Doctor has executed some pieces that would fairly gain him entrance to the guild of artists."

And then to the meat of the story: the tragedy at sea. As a survivor of the disaster—would he, asked the reporter, speak "about the incidents of the wreck of the *San Francisco?*"

The ship had drifted for days, beset by fire, Asiatic cholera, smallpox, and diphtheria. William A. described the ocean as being like "boiling water," the dreadful screams of the women drowned in the rush of water. He noted that "the entire upper cable had been swept off." "I refused a life preserver," William A. said, "crawled up the cabin steps . . . and stumbled over the corpse of the ship's carpenter."

There were dead soldiers all around him, and he saw before him a dying child. Bodies were crumpled in pools of fetid water. Finally the rescue ship, the *Three Bells*, came bobbing and pitching on the waves. Of the rescuer William A. said, "Captain Creighton [*sic*] saved my life, very near thirty years ago," while risking his own. "He was a splendid fellow." On the deck of his ship Captain Crighton held a blackboard, barely visible through the darkness. It was a common mode of communication between ships. Captain Crighton, "God bless him," William A. recalled, kept the *Three Bells* close to the *San Francisco*, almost close enough to ram the ship, and held out the blackboard for four days as the *San Francisco* was sinking.

There were shouts and screams that no one could hear, but finally some, among them William A., were able to see the precious board upon which Captain Crighton had scrawled, "'Be of good cheer. I will stand by you.' . . . The significance of those words, to several hundred of us, standing on what we thought was a sinking ship, can only be realized by those who have been shipwrecked," Winder told the reporter.

It took ten days for the survivors to get back to New York. And then William A. had to turn around and head back to California, to travel the ocean waves with much trepidation, fearing a cloudless sky might again blacken and burst upon them. Finally he arrived in the land that he made his home. There were the thanks from the Maryland legislature for native sons William A. and his cousin Charles Winder for their bravery and assistance to endangered soldiers and civilians during the tragedy. The heroic deeds of Captain Crighton, a "brave hearted Scotsman who stood by us in the storm," William A. stated, were recorded on a roll of parchment William A. held fast in his hands. He opened the fragile scroll, read the praise for Crighton's "brave and humane conduct," and said the captain "has gone to receive the reward of his noble act."

The reporter is perhaps a bit shaken, having been taken back to a time so long past, while William A. sat before him in a quiet room full of unquiet memories of the raging sea that in those moments had perhaps come back to haunt him.

But William A. must, like the longed-for California Southern Rail-

road, plod and push along. As the railroad "inches northward . . .
multitudes of Chinese toiling with pick and shovel . . . up the coast,
over bridges, creeks and tidewater lagoons," the dream of trains
for San Diego is coming closer to reality, even as wars of company
primacy and "court actions" impede it. Finally "the first train,"
bedecked with "flowers, stalks of corn and round squash[,] pulled
into San Bernardino." Soon, but not yet, San Diego will finally see
an iron horse.[26]

Around this time Winder is also concerned about the health of
his friend Alfred Wilcox. "Rumors from day to day have reached
me concerning the condition of your health[,] all causing me some
anxiety," Winder writes. Wilcox had moved to San Francisco a
few years earlier, and William A. was unfortunately too infirm to
visit him. However, he writes, "with your splendid constitution
and the great ability displayed by your medical attendants, I feel
sure you will pull through. . . . Please ask your doctor to drop me a
line." On August 15, two months after the letter was written, Wilcox died. He was a man who had helped William A. financially,
without complaint or hesitation, and who had believed in him.[27]

• • •

As 1884 began the *San Diego Union* asked its readers, "How many
good resolves have you started the new year with? And how will
you keep them?" Winder is regrouping, measuring personal losses,
seeing a dwindling number of patients; his resolutions must be
to keep going. And to paint. He has been working on a life-size oil
portrait of Judge Oliver Witherby "on exhibition at Schneider's
book store," in New Town.[28]

In this portrait the portly bachelor, Old Town lion, and diligent
drunk—captured in seeming sobriety—sits belly forward, tight
trousers near to bursting, his gavel at the ready, and a clutch of
law books behind him. His sideways gaze, at once stilted, studied, and stern, is turned to the artist, who continued to work on
the image until 1885, when the *San Diego Union* noted, "The likeness is wonderfully correct."[29]

Not wonderfully correct, however, is an old accusation that William A. felt he must fiercely protest. The perceived disloyalty of

Gen. Albert Sidney Johnston—who had been William A.'s former commander at Alcatraz just as the Civil War began—has been resurrected in the press. William A. begins a passionate correspondence with Gen. William T. Sherman in hopes of dispelling the belief that Johnston had supported a conspiracy to aid Confederate sympathizers in an effort to take control of San Francisco, its military forts, and its gold stores.

It seemed that Col. Jonathan Drake Stevenson, a Mexican War veteran who never served in the Civil War but was once stationed in California, had written a pallid and confusing defense of General Johnston in a letter sent to the *San Diego Union* and to General Sherman. Although Sherman said he did advise the removal of Johnston from his command at Alcatraz and had recommended General Sumner as his replacement, he admitted that Johnston's subsequent resignation from the U.S. Army was based on false and disproven allegations. While Stevenson confirmed Sherman's belief in Johnston's "perfect loyalty as long as he held a commission in the army," Stevenson refers to a letter William A. wrote in defense of Johnston that "puts the matter upon a proper basis."[30]

William A. writes to Sherman, saying "that Col. Stevenson's statement conveyed a false impression of Gen. Johnston's ideas and intentions, I think and hope you will admit when you have read the following. . . . I flatter myself that you know enough of me to know that under no circumstances would I make any statement not absolutely true." Of course resignation under duress is very much a sore point for William A., and he then launches into a narrative of what happened before Johnston left the service of the Union. After reminding Sherman that Johnston was stationed at Alcatraz, Winder states, "As soon as war was inevitable, General Johnston promptly ordered all of the arms and ammunition at the Arsenal at Benicia, where they were exposed to capture by any small force, to be brought to the island of Alcatraz for safety." While Johnston "was still in command, Colonel Burton and myself called on him. . . . The General said to me 'I was never in so painful a situation in my life. I owe everything to the state of Texas . . . to take up arms against her is intensely painful . . . but there is one thing very certain . . . *I will perform my whole duty while I do remain in the Army."* Of course Johnston did resign, but he had agonized over the choice. And then came William A.'s absolute defense of his own predicament while at Alcatraz. "The fact that such a man, with such a record of a soldier[,] could be suspected and disgraced because he was of Southern birth, what would be the fate of one so humble without a record as myself," Winder writes. "The result justified my fear, for notwithstanding the strict attention to and performance of all duty assigned to me, I found myself an object of suspicion in the eyes of the Sec of War, until the close of the war, and but for the fact that I was fully sustained by my military commanders, I know not what would have been the end." William A. asks Sherman to "pardon the digression," but he cannot help but remind his old comrade of what he suffered and that he, unlike Johnston, in spite of his father's threats, never went over to the South. Many years had passed since the events about which Winder wrote, but the mental torment of it had not passed at all. His bitterness and sadness were apparent in the words scrawled across the stationery, and passages were underlined. William A. in closing says that the whole story of Johnston's so-called collusion with the enemy is "bosh." He can't help but add this final note about himself: "After my return from the Army of the Potomac, Gen Wright assigned me to the command of Alcatraz where I remained until the close of the war, with the exception of about a month when I was superseded for 'feeding Rebel prisoners on the fat of the land and off of silver plates.'" To drive a final point home just so Sherman fully understands, William A. writes that, in spite of the arrests of persons who "caused some uneasiness . . . there was never a time when there was any danger of seceding on the part of this state." A note of flattery ends this remarkable cri de coeur: "Remembrance of early days recalls your love of justice, and emboldens me to inflict this scrawl on you, hoping you may see enough in it to change your views and that your great name may be enlisted in behalf of the memory of a brave soldier."[31]

Sherman replied to William A. from his home in St. Louis, saying he has received his letter, "bearing additional testimony . . . that though there was a conspiracy in California to seize the arsenal . . . the attempt was frustrated before the arrival of General

Sumner. . . . I was only too pleased to learn the truth which you now so affirm, that Genl Johnston was absolutely true to his high trust as consistent with his previous exalted reputation." Sherman tells William A. that he has "sent all previous papers to the Cincinnati Historical Club and will . . . correct the hitherto wrong information."[32]

In an immediate response to Sherman, William A. expresses gratitude for the promise to restore General Johnston's good name for the record. He states that he is not mistaken in his recollection of the "reputation for justice and truth" Sherman had in their younger days and is glad it was still present. "The authority of your great name must certainly forever set at rest the question of General Johnston's honorable intentions."[33]

Winder's passionate need for public vindication of a man once thought a traitor has become a personal, nearly obsessive quest. That said, William A. again returns in his letter to his own agonies during the war, a time that "offered full license to all malicious persons . . . to vent their enmity by stabbing in the back those who served," like himself. And then there came, without hesitation but with much rancor, the recollection of terrible days when he was under so much suspicion: "There was another class, almost if not quite as vicious, and certainly more dangerous . . . by officiously hunting up incidents, antecedents, or careless remarks, and in some underhanded manner, creating suspicions toward those who were honestly trying to perform their duties."

In this letter, earlier quoted in part, William A. is once again telling his story to his old friend, the warrior who broke the back of the Confederacy and in so doing shattered William A.'s own rebel family, defeating them utterly and forever.

If for some reason Sherman didn't know just how loyal to the Union William A. was, he must tell him again. He tells him that he was visited by Confederate spies. He does not tell Sherman that he was ordered to do his father's bidding and fight for the Confederacy or commit suicide. And though he swore his loyalty to President Lincoln, he was sent far from the front, to Alcatraz. Even then, he reminds Sherman, his post "caused resistance," but his "military superiors always sustained" him. That resistance, he writes, was "the inducement for me to quit the army at the close of the war." In a final indignity, he tells Sherman that none of his applications to serve in the field was accepted.

Alcatraz, his island prison during the war, bound him so tightly he could never cross the continent or sea and fight as he wished to fight. This letter, this rumination, this naked sadness deserved comfort from the famous general. None came. Sherman's official retirement from the army had been recorded on February 8, 1884. He was in his St. Louis home at 912 Garrison Avenue, having left active duty in the army in 1883, when he "passed his command to General Philip Sheridan." Also in 1884 Sherman "declined to be a candidate for the Republican Party nomination."[34]

In San Diego on December 25, 1884, there will be much jollity, much celebration. "With all the coldness and selfishness in the world, what would our civilization come to without Christmas," the *San Diego Union* intoned. "Our outlook as a community was never more auspicious. . . . The greetings of the day come with genuine heartiness," the *Union* trilled, waiting as always for the promised November day late in 1885 when the "through railway line of the Atchison, Topeka and Santa Fe System to the Pacific Ocean" would arrive at San Diego.[35]

Remaining in New Town among throngs of children, shops decorated with pine boughs, and ringing church bells is William A., an older man who, surely missing family and friends, likely ruminates and mourns a soldier's glory lost forever. If he could see into the future and be patient, he would know that his decision to stop making house calls, given his own health problems, would lead to an appointment that will give him new purpose. And he will have an important role in a most unusual literary work begun in 1880 by a bright and bold widow determined to tell the story of the plight of the landed Californios. María Amparo Ruiz de Burton has been finishing a new novel while living in rooms rented for free in a simple two-story frame house owned by William A. Once wealthy, she is now impoverished. She'd inherited large tracts of land in Baja but "lost her wealth in long litigation[,] . . . her holdings seized by the International Company of Mexico." She'd repeatedly fought to keep Rancho Jamul, where she'd lived with General Burton. María and William A. labored to ready her manuscript at his home at 1421 Fourth Avenue. The female author who published under a pseudonym became "one of San Diego's fabulous characters."[36]

Picture the two friends, both wearied by time and troubles— her sweep of black hair threaded with gray—their heads bent over the pages. Both felt the pain of every trial they'd faced, such as the early death of her husband, who'd been William A.'s commander at Mission de Alcalá when he first beheld María, the "stormy aristocratic beauty" he came to know and respect.[37]

The theme of loyalty—his and hers—likely birthed her pseudonym, C. Loyal. "The C. stood for *Ciudadano*, or 'Citizen,' and Loyal for *Leal*—, i.e., *Ciudadano Leal* a 'Loyal Citizen.'"[38]

María Amparo Ruiz de Burton's determination to be not just a "foreign" outsider, a Californio derided "in the gaze of the squatters" as a "greaser," somewhat resembled William A.'s grinding determination to be restored to the army, to be remembered and acknowledged as a loyal citizen of the United States. For both this was a time for reclamation of self.

• • •

"A novel of California life, which will interest anyone who takes it up," was the way the *San Francisco Chronicle* announced the publication of *The Squatter and the Don* a few days after it was released. For two dollars a copy, which came in at a fulsome 430 pages, interested readers could immerse themselves in a story many might find true to life and painful, while others might turn an indifferent or scornful eye, for the novel exposed the corruption, greed, and cruelty that San Diegans and Californios alike experienced. Noting the author's pseudonym, C. Loyal, and that the book was at least in part written by a woman, the reviewer addressed the book's main themes: "The realistic style, the grip which the railroad monopoly has got on this state, and like Mrs. Jackson's 'Ramona,' it is an eloquent and impassioned plea for the holders of Spanish grants, whose patrimony was filched from them, acre by acre, by squatters, who dubbed the real owners of the land 'Greasers.'" One of the novel's main characters, William Darrell, is a decent man but one beset with a "mania to acquire land" in Sonoma County, where he was "dispossessed." "Seduced" into going down to San Diego, he squats on the fictional Alamar Rancho, not realizing he has been deceived by friends who told him the land was available and not under litigation. "More ill-intended squatters swoop down like so many buzzards," nibbling at and finally gorging themselves on the land owned by Californio Don Mariano, slaughtering his cattle, refusing to pay him for stock or lands, and finally forcing him to drive all his cattle into the mountains, where a sudden snowstorm finishes the worldly wealth of the don. His well-bred son is "reduced to the labor of carrying a hod." The tale is told against the backdrop of the crushing of the Texas and Pacific Railroad by the Southern Pacific lobby and "the consequent death of the great expectations of San Diego as the southern metropolis of California." Of course, there is also a love story, "which springs up between the son of the squatter and the favorite daughter of the Don," told in María Burton's dramatic, flowery, romantic, and occasionally bathetic style.[39]

A second review, in the *San Diego Union*, reveals the plot and praises the book as having a "rare quality of originality." It notes with interest the two voices, one pedantic, the other, romantic. "On a few occasions C. Loyal seems to speak more like a priest than as a novelist telling a story," the reviewer notes.[40]

The authorial voice of the novel damns the railroad monopolies that buried the dreams of so many, saying, "If the Texas Pacific Railroad had not been strangled . . . San Diego would not then be the poor, crippled and dwarfed little city that she now is," María wrote.[41]

In reading the novel it is not difficult to hear William A.'s somber and sober voice. It has been suggested that Winder was "said to have been written," dictated, or merely suggested the topic to his friend María Burton or that he "helped Mrs. Burton with her manuscript." Whatever the case, the burst of publicity for her novel sputtered out, and she faded into relative obscurity, frustrated and depressed by her inability to own outright her beloved Rancho Jamul.[42]

Regardless of whether Winder was the author or just a collaborator, any profits from the book would go to María so she could continue the lawsuits that she prays will return Rancho Jamul to her family. As María fights her battles, William A. is fighting his own ill health and financial woes even as he persists in his determination to continue his medical practice. Infirmity stalks him; aching joints and a deformed hand that cannot properly hold a stethoscope have slowed the intrepid healer. As if by prestidigitation, an official announcement, an assignment for him, makes its way across the country to the *San Diego Union* office and is immediately reported: "Dr. Wm. A. Winder has received the contract for the medical, surgical and hospital care of the sick for the United States Hospital Services: his contract takes effect from this date."[43]

Although it appeared that William A.'s contract was official, it would be a few years before San Diego's Marine Hospital became a reality. Waiting to take the new position, selling plots of pueblo land as often as he could, and painting occupied him. Contrary to the rumors that he had retired from active practice, he was still listed as a "physician and surgeon" in the San Diego city and county directory for 1887.[44]

But on November 21, 1885, there was an event to hearten, gladden, and relieve residents throughout San Diego as "the first transcontinental train to arrive reached San Diego . . . with sixty passengers aboard." There followed "a parade with brass bands and marching units of the Grand Army of the Republic" as hundreds of citizens welcomed "visiting railroad officers." Wheeler-dealers, gamblers, doctors, Californios, throwaway drunks, the hotel managers, shop and saloonkeepers—the whole town erupted in celebration. "The quiet years were over," and the boom had begun.[45]

• • •

It is a moment of immense prestige for William A. Winder when he is elected chair of the San Diego Medical Society, part of the State Medical Society, on August 8, 1886. This was an honor for him and an opportunity to make new rules and enforce existing medical regulations.[46]

It was a new day for San Diego. With the arrival of the railroad, "the two years that began in 1886 and ended in 1888 were the most gaudy, wicked and exciting in San Diego's history," the historian

Richard Pourade writes with an exaggerated flourish that compares these booming days to the gold rush in northern California. In rushed all manner of new residents. There were among them literati eager to write; Mark Twain had come from the "Mother Lode Country" because the occasionally high-minded but always entertaining *Golden Era Magazine* had now relocated to San Diego. Racing to the land of a seasonally alternating lugubrious and salubrious climate and seeking fountains of youth to make the old and ailing young again, speculators, the hated squatters, criminals, and gamblers arrived. Guns, gold pieces, and greenbacks were scooped up, secreted, pocketed—dollars upon dollars—and spent on new hotels, on rooming houses and saloons, and on land, with lots and acres snapped up. "A Golden land was sold and resold, from one person to another and back again," Pourade writes.[47] All through 1887 William A.'s subdivision (known as the Winder Tract), which he had purchased in 1882, was for sale. The large parcels were long and narrow, both north and south of Pennsylvania Avenue between Kite and Jackdaw Streets. "The finest view in San Diego! Overlooking the Bay, Ocean, Roseville, Coronado Beach, Mexico, National City and San Diego," the *San Diego Daily Bee* crowed repeatedly. "Choice lots at the low figures of $250 for inside lots, and $300 for corners," were going fast.[48]

After a year of incessant promotion for San Diego and its come-hither attractions, a promotional colored lithograph, an idealized map of San Diego, with the bay and beaches washed in delicate blues and greens, is available for fifteen cents and can be seen hanging on restaurant and hotel walls. Artist Maud McMullan's perfect sweeping scenes seduce the observer with soft mountains and perfect houses nestled on shores of San Diego Bay. Boats and bathers loll in calm waters.

But amid this delicious fog of euphoria, the fugue state of a city finally seeing a real future, by 1889 William A. will again be prominent in the press. There is yet another and much-publicized petition for his reinstatement into the army; this time a curious character is making the appeal for William A.'s reinstatement. If there was any lingering misinformation or doubt about William A.'s kin, there were several articles detailing the particulars of the latest petition that had resurrected the story of firm loyalty to the United States despite suspicions to the contrary. The *Washington Post* headlined an article, "His Family Were Disloyal: How their actions hung like a cloud over Captain Winder's head." The article states that "when the War broke out Captain William A. Winder[,] whose father was a Confederate officer, General Winder, and whose two brothers were in the Confederate service[,] gave up his relatives and his home in order to serve on the side of the Union." The *Post* reported that the appeal for Winder came from the rather mysterious Col. Julian Allen, who was originally from Poland. The Julian Allen Scrapbook notes that he allegedly "aided the United States government in connection with Sherman's occupation of Savannah, Ga., and settled after the war near Statesville in Iredell County, N.C." The *Post* added that Allen had brought to Lincoln's attention the case of William A. Winder and how he was affected by the actions of his family during the Civil War.[49]

According to the *Post* article, William A. went with Allen to see Lincoln, who assured William A. that his loyalty was not in question. When he requested to be sent to the front but was instead ordered to California, William A. objected, and Lincoln promised to have the order changed. However, "Stanton refused to modify it in any way and so Captain Winder went to the Pacific Coast. To Alcatraz. Now broken down in health and fortune he seeks to be reinstated in the army and placed on the retired list." William A. never mentioned going to see Lincoln with Julian Allen; he said on a few occasions that he went on his own to see the president. Therefore the assertion in the article that Allen was his companion on the trip to the White House is questionable. Perhaps Colonel Allen sought to underscore the importance of reinstating William A., or perhaps it was a publicity grab by a dubious "colonel."[50]

In an Associated Press dispatch to the *Los Angeles Herald*, under the heading "A Grave Grievance: A Loyal Soldier under Undeserved Censure; He bore the burden of his father's disloyalty while true to the Union flag," the Allen claim is repeated together with a recitation of William A.'s service record and a disturbing sidebar: "in California the charge of disloyalty was renewed, finally resulting in a trial, by which he was honorably acquitted."[51]

Never before had there been any contemporaneous mention of a trial. Even more important is that there is no extant primary source record of such an event. From a distance of more than twenty years, a mistruth had taken center stage, one that arose from the effort to get the suffering Winder immediate reinstatement and retirement, and thus a pension.

Variations of this Allen petition were reported in newspapers around the country. One wonders if William A. had any say in what was or wasn't reported. After this surge of publicity, there was nothing more—no denials, and certainly no reinstatement.

But with an official notice from Washington on June 26, 1889, printed in the *San Francisco Bulletin* on June 27, the Marine Hospital service contract William A. had received from the government went into effect. It had taken three years. He had waited quietly in his private office, where an occasional patient would come to talk while William A. tried as best he could to hold his instruments with his good hand. He would never give up. But this time, with this new job, he would be more of an administrator, not easy work but still an official job with regular pay. This assignment came about because San Francisco's climate was considered unhealthy and potentially lethal to patients "suffering from pulmonary affections," and San Diego had grown so rapidly that it became a prime spot for a new Marine Hospital Service location. William A. would have well understood the perils of the San Francisco climate, as he continued to suffer from lung problems that developed while he was stationed at Alcatraz.[52]

The official notice of Winder's new job included information about how the Marine Hospital Service would attend to sick and wounded seamen on the Pacific coast. From San Francisco to Sitka, Alaska, there was a string of Marine Hospitals, and the new one in San Diego that would operate under the direction of "Dr. W. A. Winder [would] furnish quarters, subsistence nursing, medical attendance and medicine at $1.75 per day, and . . . provide for burial of deceased patients at $15.00 each."[53]

William A. obtained for the use of the new Marine Hospital a series of rooms at the rear of what was once a sanitarium (and later the Arlington Hotel) in downtown San Diego at Columbia and F Streets. Now the building became a sort of hospital, or at least he would make it so. He furnished it as best he could, but how could he care for half-dead sailors on $1.50 a day and make any profit at all? He hired a cook and attendants as he looked to the docks for the active seamen whom he could house apart from the old hotel's normal population of indigents—the crusty, sun-seared men sick from the seafaring life and of the sea itself, as he once had been. If they were to die in his keep he would get $15.00 to bury them, in lieu of absent or indifferent families who would not see them to their rest. He looked seaward. He must make this work. It did for several months, as from ships' holds, battered sailors with hardly a breath left in them were borne to the back of the building and placed in William A.'s care.

Later that year, "having heard all was not as it should be" at the hospital, a reporter from the *San Diego Union*, eagerly antic-ipating a scoop, went to the gabled building "around the corner from a Chinese laundry establishment." He flung open the massive door that led to the hospital room and found "nine beds, and apparently a man in each bed." When the reporter went into the kitchen he encountered a "beetle browed" cook preparing a meal of "sow bellies and liver." He asked too many questions of the cook, it seemed. With "vague rumors of mistreatment afloat" and the reporter's obvious repulsion at what he'd seen, the cook grabbed him by the back of his pants and collar and threw him out the door. With that ignominious forced exit, which landed him in a mud puddle, the limping reporter "cannot say whether there are any irregularities in that hospital or not." William A., though living at the hospital, was not there at the time of the reporter's visit. Heading sore-legged and sore-headed into the night, the reporter knew he would be back.[54]

And he was, just before Christmas. "Having laid up for repairs for several days," the newspaper reported, "he resumed his investigations of the institution [against] whose management charges too grave to be ignored had been made." Concerned that the hospital was under government supervision and "supported by a government fund; that it was a place totally unfit for the reception of sick and disabled sailors, that it was unclean and ill-kept . . . through the courtesy of Dr. Winder the reporter obtained considerable infor-mation." Perhaps still outraged at his treatment on his first visit, or genuinely concerned, the reporter indicated that the hospital was not a Marine institution and that "about four years ago Dr. Winder entered into a contract with the Government by which he is allowed so much per man per day." The reporter thus deemed the ill-kept place a "private affair." William A. said that a previous federal statute (the Coast Marine Hospital instructions) "did not apply to the hospital here," a curious and damning thing, to say the least. So what was happening? William A. said he is "allowed $180 per day, per man" and that "out of this he must pay for med-ical attendance, medicines, food, servants, provisions and inci-dentals to make a profit." With only seven men present, "several very sick, . . . some months there is no one at all in the hospital." So where is the profit? The reporter wanted to know. "The doctor claims to furnish the best of everything," but again the reporter asked himself and his readers how this could be done on such a pittance. "Who can dispute the tremendous temptation to reduce expenses" by buying inadequate provisions on the cheap and thus "increase his margin of profit?" A description follows: "moderately clean linoleum floor, the main room about thirty feet long by sev-enteen wide, three windows, coarse bedding, not overly clean, sick inmates in beds close together, no food seen in the kitchen, smok-ing permitted, exceedingly hot." Deeming the "aspect of the place unpleasant and forbidding," the reporter indicates that William A. "showed his own sleeping quarters, his room small and cheerless," and he remarks upon "offensive odors." He states that Winder's "system is bad, and though his intensions [sic] are probably good enough in their way, his forced economy to enable him to derive any profit at all lays him liable to charges of abuse." With outrage apparent, the reporter damns "the resort of men who, after long debauchees avail themselves of this place to sober up." They are not just seamen but "common vagrants." The reporter blames the government for taking in men who aren't true sailors and for pro-viding such a paltry allowance for the others.[55]

Whatever came of this very public and damning article—most all residents of both city and county read the *Union*—is not known, but on June 6, 1899, when William A. was admitted to the Southern California Medical Society, his license and post at the Marine Hospital were not withdrawn. In fact, he was formally recognized as a government doctor.

With the maintaining of the Marine Hospital, a sure burden with little compensation and much worry, the year 1889 slid to an unsatisfactory close. Would there be another job, another miracle for William A. in a new year?

• • •

On June 10, 1890, a bill to "restore William A. Winder to the United States Army and to place him on the retired list with the rank of captain of artillery" comes into play. H.R. 9057, introduced in the House of Representatives by William Vandever of Iowa, was referred to the Committee on Military Affairs. The bill's language is as follows: "Be it enacted by the Senate and House of Representatives [a subjunctive phrase indicating a hope the Congress will act] that the President is hereby authorized to appoint and restore to his proper rank in the Army . . . and to place him on the retired list, William A. Winder of San Diego, California."[56]

Again the silence that followed was deafening. Surely by now all the venerable gents, politicians, friends, military commanders, secretaries of war, and the flood of petitioners over the years well knew William A.'s restoration to the army at his former rank was an impossibility, as the vacancy his resignation had created had long ago been filled.

Undaunted, on January 7, 1892, Rep. William Wallace Bowers of San Diego, who had moved there shortly before William A. did, used the same language he had in his previous bill to double down on yet another effort to reinstate Winder, and he presented this new bill to the House Committee on Military Affairs on behalf of William A.[57]

In response, on February 5, 1892, Rep. Hugh Reid Belknap of Illinois urged the committee to place William A. on the retired list because "Capt. Winder is now an old man in feeble health, has served his country well, and deserves its gratitude," and he recommended that the bill to reinstate him (H.R. 704) be passed.[58]

No doubt in feeble health yet still moving forward, William A. is now seeking treatment for his pain in the mineral-rich waters of hot springs. The *Los Angeles Herald* reported, "Dr. Winder passed through Los Angeles on his way to the hot springs at San Jacinto. The doctor is a noted character in California. As a soldier, physician and painter, he has won recognition. He confesses to rheumatism, but in other respects is hale and well." Being hale and well would be a miracle at this point, but then Winder's powers of resurrection—at least in the moment he has greeted the journalist—seem close to miraculous.[59]

In 1893 Representative Bowers made yet another effort at gaining Winder's reinstatement by introducing H.R. 450, another bill asking Congress to "authorize the President to appoint and restore to his proper rank in the Army, as captain of artillery, and to place him on the retired list, William A. Winder, of San Diego." Winder, warmed by the waters at the hot springs, surely is also warmed by yet another try at reinstatement by his friend Representative Bowers. As have many others, Bowers presents William A.'s service record as "part of this report."[60]

• • •

On January 23, 1894, Representative Bowers offered a lengthy report he had prepared to accompany H.R. 450. It is a powerful document, an homage to Winder's long service record and undying loyalty to the Union during the war in the face of the "fanatical patriots [who] made various charges and insinuations against his loyalty" while he was at Alcatraz, and though "every act of his was viewed with suspicion and the worst construction placed upon it, through it all he bore himself as an honorable gentleman and a brave, loyal Union soldier" in spite of his entire Confederate family's treasonous stances and actions. Even when Winder was told "the vacancy made by his resignation was final and it was beyond the power of the President to reappointment him to his former grade," in spite of there being no chance for this much-needed action, and though "Captain Winder is now a broken-down invalid" and, as Representative Bowers wrote, "he has but a short time to live at best," the document pleads that Winder "served his country faithfully. It will cost his country but a very few dollars to do this act of justice." The bill did not pass. Finally and formally portrayed in the public record as a tragic figure with no future, William A. has little left but his post with the Marine Hospital. And he must now leave it because of gross infirmities.[61]

15

Round Valley

A t last, by petition or recommendation—perhaps an urgent request from Representative Bowers to save an old friend—William A. was appointed by Pres. Grover Cleveland to be "a special government agent to make allotments of lands in severalty to Indians at the Round Valley Indian Reservation," located in Covelo, California. This presidential appointment, announced in the *Washington Post* on January 30, 1894, was of course not a medical position; it was too late for that. But it is true that Winder is a man who is well acquainted with Native Americans. This is yet another new career for him, when he is infirm, broke, and toppling toward the age of seventy-two with no retirement in sight. Weary and perhaps wary, he must move forward. With what appeared to be a grim and short future, at least in Representative Bowers's dramatic declaration that William A. had but a short time to live, the government, it seems, is taking care of him at last.[1]

Winder's position was made possible by a controversial act of the Forty-Ninth Congress approved on February 8, 1887, and named for its sponsor, Sen. Henry Laurens Dawes, who chaired the Senate Committee on Indian Affairs. The General Allotment Act—also known as the Dawes Severalty Act—at its most positive addressed the idea that the federal government "believed that individual land ownership was the starting point for assimilation." But the act allowed the president to break up reservation land that was held in common by members of the tribe and then to parcel it out to individuals. There were other purposes and mandates seemingly meant to enrich the lives and welfare of Native Americans. According to the mandates of the act, "The head of each family shall receive one hundred and sixty acres . . . single persons and orphans under the age of eighteen were granted eighty acres, natives under the age of eighteen would receive forty acres each." Eligible natives had four years to choose their allotments, "or if this time passed, the selection would be initiated for them by the Secretary of the Interior." It was the law of a white government—compulsory—but thought to be of economic benefit to the Indians by making Christian landowners of them. While the provisions of the act would ultimately efface the well-established tribal communities, the goal was assuring their safety from white settlers and assimilating them into "white culture." However, many Native Americans were assigned to often unworkable, nonarable parcels not of their choosing. Keeping them on the reservation but making them farmers and "civilizing" them—seen as more acceptable than slaughtering them—was the declared intent. But to a man like William A., who from his earliest army days had never by word or deed intended harm to indigenous peoples, this was not only a much-needed job but an opportunity to help and perhaps build a path to citizenship for a people long devalued, long brutalized, long massacred. It was a formidable task for William A., who never believed any Native American was a true enemy.[2]

Winder will leave San Diego behind, as he has in his various past lives as a military man, a mining hopeful, a husband, a father, and a doctor. He must summon what little remaining strength he has and reinvent himself yet again. That will be a mighty task. He will take as devoted assistants two much younger men: Charles Reiter, the husband of Andrea Moro, a full-blooded Luiseño Indian who lived on the Warner Ranch in San Diego County until Reiter married her, and John Chew Minor, a former Confederate soldier whom William A. had met at María de Burton's Rancho Jamul cement works, one of her last attempts at a money-making enterprise.

With these younger men perhaps imbuing him with a stronger spirit, they headed north to the Round Valley Reservation, a grueling distance of six hundred miles, over a mountain range and along perilous and twisted roads, to a remote sweep of "hunting grounds and fishing camps" in California's Sacramento Valley. Winder finds great natural beauty—wildflowers and sweet grass in the hot summer and a dry, chilly, but bearable climate in winter—colliding with a heartbreaking history. The elders have passed on to their descendants tragic stories of massacres, rapes, and lost lands focusing on 1856, when bullwhip-wielding men rounded up thousands of disparate tribal peoples—"the Concows, the Pit Rivers, the Nomlackis, the Nisenans, the Wailackis, and the Pomos"—and forced them onto what was called the Nome Cult Indian Farm.[3]

If these dislocated tribes survived the death marches to the reservations—many did not, and they continued for years—they came to the ancestral homeland of the Yuki, whose traditions, ceremonies, language, and culture were foreign, and forbidding, to them. But coexistence was unavoidable, as there was no other choice. In 1870 Nome Cult officially became the Round Valley Indian Reservation at the order of Pres. Ulysses S. Grant. But according to *Albion Monitor* reporter Jeff Elliot, "Angry whites protested by tearing down the reservation fences so that their cattle and pigs would destroy Indian crops. Although Congress expanded the reservation to more than 100,000 acres, the Indians saw little benefit. Restricted to 5,000 acres in the undesirable northern end of the valley, most of their land was illegally occupied by white ranchers."[4]

Twenty-four years after the Round Valley Reservation's establishment, William A. must now make the Dawes Act allotments and "confirm the land choices of Round Valley Indians." It was a difficult, often grueling procedure. "First, the General Land Office conducted a detailed survey paid for with money transferred from the Indian Office appropriations." An agent like Winder would "prepare a roll of all Indians entitled to allotments, and direct the process."[5]

He would learn that some reservation residents did not want the allotments, while others, especially those working outside the reservation—by choice or for pay—lobbied hard to receive the gift of land, especially if it was near good, clear water and would bring economic security. Winder worried that "in some cases . . . these so-called streams are in winter mountain torrents and in summer dry rocky beds, absolutely worthless."[6]

In order to try to be fair—fairness to Native Americans in the face of injustices was always his concern—he at first gave allotment priority to "Indians who had made engagements to shear sheep [and] would lose the work by which they earn a little money."[7]

Others wanted to "avoid the federal government" and despised the idea of taking orders from any white man, especially when, as the need for more allotments grew, Daniel Browning, the commissioner of Indian Affairs, ordered Winder to mandate that married women who'd already received ten acres must now give back five acres, as he believed that a woman's work was unimportant and that "only men farmed and contributed to the household's economy."[8]

Winder waited until after the Fourth of July, which the reservation Indians—likely mandated to do so—celebrated as a feast day replete with fireworks, to deliver the edict. "Before informing them ... I called their attentions to the many and great benefits the Government had conferred on them, and their desire to give them a good start in their new life," he wrote. When the Indians didn't happily respond to this new start in life, "some avoided me and could not be found," William A. wrote.[9]

William A. and the local agent, Lt. Thomas Connelly, "in whom [Round Valley Indians] have great confidence," were able to calm a potentially dangerous situation with the help of "Yuki Captain John Brown ... who accepted his allotments." Perhaps, as author William J. Bauer Jr. posited, Brown had done so to be a "good example for other reservation Indians." For whatever reason, major conflict was avoided.[10]

The job William A. so desperately needed involved not only parceling out allotments but also taking away some of the land the Indians loved and needed. Winder's time at Round Valley had ended by 1895, when "601 allotments with an average size of eight and a half acres" had been made.[11]

The job was done; the lands were allotted, for better or worse. William A. had managed to fulfill his obligations. By that time also he has most likely received news of the passing of yet another family member, his third cousin Richard Bayley Winder, on July 18, 1894. After his release from Richmond in 1866, R. B. Winder—indicted for war crimes, jailed, and finally paroled—began a new life. He "took up the study of dentistry and twenty years later became the dean of the Baltimore Dental College." This Winder had survived and thrived; he was a success.[12]

What was next for William A., frail and silver-bearded, hunched and weary? On February 5, 1895, before he can shamble back to San Diego, banish the old ghosts, and begin again, there is this: "Special Agent George C. Crager"—an Indian fighter-turned linguist and interpreter living among the Lakota Sioux—was directed to "turn over his work to Special Agent William A. Winder who has been appointed to succeed him." The assignment is familiar. The language is familiar. William A. has again been appointed a "special agent to make allotments of land in severalty to Indians," this time at the Rosebud Reservation in South Dakota.[13]

Again the government has come to William A.'s rescue. And he will again try to do what will be required of him in the year 1895, and in winter on the Great Plains. As he is elderly with severe rheumatism, it will be a winter harsher than any he has ever endured. Minor and Reiter will accompany him on this long journey to sacred lands that once belonged to warriors both princely and ferocious.

16

Rosebud

Now embarking on a nearly two-thousand-mile journey, the trio of Winder and his assistants boards a train on the Central Pacific Railroad line. It had been built by the herculean labors of Chinese immigrants: blasting and tunneling through mountains, laying miles of track. In 1869 the Central Pacific Railroad line met up with the Union Pacific line at Promontory Point, Utah Territory, and the Golden Spike driven into the ground there finally connected the East and West Coasts by rail. The Union Pacific line was built westward from Council Bluffs, Iowa, a town that was roiled by labor strikes in the late nineteenth century. Strikebreakers, meatpackers, and cattlemen fought and rioted there. Beyond the town, trains clattered through a sparsely populated landscape bleached and parched by a killing drought that began in 1891. There are dust clouds, fields of parched crops, and starving animals that forage for the sparse nubbins of anything that remains. The dead landscape stretches along the prairie past sod houses and log houses of the once hopeful settlers, desperate now, hungry, and, while waiting for government assistance, forced to sell or eat their remaining livestock.

At Omaha the trio from California transfers to the Fremont, Elkhorn & Missouri Valley Railroad bound for Valentine, Nebraska, a twelve-hour leg.[1]

At last they arrive in Valentine, population seven hundred. It is a rough, lawless town of miscreants, robbers, prostitutes, and gamblers. Also journeying through drought-stricken Nebraska and South Dakota around this time was the intrepid *New York World* reporter Nellie Bly. From Fairfax, South Dakota, on January 21, 1895, she wrote, "They have only one train a day out of Valentine and that's at 4 a.m. I really believe they have it at that hour for fear everybody would leave if the time were more convenient."[2]

From Valentine to the reservation is a distance of forty-four miles—about six to eight hours by horseback or carriage—and there is the Niobrara River to cross. Along the river is Fort Niobrara, an army garrison "established in April 22, 1880, to protect settlers from hostile Sioux Indians and to oversee the Spotted Tail Indian Agency" (the former name of the Rosebud Indian Reservation) just across the Nebraska state line in South Dakota.[3]

According to tribal information sources, Rosebud "was established in 1889 by the United States' partition of the Great Sioux Reservation," and thus that partition occurred the same year South Dakota became a state. The reservation had originally been "created in 1868 by the Treaty of Fort Laramie," and it "originally covered all of West River, South Dakota (the area west of the Missouri River), as well as part of northern Nebraska and eastern Montana." It also "included Todd, Mellette, Tripp, and the eastern two thirds of Gregory County." Now the reservation was smaller, the lands around it snatched or sold away. Its people had been worn down by war, dislocation, and genocide for generations.[4]

Tall, craggy buttes—stark, brown, and magnificent—loom as the Californians quicken their approach to Rosebud and the Lakota Sioux branch known as the Sicangu Oyate or Brulé ("Burnt Thigh") people. There in tents, tepees, and camps, along the drifts of snow and frozen grasses, many Brulé hold sacred the memory of Chief Spotted Tail (Sinte Gleska). He had been a fierce warrior, a visionary, an icon, and finally a controversial conciliator who willed his people to bow to the white man, saying, "In the long run they could not win against the power of the Americans."[5]

In 1877, a year after his nephew Tasunke Witko, better known as Chief Crazy Horse, had ended the life of George Armstrong Custer at the Battle of the Little Bighorn and the U.S. Army had retaliated by sending a raging army to wipe out all the Sioux, Spotted Tail concluded it was better to go to the reservation. Better to survive. Better not to join the Ghost Dance to pray, sing, and summon the Indian messiah who would calm the wrath of the gods by spitting fire at the Sioux who had ceded the land to the white man. Forbidden but performed in secret, the whirling, swooning Ghost Dance called on the "spirits of all the dead . . . to join their living relatives and assist them in a return to the old happy life . . . in a land from which all whites had disappeared."[6]

Ghost Dancers prayed for clouds of dust to envelop the invading white men and make them magically vanish from the Black Hills, from the sacred Sioux homeland that had been decimated and desecrated by settlers streaming in by land and rail to mine the Black Hills gold, to squat, camp, and commandeer the territories where the great buffalo herds the Sioux relied on for sustenance had been hunted to near extinction.

Although Spotted Tail was murdered on August 5, 1881, by rival chief Crow Dog in a struggle for power and primacy on the reservation once named for him and whose residents both venerated and resented him, in William A.'s time it was the reluctant home of the Rosebud Brulé. Even to this day it spans rivers that border the land: the White River, the Missouri River, the Ponca River crossing Bull Creek, and the Keya Paha River, which led to the prominent Christian mission close by the Rosebud Agency buildings where Winder, Reiter, and Minor will live. Sprawling across the reservation are districts named for "physical features such as creeks, or for tribal leaders."[7]

On unfamiliar ground that must be made familiar, on horseback or at times by wagon, Winder, Reiter, and Minor will travel the "districts or communities" of the reservation as recorded by a white photographer and regular Rosebud visitor, John A. Anderson.[8]

These districts were "Rosebud (or agency), Spring Creek, Ironwood Creek, Upper Cut Meat, Cut Meat, Lower Cut Meat, He Dog's Camp, Red Leaf, Black Pipe, Corn Creek, Little White River, Pine Creek, Upper Pine Creek, Ring Thunder's Camp, Butte Creek, Oak Creek, White Thunder, Little Crow's Camp, Ponca Creek, Whirlwind Soldier, and Milk's Camp."[9]

In the field, the work of Special Allotting Agent William A. Winder was to do just that—allot lands to the Brulé Sioux, and when meeting resistance, he would try to resolve conflicts as best he could. The agency superintendent, Charles E. McChesney, was "the link between the people of the reservation and the govern-

ment in Washington," as well as the person charged with overseeing the issue of staples such as "salt, bacon, green coffee, sugar,
navy beans, rice, hardtack, flour, baking powder and yellow laundry soap," brought by railroad cars and "hauled to the Agency by
the Indians." There was a police force on the reservation as well.
The mounted officers "guarded the issue of rations[,] . . . protected
government property, carried mail and messages to the reservation" and "found and returned truant children to school," many
of whom couldn't abide the strict, unfamiliar, and often humiliating rules. A truant child was a bad child, a bad Indian child, as
William A. would come to see.[10]

There were twenty-one day schools spread over the reservation, most in the same camps Winder must visit, as well as "two
mission boarding schools, one Roman Catholic, one Episcopal,
. . . about seven miles south of the agency."[11]

At most schools Winder will see children's tribal identities
effaced, as they are required to "wear white man's clothing. The
boys were given haircuts, and all were given Christian names,"
but they "were allowed to retain their father's surnames." No haircuts were allowed for the girls, but usually a "single braid" was
required. This effort to "whiten" the youngest tribal members was
a practice encouraged by the U.S. government. Future generations
confined to the reservation, having undergone these indoctrina-
tions, instructions, and regulations, might be more manageable
than their wary, angry, heartsick parents, who would wish them
free, riding across the prairie toward a bountiful bison herd.[12]

Apart from medicine men and natural remedies for illness and
disease, there were only two reservation physicians. Winder is not
one of them. Because of his own infirmity or choice or because
the government does not need another doctor, his life as a doctor has passed. Now he is an agent, an official agent. Allotments
must be offered to the former "hunters and warriors who must
not demean themselves by working with their hands." To feed and
sustain the Sioux of Rosebud, rations were supplied; "beef was
regularly issued to the Indians . . . to keep the people from leaving
the reservation in search of meat." In addition, branded cattle on
the hoof would be driven from corrals to the prairies, where the

Indians could shoot the animals and butcher them, after which every part of the animal was used.[13] And though it was deemed "a betrayal of the tribe's honor for any Brûlé to attempt to make a living like the white man by scratching the ground," they must do just that. If they did not engage in farming, it was the rule across the country and on most if not all reservations that the land would be sold by the government and their allotment would be gone.[14]

As Winder came to better know the Sicangu, he would hear firsthand of the tragedy of five years earlier. It happened near Pine Ridge after the arrest and killing of the Hunkpapa Sioux chief, Sitting Bull, whom the army mistakenly believed was performing the banned Ghost Dance. Amid confusion and chaos, soldiers of Maj. Samuel M. Whitside's U.S. Seventh Cavalry pursued Chief Spotted Elk's tribe to Wounded Knee Creek. Perhaps as many as three hundred Sioux, including fleeing women and children, were massacred—gunned down at close range. It was these lost ones whose spirits were still believed to swirl in the racing wind over Pine Ridge and Rosebud, over tepees, schools, stockades, and log houses, through snow and summer sun, over canyons and pine forests and along endless prairie.

There are those among the Sioux of Rosebud who, when summoning the lost, mourn their tragedies and long for the days when defeat of the white man was an honorable and necessary fight, when the great hunts, the pride in the hunts, when the skins, sinews, bones, and flesh of the buffalo were not wasted, as the white man wasted them.

Winder would meet the "traditionalists"—wanting nothing to do with the allotments, as they were once warriors—struggling with the "progressives" who, inspired by the deeds of Spotted Tail, accepted the mandates of the Indian agents and their promises.[15]

There was much work and much convincing for Winder to do.

"Since entering upon duty, Special Agent Winder has for the most part been engaged in correcting and revising the work done by Special Agent Crager, but is now engaged in making new allotments," a government report noted.[16]

And he has asked for more much-needed help, knowing his stay at Rosebud would not end quickly.

The *San Francisco Call* reported, "Colonel Chalmers Scott will leave here tomorrow for South Dakota, in response to a telegram from Dr. William A. Winder, allotting agent for the Rosebud Sioux, appointing Colonel Scott chief engineer. There are some 3,500,000 acres in the Rosebud agency to be allotted, and the work will consume three or four years. Three surveying parties are now in the field." This Colonel Scott was an engineer and surveyor from San Diego and also Winder's dear friend. The article also noted that "the standard and base lines and township lines are all to be run, and sectionizing is to be done. Then subdivisions are to be made of the land into twenty and forty acre lots. Each Indian will get about that amount where the land is good, but where it is bad it will be allotted in larger tracts."[17]

The summer of 1895 at Rosebud brought the usual persistent heat, but there also came news of the passing of Winder's dear old friend María Amparo Ruiz de Burton on August 12. After struggling and petitioning the government to return her beloved Rancho Jamul, the place John C. Minor called home, she died in poverty in Chicago. She had been there for almost a year, trying also to sell her land in Mexico. She died at the Sherman House of gastric fever, and her remains were embalmed and sent back to San Diego, where the funeral was held. William A. would remember the days he spent working with her on *The Squatter and the Don*, days sequestered in his frame house in New Town with the friend of his youth at Mission de Alcalá, the friend of his later years when he was writing, painting, and doctoring—the special times with his special friend, the widow of his revered superior officer, Gen. Henry Burton.

Once again, grieving and loss cannot be allowed to interrupt his work. He has made 345 allotments and offered the "allottees some timber for use in connection with their agricultural and grazing lands."[18]

William A.'s time at Rosebud, with its hard, demanding work, insulates him from the family circle from which he has long been absent. Slowly the remnants of his Confederate kin are dying without ever having been in contact with him, forever firm in the belief that he was a traitor to the rebel cause. On March 22, 1896, a little more than a year after William A. arrived at Rosebud, his half brother John Cox Winder died in Raleigh, North Carolina, while serving as the vice president of the Seaboard Air Line Railroad. He had made a proper life for himself as a well-paid railroad engineer. No such prominence has come to William A. His current work, so often drudgery but bringing him a much-needed salary of about $1,000 a year, continued as grass fires, snow, and rain whipped the reservation. And if the days and nights in camps—allotting, bargaining, soothing, and helping—tired and weakened him, he managed. He continued.

The *Valentine Democrat*, a chatty sort of newspaper, was glad to follow the reservation happenings, as well as to agree that the work of men like Winder was beneficial:

> Uncle Sam is generous. Up to date, 175 Indians from the Rosebud Agency have received their allotments of wagons, etc., from the depot here. Each Indian receives a wagon, complete with top box, bows and cover; set of harness, harrow, hoe, axe and pitchfork. A team of mares, one with foal, two cows, one with calf by her side, and $50 in cash, will complete the Government gift to those Indians who have taken land in severalty, and will give them a good start on their farms. The outcome of this experiment is difficult to determine, but we hope 'twill prove successful.[19]

Winder surely knew the hardscrabble life of the Brulé as he toiled among them over this long year. But to many in the United States the vanished days on the plains frontier, when news of massacres by both Indians and whites was still alive in mind and memory, aroused a hunger to see "savages, for titillation, pleasure and profit," and excited crowds would pay to view them. So, "after signing federally approved contracts . . . officials at the Cincinnati Zoological Society" arranged for eighty-nine Sicangu Sioux men, women, and children, along with two boxcars transporting their tepees and horses, to travel from Rosebud to Valentine and then proceed by rail to Cincinnati. They are encamped and exhibited at the city's zoo in "a spectacular event [that] lasted three months." Prodded to show fearsome displays, the Rosebud people face huge crowds who watch them participate in "reenactments of legendary western battles, an attack on a stagecoach, war dances and Indian pony races." Indians in war paint wielding tomahawks, sounding war cries, and speaking in native tongues galloped along as Cincinnatians traveled vicariously through time and space. Much like other raucous displays throughout the country—Buffalo Bill's Wild West Show comes to mind—the shows are huge draws. Sellouts. They are at once degrading exploitations but a chance for a select, perhaps coerced group of Indians, enticed by the promise of a salary and subsistence (as long as they consumed no alcohol) to leave the reservation—for a world of white gawkers who applauded the stereotypes as their "love affair with frontier events grew, thus immortalizing the vanished frontier and the mythical West."[20]

No such stunning displays blazed though Winder's days as he traveled the reservation, wooing, winning, and convincing the more compliant Brulé to accept the allotments, surely believing his work has merit. He must believe this.

According to the report of the commissioner of Indian Affairs, the year ended with "four hundred and eleven allotments made by William A., making "a total of nine hundred and ten allotments . . . quite a number of Indians are now waiting for government surveys to be made so they can take their land in severalty also."[21]

• • •

At the beginning of 1897, with the departure of Chalmers Scott from Rosebud due to illness, Winder, Reiter, and Minor must now work without him, and even though the *Valentine Democrat* is now referring to William A. as a doctor, there is worrisome news. The newspaper reports that "Dr Winder, of Rosebud, has been quite ill for several days past."[22]

While the specifics of Winder's infirmity are unclear, the devoted Charles Reiter has been helping him by surveying and selling Indian lands refused by the allottees. And there was a glimpse of the old healer Winder. There was this: "Professor Hadden came in from the Boarding School, Sunday, with his son, Rob, who dislocated his arm at play. In the absence of the Agency physician, Dr Winder, with the assistance of Miss Kleine, put the troublesome member on the road to speedy recovery."[23]

With Winder briefly returning to his beloved doctoring, one might ask why he does not continue the healing when he is in a place where there is such need. As summer arrives with unremitting heat he will pause to rest, to reflect on the days when killing Indians was the daily activity of many of his compatriots, activities he had notably refused. Picture him now among the thousands gathered for the grand Fourth of July celebrations on the reservation, which are curiously protracted and massive displays of patriotism.

"In 1897, for the first time, the [Brulé] placed special emphasis on an occasion important to the white man's history," authors Henry W. Hamilton and Jean Tyree Hamilton write. Two days before the holiday the Brulé, the local traders, and people from across the Niobrara River valley pour into the fairgrounds just north of the Rosebud Agency. Six thousand were in attendance to see "the Squaw Dance, the Corn Dance, and chief's dances," followed on the Fourth by a reading of the Declaration of Independence. The celebrations lasted six days and included a "mock attack on the stockade," recreating actual events that occurred in 1889—and this mock attack "was to become a Rosebud Institution." A mock attack, a practiced and prolonged celebration, "bronc riding and steer riding, horse races, foot races and cash prizes"—what to make of it? It is likely that for some of the Sioux, displays of their traditions mingled with their relatively new independent lives as farmers—like the white man—made the time of great celebration uniquely their own.[24]

With Winder still at his labors by year's end, a bit of praise came to him in the form of the usually terse Indian Affairs report: "The work on this reservation is progressing satisfactorily under the direction of Special Agent William A. Winder . . . who had made one thousand four hundred and twenty-eight allotments; the whole number of Indians on the reservation entitled to allotments is approximately three thousand five hundred." The allotments are numbers, to be sure, but the reservation is large. And of the other tribal members not entitled to allotments—whether holdouts, renegades, or simply not on the proper rolls—their fate is unknown. Perhaps the news that "five hundred" Indians have come to Rosebud from south of and near the White River and an additional "five thousand dollars for surveying" will bode well for them, and for their agent, William A.[25]

There is more to do on the reservation, but at least he has help. "Special Agent John H. Knight has been recently assigned to assist" William A., who "has made two thousand three hundred and five allotments." And according to the commissioner of Indian Affairs, William A. was "instructed in regard to making allotments to an Indian named John Bob Tail Crow and his children on the Sioux ceded lands." William A. must protect John Bob Tail Crow and his family from "several white men" who "filed homestead claims." This was not uncommon, but in this case, and with William A.'s intercession, a dispute before the "local land office" ensued as the white men tried to buy the land for "a paltry consideration." But after a "decision of the Commissioner of the Land Office in favor of the Indians," the land was finally allotted to John Bob Tail Crow and his family. The occupation of land by squatters, or settlers as they would have preferred to be called, was not uncommon. But here was a victory. Here was a family.[26]

• • •

It is 1899, and it is spring. William A. has survived a hard Rosebud winter. Should he remain well, William A. will see a new century, a time of change and promise, but at the Rosebud Reservation life continues as it has continued, with the exception of a reported Indian uprising in Crookston, Nebraska. From his home in Valentine, the photographer and diarist John Anderson, who was photographing the people of Rosebud during the time William A. was there and would have known him, wrote of news that sent "hundreds of frightened settlers [running] . . . scared almost to death. . . . The scene was never to be forgotten." Anderson reminded himself and other whites that no matter how well he was received as he lugged his camera though the camps, restive and angry Indians were always to be feared, no matter how many had duly acquiesced to a "civilized" life.[27]

• • •

As summer descended on the reservation, William A. travels to Omaha on "reservation business." On August 1, 1899, the *Omaha World-Herald* reported on his friendship and kindness to the Indians in his keep. And to animals. It seemed that he had been raising and taming squirrels and decided to give some to a local park so others might enjoy the little animals, so often hunted for fun:

Riverview Park was enriched last evening by a big cage of squirrels. Under ordinary circumstances, and if they were ordinary squirrels, this addition to the big park menageries would hardly be worth passing notice, but these are extraordinary squirrels, they being the possessors of the spirits of little Brule children who have died. Or, at least, such is the belief of the Indians, who treat them with the greatest veneration. . . . The squirrels are the gift of Dr William A. Winder, who has been at Rosebud Agency for a number of years and collected them at and near the agency. They have been the subject of considerable correspondence between Dr Winder and park Commissioner Cornish, who is always active in behalf of the menagerie, and yesterday the latter received a telegram from the former saying that he [Winder] and the squirrels would arrive at the Webster street depot during the afternoon. They were met and at once taken to the park. The squirrels have always been pets, and are very tame, both Dr Winder and the Indians always treating them kindly, the latter often coming long distances to feed and talk to them. Whether the small white boy will treat them as gently is a question now worrying the park commissioner.[28]

From Omaha, William A. and his assistant John C. Minor then travel to Chicago.

On the way, at Sioux City, Iowa, William A. gives a rare and reluctant interview to the *Sioux City Journal.* The newspaper may be interested in him because Winder's brother-in-law is Adm. George Dewey, who gained fame and public adulation during the Spanish-American War, when on April 27, 1898, he crushed the Spanish fleet at Manila Bay. Winder's son, Willie, now a captain, is in Admiral Dewey's fleet, and Dewey's son George was a resident at the Goodwin home in Portsmouth, New Hampshire, during his early years. When urged to speak about his now deceased Confederate family, Winder was discomfited. He is being called upon to remember what the journalist perhaps thinks are glowing times, but they are dark days to Winder. And he is old, his memory of names and dates smudged with time.

The *Sioux City Journal*'s attention-grabbing headline is "Brother-In-Law of Dewey . . . Winder fought on the Union side . . . His Father the Andersonville Jailor." And the interview proceeds: "A brother-in-law of Admiral George Dewey, the hero of Manila[,] arrived in Sioux City last night. General William H. Winder [the reporter misstates his rank and middle initial], is United States special agent in charge of the allotment of Indian lands. It was with considerable hesitancy the general consented to talk of himself and the days of long ago when he and Lieut. Dewey were courting sisters in New Hampshire."[29]

"'Yes,' he said, stroking his white beard, 'Dewey and I married daughters of Gov. Ichabod Goodwin of New Hampshire,'" referring to Dewey's late wife, Susie, "'while the governor was in office. I had married two years before his election. Dewey was a lieutenant commander in the navy; I was captain of the Third Artillery. His wife's first name was Sarah [he means Susie Dewey, who died on December 28, 1872, five days after their son George was born]. My wife was Abbie [Abby] Goodwin. She still is living and at present is visiting at Portsmouth, the old family home.'" Of course, after Winder went back to California in 1866, Abby returned to her father's home and never lived anywhere else. William A. continued.

"'After Mrs. Dewey's death a few years after her marriage, my wife took the young George Dewey and he lived with us until he entered Princeton.'" Winder went on to praise Dewey, saying his "'great trait is carefulness. . . . I cannot remember of him ever being unprepared.'" And of his attire, he stated, "'While he was never dudish he always faultlessly dressed.'"

Winder also spoke of a letter written to his wife, Abby, by their son, Willie, about the Battle of Manila. "'He began the letter the night of the battle and added a few pages every day thereafter,'" William A. said. "'He told his mother he always wondered how he would act in a fight, "and mother," Willie wrote, "I was astounded at myself. I had felt that I would be frightened. When we entered the bay I kissed your dear photograph and then saluted the dear old flag. After that I had no thought of fear and when the fight was hottest I watched the shells strike without realizing any danger.""

When "reminded that his name sounded like that of Gen. John Henry Winder, of the Confederacy, who during the war of the rebellion had charge of Andersonville and the other southern prisons, and in reply to a question as to whether he knew the man"—one can almost hear an intake of breath at this point in the interview, or see a flinch, a quick closing of the eyes—"'Yes, sir, he was my father.'" And Winder related their shared histories, their births in Maryland: "'My father united himself with the Confederacy and I fought with the Union army.'" And does he pause then, to hear his father's voice through the message he gave to the spy Timothy Webster: Come to me, come south now, fight with me or, if not, Yankee son, desert the Union, be jailed for the whole war, or commit suicide. Those hard words he does not speak of. Instead he tells the reporter, "'The last time I saw him [Gen. John Winder] was a year before the war. He dropped dead in 1864 [1865].'" He goes on as he has gone on before to speak of loyalty, to forcefully deride the "unjust charges" against General Johnston when he was accused of "'attempting to turn the state of California over to the Confederacy,'" and he quotes from a letter he wrote to Sherman, before again defending Johnston.

Sherman's reply must have been a comfort, as Winder truly believed in Johnston, his late rebel friend and former commander at Alcatraz. "I was only too glad to hear the truth, which you now so simply affirm," Sherman had written to him, "that Johnston was absolutely true to his high trust."

The interview concluded with the newspaper reminding the readers of Winder's appointment as special allotting agent by Grover Cleveland in 1892 and that he was assigned to service in California. "Three years ago, he was transferred to South Dakota. He is now accompanied by his clerk . . . [J.] C. Minor."

According to a Duluth, Minnesota, newspaper, William A. and Minor also stopped in Chicago. "General [sic] William A. Winder, a brother-in-law of Admiral Dewey, accompanied by Major J. C. Minor, was at the Palmer House today," the newspaper reported.

"General Winder married a sister of Admiral Dewey's wife in 1851. General Winder is special allotting agent of the government at the Rosebud Indian Reservation agency, in South Dakota. Major Minor is the government surveyor at the reservation. General Winder has been located there for five years. . . . 'We have been ordered to report to Washington by the secretary of the interior,' said General Winder . . . 'We hope while there, to see Admiral Dewey.'"[30]

That November, while at the reservation, William A. received a letter from his subordinate allotting agent, Charles H. Bates, reporting a concern he has for the family of tribal elder Jack Sully. This elder has told Bates that he wanted to talk about how they should proceed to gain their allotments.

Sully was in great distress, Bates wrote:

> He told me that they were not drawing rations anywhere, and had not been for a number of years. . . . I found that his people was not on any of our lists, and I told him I thought if his people were allotted the matter for good and all, that is Major McChesney [Charles E. McChesney, William A.'s superior] would not act in the matter to subject it to one of the congressmen for action before the Comm., and to do it as soon as possible so that if they were recognized on the Rosebud Res., then allotments could be made to go on this year[']s schedules. . . . All that I know about his being ordered off the Res . . . I suppose they still imagined as Sully had told me, that they were to be ordered off. Gamble says McChesny [sic] wrote him that he did not know anything about a man named Sully from the rolls.[31]

Apparently this was not an uncommon problem. But without rations, the Indians would starve. Bates then wrote, "I told him, if he would go to work right away to find out where he was at, I would set a stake for anybody on the land he claims for his family, unless especially ordered to do so by you. The foregoing is all I know in the matter." The fate of Sully and his family remained uncertain. Perhaps that was the reason William A. needed to go to Washington. And Bates, who knew that William A. had seen his son and Admiral Dewey while in Chicago, wrote, "I was very much pleased to learn in your letter that your trip to Chicago did you so much good, you certainly enjoyed your visit with your son and I don't know of anything that would make a man enjoy the good things to eat, and the big crowds of people, and excitement after more than 5 years of life at Rosebud Agency." Bates added wearily, and clearly tired of paperwork, "I am at work on my field notes and it [illegible] pretty hard to be housed up in this fine weather and I wish every day I was out with your party in the field."[32]

$$\bullet \ \bullet \ \bullet$$

William A. has toiled to a new century. With winter past, he has once again traveled to Chicago for a much-needed break. The *Valentine Democrat* offered this on May 17, 1900: "Major Minor and Dr Winder, of the Rosebud Agency, started Wednesday morning for Chicago, where they expected to be gone for ten days or a couple of weeks as a means of recreation after months of toil. The *Democrat* wishes them an enjoyable time."[33]

In early June William A. and Abby were briefly reunited at the Palmer House Hotel in Chicago—the *Portsmouth Herald* referred to them as "Gen. and Mrs W. A. Winder"—as they awaited the arrival of their son, Willie, who was coming in on the USS *Michigan*. It was a fleeting reunion.[34]

And again, as though slipping through the fog, William A. has gone back to Rosebud. And has been ailing. Then this odd item from the *Valentine Democrat* on November 1, 1900, reports that William A. has been on the move: "Major Minor and Dr. Winder of Rosebud are making their home in Valentine now. The Dr. has been feeling unwell for some days but is now better."[35] Here in a November 14, 1900, letter to William A. from his superior, U.S. Indian agent Charles E. McChesney, is more information about William A. needing to be on the move: "I was talking with Major Miner [sic] over the phone yesterday and he seemed to have the idea that it was imperative that both you and himself return to this Agency in the near future." Apparently there is a smallpox epidemic in Valentine. McChesney urges William A. to leave Valentine for Crookston, where it seems that smallpox is not a problem, and "at the end of two weeks absence from Valentine . . . you would be able to come through without trouble. You could advise me a few days before by telegraph and I could then inform you whether there are any cases of smallpox in Crookston." He adds, "If I raise the embargo on you I might as well raise it on everyone, which I do not feel justified in doing so long as there is a case of smallpox in Valentine. . . . I regret the delay and inconvenience it has been to you, but I have something over 5,000 people here to consider and I do not wish smallpox or any other contagious disease to come among them, and deem it to be only my duty to take all ordinary precautions in the matter." Thus, it would seem that the authorities took all ordinary and extraordinary precautions to protect for the welfare of the Indians, as an epidemic would rage unabated.[36]

Eager as William A. is to continue his allotments, he must stay away. If necessary, he could communicate by telephone. The McChesney letter is the first mention of its use at Rosebud.

• • •

By 1901 William A. is spending time both on and off the reservation. In summer, on June 13, the *Valentine Democrat* reported that "Dr Wm A Winder and Major J. C. Minor came down from the agency last Saturday to look after business matters. They are very busy with the allotting of lands to the Indians[,] which will occupy considerable time yet."[37]

And it does, for a good period of time. Although there is no evidence of William A. attending patients at this time, he is referred to as Dr. Winder. Perhaps it was just a nod to his years as a healer. In the meantime the *Portsmouth Herald* announced Willie's engagement: "Lt. Cdr. William Winder, of the USS *Michigan*, only son of Mrs. Abbie Winder, of this city and Miss [Ethel] Taylor, a well known society lady of Erie, Pa." William A. is not even mentioned.[38]

• • •

In early 1902 it appears that William A. is no longer in the field among the Indians at the camps. The ever-faithful and diligent Charles Reiter has taken over some of William A.'s duties. Reiter wrote about "a case I wish to submit to you for your decision of the amount of land that Medicine Owl, the widow of Spotted War

Bonnet . . . has not been allotted." After the death of Spotted War Bonnet, his widow, who is in "the census with three children," remarries Wolf (last name illegible), and Reiter wants to know if she gets "640 acres, or 320 acres," and benefits. Apparently there is also a similar case involving "Charging Hawk and Not Standing Hawk [and] . . . War Horse Comes Out and Dog Track." These Indians have numbered stakes on their desired allotments, but some allotments, including those of Kill in the Water and Blanket Long Pheasant, were transferred to the Rosebud Reservation's territory. Confusion abounded as to these Indians named by Reiter and their entitlements to land. Unfortunately, resolution of these cases is unrecorded.[39]

• • •

On April 26 John C. Minor, William A.'s companion, friend, and associate, died in Valentine, Nebraska. A grieving William A. sent a "card of thanks" to the *Valentine Democrat*: "I wish to extend my thanks to my friends who rendered aid, and to those that offered their services through the sickness of my friend, Major Minor."[40]

On May 1 the *Valentine Democrat* offered this obituary, worth recording in full. It illuminates the life of John C. Minor and allows a glimpse into the increasing frailty of William A.:

> Last Thursday morning, about three o'clock, Major John Chew Minor breathed his last after an illness of several weeks from cirossis [sic] of the liver. Thus passes away an eventful and useful life of a man who was modest, gentlemanly, and kind, courteous to all alike, and was untiring in his devotion to Dr Winder, of whom the major frequently spoke and referred to as the "venerable old man." No less was the devotion of Dr Winder to his friend the Major who has been in the employ of the government with the Doctor and Chas Reiter during the past ten years and their constant association has endeared them one to another.

The obituary then notes that the two men met when Minor was in charge of the Jamul Cement Works in Southern California and was chief deputy collector at the Port of San Diego. As the two traveled together in the area of Rosebud, "our people have seen the familiar forms of the Doctor and Major and noted their devotion to each other. Their fathers were fast friends before them, and they seemed like father and son, the Major always attentive and striving to make the Doctor comfortable, who was nearly 20 years older and though more feeble from age has survived the Major and may yet live another 10 years or more. The Doctor has the sympathy of all who know him and all will feel that he is more endeared to them because of his age and recent bereavement."[41]

• • •

On June 29, 1902, came important news from the *Omaha Daily Bee*: "Captain William A. Winder . . . lies seriously ill at an Omaha hotel." His condition was precarious because of the "infirmity of his advanced age. . . . He is now in his 77th year."[42] (He was actually seventy-nine.)

The article contained something more than a health report, however. It also contained a statement from the patient himself: "'I want to tell the world a story before I leave it to vindicate the name and memory of an honorable man who suffered from a cruel slander during the last few years of his life and whose memory has been defamed by ruthless, baseless utterance.' . . . This statement was made by the stricken veteran to a reporter for the *Bee* one day during the week. The man he wanted to exonerate of false charges had been his enemy and [an] enemy of the United States." It was, of course, Albert Sidney Johnston, the Union officer who became a Confederate general at the beginning of the Civil War and whom William A. repeatedly defended as a man of honor because he never acted against the Union while stationed at Alcatraz.

Described as "emaciated," William A. had something very important to say: "As for me there was never any doubt in my mind as to what my course would be, though I confess that it cost me many a severe struggle to take sides against my own relatives, as much as I loved the Union, and what it stood for."

And there it was, his final declaration of loyalty, at what he sensed would be the end of his life.

• • •

William A. was incapacitated and bedridden at the Henshaw Hotel in Valentine when he got a letter from Charles Reiter suggesting he was still needed, at least on paper.

May 31, 1902

Department of the Interior
U.S. Indian Service
Rosebud S.D.
Wm. A. Winder
U.S. Special Allott. Agt.

My Dear Sir:

Indian agent, Chas. McChesney told me to send you the schedule for your signature, which I have addressed to the Henshaw Hotel. I also enclosed four blank schedule sheets so that in case the ones I send do not prove satisfactory you can make them out again. The schedule is closed again so the Indians that come in from now on will have to wait. Your signature is on several sheets and as there are not enough to reach it I thought it best to send them to you and you can then send them back again for the agent's signature. It seems that we have about all the allotments we can get, for the Indians had a chance again to take land and receive their benefits but, there was not any to come around and take it. I will commence on the Township Plats and work them through as fast as I can. I trust you stood the trip to Omaha in good shape and that I will hear from you soon. I have no news to write so will wish you good health and remain.

Very Respectfully
Charles Reiter.

P.S. Mr. Jordan sent by registered mail to the Clarkson Hospital, your moccasins. It was done without my knowing it.[43]

By August 14 the *Valentine Democrat* was reporting that "Dr Wm Winder departed for Omaha last Thursday morning, where he will try to regain his health. The Doctor is remarkably strong for one so advanced in years and having endured so many hardships."[44]

And then the truth of his sickness was reported: "Dr. Winder, accompanied by a trained nurse, returned from Omaha last week. The Doctor is suffering from a cancer on the tongue."[45]

And this: "Dr. Wm A. Winder and his nurse from the Clarkson Hospital, Miss [Louisa] Key, returned to Omaha Tuesday to consult the doctor who is attending Mr. Winder. A week or ten days will be their stay, possibly longer. It is hoped that Dr. Winder will be benefitted and return soon," reported the *Valentine Democrat*.[46]

Finally came the news that "Chas Reiter came down Monday [Nov. 3] expecting to go to Omaha to see Dr. Winder, who is not improving in health."[47]

In fact he was dying. But what has been the worth of his work?

• • •

Despite all of William A.'s diligence and well-known humanity, along with his years of caring and careful allotments to the Rosebud Sioux, it seemed that little had changed about the white authorities' concept of "civilizing" a people and effacing a cherished culture. The words of Winder's correspondent, agent Charles H. Bates, now "in charge of allotments at the Pine Ridge Reservation," were recorded by the *Daily Deadwood Pioneer-Times* well after Winder left Rosebud. His letters to William A. expressing concern for the Indians in his keep appeared to have devolved to common prejudice. When asked if Indians are still "painting their faces . . . each decade," Bates replied laughingly that he is "seeing a great advance in the character of the red fellows. Their type is advancing, and they are being improved in many ways, but will always be Indians. The general tendency is for a pure blood Indian to marry a blood Indian. In the same way it is the tendency of half-bloods to marry half-bloods, and of quarter-bloods to marry quarter-bloods."[48] William A. would have been disheartened to see such an opinion and would have commented if he'd had the chance. But it was too late.

• • •

It is 1903, on February 26 to be exact. Abby Winder had just learned of her husband's grave illness. Although William A. and Abby have been living apart since 1865—there are only two or three occasions of record during those long years that they have seen each other when visiting their son Willie—here came a rare and intimate glimpse into Abby's heartbreak upon hearing her husband was gravely ill in Omaha.

From Portsmouth, in a letter to her cherished cousin Elizabeth "Lizzie" Blanchard in Santa Paula, California, Abby thanks Lizzie for her letter of concern about her "dear brave courageous husband. Oh it is *dreadful* and since last April, I have had a sad life of sympathy, which does little good. And the [illegible] between hopes that recovery might come—and now the certainty that the end is close at hand. The only consolation is, that he has had such care as only goes to the most favored sufferer[,] a god given nurse [Louisa Key] who has been with the dear soul since April."[49]

Abby feared her husband "does not miss me," but "every day, his nurse wrote, when he did not, I wrote him." She expresses her sadness in knowing she has lost him forever, is truly losing him—the young soldier she married, the father of their only son, the trying times at Alcatraz they endured together. Perhaps she is mourning the lost years spent apart.

Far away in Portsmouth, Abby feared her "touch was like a sledgehammer," and if she could touch him and say "poor sufferer," he "might say yes." But William A. could no longer speak. As Abby noted, Nurse Louisa Key wrote to her that "except for moaning, he never complained."

Abby was relieved to know that her son "Willie at last managed to get a week[']s leave to go to his father—about this time his father expressed a most earnest longing to see him . . . and it was such a comfort to both the dear souls." Willie consulted with a "Dr. Summers in Omaha who pronounced his malady a *cancer of the tongue*—and he thought the tongue must be mostly removed. Then it was decided to try a system called the 'Alexander,' a very painful treatment but endurable with the hope of recovery." The Alexander technique involved injections into the tumor. In some cases, it was a cure. Not in this case. "Of course," Abby wrote, "it was impossible for me to think of going there . . . alas for so many years he has been unaccustomed to my ministrations."

Nourishment, Abby was told, could not be taken by her husband "except by enema, it seems impossible that it should last long. Oh—*if only he could be at rest!* . . . But he is so brave—so absolutely uncomplaining."

Abby also relates what Willie wrote his mother from his father's bedside: "'I often tried to hold his hand—or smooth his beautiful silver hair'—but he [Willie] wrote on his pad, 'I hope I have been a good son' . . . and his father wrote, 'you are and have always been the apple of my eye.'"

Abby then tells her cousin how Willie wrote that his father scrawled on the pad, "You have devoted your life to your dear mother." Willie spoke of "the devotion of Miss Key and Charlie [Reiter] as beyond belief." There was little more to be said.

On March 6, 1903, William A. died at "four [a.m.] in his apartments at the Millard Hotel. The cancer had compelled him to retire from active service and seek rest and quiet some weeks ago. The cause of death was carcinoma hemorrhage," reported the *Omaha Daily Bee*.[50]

Obituaries and death notices came quickly.

On March 7 the *Omaha World Herald* reported that

Dr. William A. Winder, Indian fighter and friend of the Red Man, dead. Brother-in-Law of Admiral Dewey and Father of a Battleship Commander. Dr. William A. Winder, veteran Indian fighter, scout, traveler and gentleman, who has many times won medals and trophies of gallantry, and whose acquaintance over the west for the past forty years has included all the prominent men of his time, is dead at the Millard Hotel. He was a brother-in-law of Admiral Dewey. . . . The death of Dr. William A. Winder, of Rosebud, South Dakota, removes from the west one of the most interesting individuals and lovable of characters. For a long time he has been allotting agent for the government in South Dakota. It was largely through his influence . . . that the Indians of the Northwest were made to feel that they had an interest in the country in which they lived. He was always kind to the red men, yet stern, and these two characteristics caused him to be respected wherever known.[51]

The newspaper went on to relate the particulars of William A.'s family, the generals—grandfather, father, and cousin Charles S.

—without condemnation and noting the latter two's Confederate service.

Also on March 7 the *San Diego Union* reported that "W. W. [William Wallace] Bowers received a telegram yesterday from Omaha announcing the death of his old friend, Dr. Wm. Winder at that place. Dr. Winder was well known in this city[,] having been an old-timer. He was a practicing physician here for a number of years, and won many friends. He was a veteran of the Civil War holding the rank of captain of artillery. For a long time he was stationed at Alcatraz Island, San Francisco. In recent years he has held the position of United States allotting agent at the Indian reservation of Rosebud, S.D."[52]

The *San Diego Union* reprinted the text of the "telegram received" informing the newspaper of William A.'s passing: "Omaha Neb. March 5[6], 1903. Mr. W.W. Bowers Collector of Customs, San Diego Calif. Doctor Winder died tonight. Body will be embalmed and taken to Portsmouth. Notify friends. Charley Reiter."[53] With Winder's body scheduled for transport to Portsmouth, it seemed that finally and forever, he was returning to Abby and Willie.

Also on March 7, 1903, the *Baltimore American* reported that "Capt. William A. Winder formerly of this city and a member of the well-known Winder family of this state died yesterday in Omaha, Neb. Aged 79 years." The piece mentioned his father, John H., and that he was "a brother of W. S. Winder . . . his father was a Southern sympathizer . . . and joined the Confederate Army." A recital of William A.'s career followed, including his heroism in the wreck of the *San Francisco*, his army resignation, and his mining ventures, as well as his last job, at the Rosebud Reservation. "Mr. W. S. [Sidney] Winder of this city said last night that he received a letter from his brother's wife, in which it was stated that Captain Winder was seriously ill," the article stated.[54] When Sidney Winder heard that William A. was dead, he said he had not seen him since 1866. That is probably not true, as Sidney had fled to and remained in Canada the whole of 1866. Perhaps he wished he had seen the half brother who had tried to intercede with President Lincoln in 1863 when William A. thought Sidney might be executed.

Another notice from the *Omaha World-Herald* was published

March 9, 1903: "The body of Dr. William A. Winder, who died suddenly at the Millard hotel Friday morning, will be taken this evening at five o'clock over the Northwestern to his old home at Portsmouth, N.H., by members of the Loyal Legion of the United States. Mr. Winder's son, who is at Erie, Pa., will meet the body there, and will accompany it to Portsmouth, where the funeral will be held. This is the home of Mrs. Winder and the body is to be taken there on her instructions and those of the son."[55]

This from the *Portsmouth Herald* of March 12: "The funeral of Capt. William E. [sic] Winder was held today at the Gov. Goodwin mansion on Islington street, and was private. Rev. Alfred Gooding of the Unitarian church officiated. The body was placed in the Goodwin tomb in the Proprietor's cemetery by Undertaker Ham."[56]

Probably one of the most compelling headlines about William A.'s death appeared on March 15, 1903, in the *Omaha Sunday World-Herald*: "Touching Feature of Captain Winder's Life and Death . . . Because his father and brother were Confederates the distinguished Veteran was pursued by insinuation. . . . Although President Lincoln personally assured him there was no question of his loyalty, disappointment pursued him." Accompanying the piece is a photo of William A. at the end of his life, when he appeared very aged, somber, and sunken-cheeked. It was his final portrait.[57]

The last record of Winder's time at Rosebud came in a letter from the Office of Indian Affairs in Washington dated March 28, 1903. Acting Commissioner A. G. Tonner wrote to Charles E. McChesney, now the Indian agent at Rosebud, "The administrator of the estate of Special Allotting Agent William A. Winder, deceased . . . has been instructed to turn over to you all government property, including books and records, which was in Mr. Winder's hands at the time of his death."[58] These were important documents that would need to be preserved.

Consider this: the aged Winder spent hard years in South Dakota, with long hours slogging along rutted roads, or in snowdrifts snagging buggy wheels in the long cold winters, or traveling about in the summers amid thigh-high grasses, prairie fires, droughts, and the occasional flood. If on one of those long nights before a warm hearth, or when restless as he grew sicker and sicker, perhaps he saw over those vast hills, over the rivers, visions of long-gone days, visions that came in the dreams, ceremonies, and songs of the Sioux, the ghosts of buffalo dotting the plains and the warriors on fleet ponies charging after them. Or were there warships and cannonade at Alcatraz, a tangle of seabirds and seaweed covering drowning men? His fate was not to drown, never to drown in rumors, in failures, or in rough waters.

17

Of Lives Lost

Two years after William A.'s death, his half brother Sidney committed suicide at his Baltimore home on February 26, 1905, at the age of seventy-one. "Old, alone and almost blind," his father's devoted acolyte, adjutant, and defender at Richmond and Andersonville never gave up trying to clear John H. Winder's name, or his grandfather's.[1]

"Was 71 and Shot Himself," the *Baltimore Sun* headlined its coverage in the February 26, 1905, edition. Among Sidney's papers, the *Sun* reported, was a "clipping of an address by Dr. William Osler of Johns Hopkins University in which reference was made to the uselessness of men over sixty years old." In a farewell speech to colleagues at the university as he was about to assume a post at Oxford College, Dr. Osler, a famous and innovative medical practitioner, had suggested that men achieve their best work before forty. After sixty, he said, death by chloroform might be a mercy. The outcries and condemnations after these remarks were instantaneous. They were intended to be tongue and cheek, Osler was alleged to have said. It seemed that Sidney Winder took them to heart. He shot himself in the head two days after Osler's address.[2]

On May 9, 1906, in the *Portsmouth Herald* came notice of the death of "Mrs. Abbie [*sic*] Rice Winder ... at the home of her sister Miss Hope Goodwin, on Islington Street at the age of seventy-seven years, two months and twenty days." Abby was a beloved Portsmouth fixture, adored and respected: "A lady of fine presence and of distinguished talent. Her kindness of heart and generous impulses were proverbial and she leaves precious memorials to kinship and to the community."[3]

Once, long ago, her "community" had included Alcatraz, Old

Town, and New Town in San Diego, places of confinement and pain for Abby as well as for William A. "On returning from San Francisco with her husband . . . she remained in the East and passed her life in her native city, the intimate companion of her parents and oldest child," the obituary stated. Abby "endeared herself to young and old . . . a friend to the friendless," helping to raise the children left in her family's care after the death of their mothers. "Nor was there any patriotic or charitable movement in the city which did not enlist her interest," the *Portsmouth Herald* noted.

And Willie, "the beloved son, knit to her heart by stronger than ordinary ties . . . was able to return in time to be at his mother's bedside and witness the passing." It had been of great comfort to Abby, as her husband lay mute and suffering on his deathbed in the Millard Hotel, that Willie had spent time with his father during those last days. The little boy grown to become a naval commander saw both of his parents buried side by side, his life growing more and more troubled when his wife frequently left him to travel in Europe, eventually separating from him completely.

On October 3, 1922, "Capt. William Winder, U.S. N., retired formerly of this city, committed suicide in Brookline [Massachusetts]. . . . Beside the body was found a 32-caliber revolver." Shortly after his mother's death Willie had "retired as a captain on June 30, 1907 . . . after having had 18 years sea service to his credit." Even as his father loathed and feared the sea, his son soared and flourished on the water until his demons descended and his life ended on a street in Brookline.[4]

By 1922, for those who remembered anything of Willie's father or the family name that had been besmirched, cursed, and damned, William A. would always be a Winder. But the sum of the man was more. Father to one, husband to one, son of a war criminal and brother to same; shipwreck survivor—notable brave, rescued and rescuer—he was a Union loyalist, a thoughtful and innovative defender of a madman who, because of him, did not hang for his crime. He was a healer, exile, and maker of new paths forward, reborn in the West; a San Diego notable striving in vain again and again for his place in the army, and finally, at the Rosebud Reser-

Notes

1. Bedeviled Winter of War

1. Albin J. Kowalski, "The Storm That Nearly Lost the War," *New York Times*, November 2, 2011.

2. "Arrival of Regulars from California," *New York Evening Post*, November 15, 1861.

3. "Splendid Military Sight," *New York Herald*, November 16, 1861.

4. Stiles, *First Tycoon*, 319.

5. McArthur, *Man Who Was Rip Van Winkle*, 184–85.

6. Manifest of the *Champion*, November 15, 1861, in New York Passenger Lists, 1820–1957, accessed at Ancestry.com. Although the ship's manifest recorded William A. as a captain, he left Alcatraz as a first lieutenant. Thus, he would have received notice of his promotion to captain when his ship reached Aspinwall, where official mail would have been picked up.

7. "Arrival of Regulars from California," *New York Evening Post*, November 15, 1861.

8. Stewart, *Wreck of the "San Francisco,"* 201.

9. Hill, "Winder's Reminiscences of Early Days."

10. Matthews, *Golden State in the Civil War*, 109.

11. Matthews, *Golden State in the Civil War*, 192.

12. Matthews, *Golden State in the Civil War*, 193.

13. Matthews, *Golden State in the Civil War*, 193.

14. Matthews, *Golden State in the Civil War*, 192.

15. Matthews, *Golden State in the Civil War*, 193; Ron Soodalter, "The Day New York City Tried to Secede," *History.net*, October 26, 2011, http://www.historynet.com/the-day-new-york-tried-to-secede.htm.

16. Soodalter, "Day New York City Tried to Secede."

17. Strong, *Diary of George Templeton Strong*, 3:363.

18. Abraham Lincoln, "First Inaugural Address," March 4, 1861, *History Now*, Gilder Lehrman Institute of American History, https://www.gilderlehrman.org/content/president-lincoln%E2%80%99s-first-inaugural-address-1861.

19. Blakey, *General John H. Winder, C.S.A.*, 48.

20. Jones, *Rebel War Clerk's Diary*, 60.

21. Blakey, *General John H. Winder, C.S.A.*, 25, 27.

22. "Confederate States of America, Jefferson Davis Message to Congress," April 29, 1861, Avalon Project, Lillian Goldman Library, Yale University Law School, New Haven, Connecticut.

23. Blakey, *General John H. Winder, C.S.A.*, 47.

24. Casstevens, *George W. Alexander and Castle Thunder*, 39; Blakey, *General John H. Winder, C.S.A.*, 120.

25. Blakey, *General John H. Winder C.S.A.*, 142.

26. "An Act Respecting Alien Enemies," in *War of the Rebellion*, ser. 2, 2:1361–62.

27. Golden, "Castle Thunder," 21.

28. Blakey, *General John H. Winder, C.S.A.*, 122.

29. Kelly, *Sarah—Her Story*, 195.

30. "New Hampshire Appointments," *New Hampshire Sentinel*, April 11, 1861.

31. Ichabod Goodwin to Abraham Lincoln, June 24, 1861 (see below); Charles G. Brooks, "Historic Find for 50¢," *Evening Star* (Washington DC), August 9, 1960. The article in the *Evening Star* reported that this Goodwin letter with Lincoln's response on it was among several valuable old documents—letters from Ulysses Grant to Secretary Stanton and others—discovered by Joseph F. Thompson of Arlington, Virginia. The Lincoln endorsement was deemed authentic by Dr. Percy Powell of the Manuscript Division of the Library of Congress. The Goodwin letter with the Lincoln endorsement was auctioned in 2010 and to this author's knowledge has never before been published with the exception of the transcript made available on the auction site, which is no longer accessible. Of interest, it appeared that Lincoln knew William A. was a captain, not a first lieutenant. Neither William A. nor Ichabod Goodwin had yet been informed of the promotion, although the United States War Department, *General Orders of the War Department*, 1:184, does record William A. as a captain, Third Regiment of Artillery, on May 14, 1861. He is also listed as captain in United States Adjutant General's Office, *Official Army Register for 1866*, 35, 85. President Lincoln must have been informed by his secretary of war, Simon Cameron, or another official, that William A. had been promoted.

32. Teschemacher quoted in "The Overland Telegraph," *New York Times*, October 26, 1861.

33. "Suspected and Disloyal Persons," in *War of the Rebellion*, ser. 2, 2:721.

34. E. J. Allen, interrogation of Charles H. Winder, September 9, 1861, Union Provost Marshal's File of Papers Relating to Individual Civilians, 1861–67, Record Group 109, National Archives and Records Administration, Washington DC (hereafter cited as Union Provost Marshal's File, NARA-DC).

35. Charles H. Winder to John H. Winder, August 20, 1861, Union Provost Marshal's File, NARA-DC. Although Charles H. Winder denied having had any correspondence with his brother or any other Southern acquaintances, the

letter the provost marshal had in hand may well have been a copy of a letter Charles H. Winder did send.

36. Charles H. Winder to William H. Winder, April 17, 1861, in *War of the Rebellion*, ser. 2, 2:721.

37. Statement of George McGlue, September 10, 1861, Union Provost Marshal's File, NARA-DC.

38. Statement of W. H. Parker, September 10, 1861, Union Provost Marshal's File, NARA-DC.

39. William Seward to Andrew Porter, in *War of the Rebellion*, ser. 2, 2:734.

40. Secretary [of War] Simon Cameron to William Millward, September 11, 1861, in *War of the Rebellion*, ser. 2, 2:725.

41. George A. Coffey to Simon Cameron, September 11, 1861, in *War of the Rebellion*, ser. 2, 2:725.

42. Speer, *Portals to Hell*, 35, 38.

43. "Splendid Military Sight," *New York Herald*, November 16, 1861.

44. "Military and Naval Intelligence," *New York Commercial Advertiser*, November 16, 1861.

45. "A Rare and Most Brilliant Sight," *New York Evening Post*, November 16, 1861.

46. "The *Champion*'s Passengers; Particulars of the Arrests," *New York Times*, November 16, 1861.

2. The Double Agent and the Captain

1. "Sick and Wounded Soldiers in Hospitals," *Evening Star* (Washington DC), November 16, 1861.

2. "Entertainments," *Daily National Republican* (Washington DC), November 25, 1861.

3. "Dr. Johnston: Baltimore Lock Hospital," *Evening Star*, November 16, 1861.

4. Furguson, *Freedom Rising*, 144.

5. George McClellan to Mary Ellen McClellan, November 2, 1861, in Sears, *Civil War Papers of George B. McClellan*, 123.

6. George McClellan to Mary Ellen McClellan, November 17, 1861, in Sears, *Civil War Papers of George B. McClellan*, 123.

7. George McClellan to Samuel L. M. Barlow, November 9, 1861, in Sears, *Civil War Papers of George B. McClellan*, 128.

8. Cameron Addis, "Secession Winter," *History Hub*, accessed July 23, 2016, http://sites.austincc.edu/caddis/secession-winter.

9. Pinkerton, *Spy of the Rebellion*, 95–98. While Pinkerton often confabulated or embellished the escapades of his operatives, and though portions of his works should be viewed with skepticism, there are ample primary sources to confirm or disprove many of his claims. In the cases of the aforementioned quotes as well as the ones that follow from Pinkerton's extant letters to Gen. George B. McClellan, it is safe to assume facts prevail.

10. Pinkerton, *Spy of the Rebellion*, 245.

11. "Beware of Telegraphic Inventions," *Washington National Republican*, July 24, 1861. The newspaper condemned the "whole world of outside barbarians" who lurked in the city and favored slavery.

12. "Captain William A. Winder[,] accompanied by wife and child, January 9, 1862," #4291, in U.S. Passport Applications, 1795–1925, accessed at Ancestry .com. Parts of this description are also taken from portraits of Winder viewed by the author as well as an original portrait in her possession.

13. Captain Winder to Brigadier General Thomas, November 22, 1861, Letters Received by the Office of the Adjutant General, NARA-DC.

14. Birkheimer, "History of the 3rd U.S. Artillery," 347.

15. Horatio Nelson Taft, "Washington during the Civil War: Diary of Horatio Nelson Taft, 1861 to 1865," entry for January 11, 1861, Library of Congress, Manuscript Division, Washington DC (hereafter cited as LOC).

16. Pinkerton, *Spy of the Rebellion*, 247.

17. Abraham Lincoln, "First Annual Message," December 3, 1861, *The American Presidency Project*, compiled by Gerhard Peters and John T. Woolley, http://www.presidency.ucsb.edu/ws/?pid=29502.

18. William F. Barry to George McClellan, December 3, 1861, Letters Received by the Office of the Adjutant General, NARA-DC.

19. Casstevens, *George W. Alexander and Castle Thunder*, 46.

20. Pinkerton, *Spy of the Rebellion*, 110.

21. Recko, *Spy for the Union*, 6.

22. "Memoirs of Pryce Lewis as told to Major David E. Cronin," 55, in Pryce Lewis Collection, St. Lawrence University Archives, Owen D. Young Library, St. Lawrence University, Canton, New York.

23. Pinkerton, *Spy of the Rebellion*, 480.

24. Pinkerton to McClellan, December 27, 1861, in George Brinton McClellan Papers, LOC.

25. Assistant Adjutant General Townsend to Lieutenant General Grant, December 22, 1865, Letters and Their Enclosures Received by the Commission Branch of the Adjutant General's Office, NARA-DC. This is one of several records of W. A. Winder's U.S. Army service.

26. Pinkerton to McClellan, December 27, 1861, McClellan Papers, LOC.

27. Pinkerton to McClellan, January 31, 1862, McClellan Papers, LOC.

28. Pinkerton to McClellan, December 27, 1861, McClellan Papers, LOC. Pinkerton's emphases and punctuation are reproduced as in the original document.

29. Pinkerton to McClellan, December 27, 1861, McClellan Papers, LOC.

30. U.S. Military Academy Cadet Application Papers, 1840–45, within Application Papers, 1805–66, M688, Records of the Adjutant General's Office, 1780s–1917, Record Group 94, NARA-DC.

31. Pinkerton to McClellan, December 27, 1861, McClellan Papers, LOC.

32. Pinkerton to McClellan, December 27, 1861, McClellan Papers, LOC.

33. Pinkerton to McClellan, December 27, 1861, McClellan Papers, LOC.

34. William Winder to Lieutenant General Sherman, December 15, 1884, William T. Sherman Papers, LOC.

35. Captain Winder to Colonel Colburn, December 27, 1861, Letters Received by the Office of the Adjutant General, NARA-DC. The emphasis in the initial quotation from the letter is Winder's, but the exact nature of the "urgent personal business" is unknown.

36. Speer, *Portals to Hell*, 41.

37. W. H. Winder, *Secrets of the American Bastille*, 26.

38. Frederick Seward to Col. Justin Dimick, January 11, 1862, *War of the Rebellion*, ser. 2, 2:736, 737.

39. W. H. Winder, *Secrets of the American Bastille*, 28.

40. Frederick Seward to Col. Justin Dimick, January 17, 1862, *War of the Rebellion*, ser. 2, 2:736, 737.

41. W. H. Winder, *Secrets of the American Bastille*, 39.

42. Charles H. Winder's parole statement and pledge, *War of the Rebellion*, ser. 2, 2:739.

43. Assistant Secretary of State Frederick Seward to Brig. Gen. Andrew Porter, "Suspected and Disloyal Persons," January 14, 1862, *War of the Rebellion*, ser. 2, 2:737. The aforementioned memorandum, according to an afterword on the same page in the *War of the Rebellion* official records was not located. It might be assumed that it contained a portion of Pinkerton's letter to McClellan or a note from McClellan himself.

44. "Arrival of the 'Orizaba," *San Francisco Daily Evening Bulletin*, February 15, 1862. Details of the stops of the *Champion* are recorded in this article.

45. "On Equal Terms," *Milwaukee Sentinel*, April 12, 1889.

46. E. J. Allen to McClellan, January 31, 1862, McClellan Papers, LOC.

3. Of Toil, Treason, and the Golden Land

1. Hayes et al., *Emigrant Notes*, 281.

2. Dana, *Two Years before the Mast*, 111.

3. Graves, "A Doctor Comes to San Diego," July 1970.

4. Engstrand, *San Diego*, 78.

5. Lt. William Winder to Maj. W. W. Mackall, August 23, 1856, quoted in Heizer, *Destruction of California Indians*, 105. John Ellis Wool was an Indian fighter and advocate of their extermination. During the Civil War he was in command of the Department of the East. William Whann Mackall resigned from the U.S. Army and became a Confederate general.

6. Lt. William Winder to Capt. H. S. Burton, Old Mission, San Diego, April 29, 1856, quoted in Heizer, *Destruction of California Indians*, 87.

7. Hayes, *Pioneer Notes from the Diaries of Judge Benjamin Hayes*, ix, 163.

8. Dana, *Two Years before the Mast*, 173.

9. Quoted in Matthews, *Golden State in the Civil War*, 187.

10. Chandler, "Velvet Glove," 38.

11. Quotations from Chandler, "Democratic Turmoil," 36.

12. Chandler, "Uncertain Influence," 225.

13. Martini, *Alcatraz at War*, 13.

14. Hunt, *Army of the Pacific, 1860–1866*, 301, 303.

15. Harpending, *Great Diamond Hoax*, 24. The passionate secessionist and would-be Confederate pirate and privateer Asbury Harpending allegedly heard Johnston declare his full-throated opposition to a conspiracy helmed by the secret and seditious Knights of the Golden Circle. Their goal was to arm like-minded citizens who would overtake Alcatraz and create a separate nation, the Pacific Republic. For a good explanation of Johnston's dilemma, see Martini, *Fortress Alcatraz*, 36–39. Johnston's loyalty to the Union until his resignation was common knowledge to those who served under his command, including William A., one of his most passionate defenders, as will be seen. Even though Johnston ordered the removal of tons of ordnance to Alcatraz in an effort to protect it, his very presence in California at the beginning of the war caused rumors and suspicion, as he was born in Kentucky and raised in Texas. Fearing arrest, Johnston made his way to Los Angeles and subsequently fled to Texas to join the Confederacy. Highly valued by Robert E. Lee, General Johnston was killed at the Battle of Shiloh on April 6, 1862.

16. Matthews, *Golden State in the Civil War*, 87.

17. Kroll, *Friends in Peace and War*, xii, xiii.

4. A Godforsaken Fortress

1. Martini, *Fortress Alcatraz*, 11.

2. "Civil War at Alcatraz," National Park Service, accessed March 19, 2015, https://www.nps.gov/goga/learn/historyculture/civil-war-at-alcatraz.htm.

3. Martini, *Fortress Alcatraz*, 28; Strobridge, "California Letters of Major General James McPherson, 1858–1860," 38.

4. Gordon Chappell, "The Citadel of Alcatraz," Historic California Posts, Camps, Stations and Airfields, 1981, www.militarymuseum.org /Alcatrazcitadel.html.

5. "The Army of the Pacific," *Sacramento Daily Union*, February 19, 1861.

6. Martini, *Alcatraz at War*, 26–27. My visits deep underground to what remains of the Citadel basement were both memorable and unnerving. Hardhat in place and with trusty guide, the historian John A. Martini, leading the way, we went down a steep flight of stairs into a world of buckling concrete and hanging metal rods. John Martini pointed out the original herringbone-patterned brick floors, thick walls growing thicker along dark passageways to the dungeons, where the sound of waves or anything else could not be heard, then or now.

7. Twain, *Gold Miners & Guttersnipes*, 5.

8. "Platt's Music Hall," *San Francisco Bulletin*, May 27, 1862.

9. Martini, *Alcatraz at War*, 20, 26.

10. W. H. Winder, *Secrets of the American Bastille*, 28–30.

11. Speer, *Portals to Hell*, 91.

12. Putnam, *Richmond during the War*, 113. Originally the title page of this source identified the author as "A Richmond Lady"; her name at the time was Sallie A. Brock. Later she wrote under her married name, Sallie Brock Putnam.

13. "Local Matters," *Richmond (VA) Dispatch*, April 30, 1862.

14. Pinkerton, *Spy of the Rebellion*, 496.

15. Casstevens, *George W. Alexander and Castle Thunder*, 122; "First Minority Report on the Management of Castle Thunder," *War of the Rebellion*, ser. 2, 5:919–24.

5. Treason at Alcatraz

1. "The Court Martialed," *Sacramento Daily Union*, May 3, 1862.

2. "Alcatraz Island," *San Francisco Bulletin*, June 12, 1862.

3. Chandler, "Uncertain Influence," 248.

4. Wright quoted in Schlicke, *General George Wright*, 211, 228.

5. Cutler, "Your Nations Shall Be Exterminated," 3.

6. "The Battle between Gen. Banks and Jackson, Gen. Winder Killed," *Sacramento Daily Union*, August 14, 1862.

7. "Remains of Brig. Gen. Charles S. Winder," *Richmond (VA) Dispatch*, August 19, 1862.

8. Matthews, *Golden State in the Civil War*, 185.

9. Chandler, "Uncertain Influence," 248.

10. Capt. William A. Winder to Maj. Richard Coulter Drum, September 10, 1862, Letters Received by the Office of the Adjutant General, NARA-DC.

11. Martini, *Fortress Alcatraz*, 51.

12. Asst. Adj. Gen. R. C. Drum to Lt. Col. Harvey Lee, September 12, 1862, Correspondence, Orders and Returns relating to Operations on the Pacific Coast from July 1, 1862 to June 30, 1865, *War of the Rebellion*, ser. 1, vol. 50, part 2.

13. "General Wright and His Late Orders—A Military Prison to Be Erected; Captain Winder under a Ban of Suspicion," *Sacramento Daily Union*, September 13, 1862.

14. "Captain Winder of That Post," *San Francisco Daily Evening Bulletin*, September 13, 1862.

15. Col. R. C. Drum to Lt. Col. Caleb Chase Sibley, with "fair copy" sent to Captain W. A. Winder, September 12, 1862, Letters Received by the Office of the Adjutant General, NARA-DC.

16. Cullum, *Biographical Register of the Officers and Graduates of the U.S. Military Academy*, 2:331–32, 3:71.

17. "General Wright and His Late Orders—A Military Prison to Be Erected; Captain Winder of That Post," *Sacramento Daily Union*, September 13, 1862.

18. Capt. William A. Winder to Asst. Adj. Gen. R. C. Drum, September 13, 1862, Letters Received by the Office of the Adjutant General, NARA-DC.

19. "City Items—Disloyalty Disproven," *Daily Alta California*, September 17, 1862.

20. "City Items—Disloyalty Disproven," *Daily Alta California*, September 17, 1862.

21. Brig. Gen. George Wright to Asst. Adj. Gen. R. C. Drum, October 8, 1864, Letters Received by the Office of the Adjutant General, NARA-DC.

22. Capt. W. A. Winder to Asst. Adj. Gen. R. C. Drum, September 10, 1862, *War of the Rebellion*, ser. 2, 2:108.

23. Quoted in "City Items," *Daily Alta California*, September 16, 1862.

24. Capt. W. A. Winder to Brig. Gen. R. C. Drum, September 28, 1862, Letters Received by the Office of the Adjutant General, NARA-DC.

25. Capt. W. A. Winder to Brig. Gen. R. C. Drum, September 28, 1862, Letters Received by the Office of the Adjutant General, NARA-DC.

26. Brig. Gen. George Wright to Asst. Adj. General R. C. Drum, October 20, 1862; Capt. W. A. Winder to Brig. Gen. R. C. Drum, September 28, 1862, both in Letters Received by the Office of the Adjutant General, NARA-DC.

27. "Preliminary Emancipation Proclamation," September 22, 1862, 1, Abraham Lincoln Papers, LOC.

28. "City Items," *Daily Alta California*, September 16, 1862.

29. "Effect of the Order—The First Arrest," *Santa Cruz Weekly Sentinel*, September 20, 1862.

30. "Disloyalty Disproven," *Daily Alta California*, September 17, 1862.

31. Chandler, "Uncertain Influence," 248.

32. "Another Rebel under Arrest," *Daily Alta California*, October 11, 1862.

33. "News of the Morning," *Sacramento Daily Union*, October 16, 1862.

34. "What Is Treason?," *Sacramento Daily Union*, October 21, 1862.

35. *War of the Rebellion*, ser. 2, 4:359; Chandler, "Uncertain Influence," 249. There are no recorded lists of the number of prisoners sent to Alcatraz during the war, but it is safe to assume there were many unrecorded arrests and short stays after the oaths of allegiance were taken.

36. W. H. Winder, *Secrets of the American Bastille*, 43, 47.

37. Blakey, *General John H. Winder, C.S.A.*, 50.

38. Mary Lincoln to Abraham Lincoln, November 2, 1862, Lincoln Papers, LOC.

39. U.S. Returns from Military Posts, December 1862, from information in Returns from U.S. Military Posts, 1800–1916, Microfilm Publication M617, 1,550 rolls, Records of the Adjutant General's Office, 1780s–1917, Record Group 94, NARA-DC, accessed at Ancestry.com.

6. A Rebel Cell

1. Harpending, *Great Diamond Hoax*, 53.

2. Matthews, *Golden State in the Civil War*, 191.

3. "Piratical Chivalry," *Sacramento Daily Union*, March 18, 1863.

4. Harpending, *Great Diamond Hoax*, 16.

5. "Case of the 'Chapman': Culpableness of Parties Selling Munitions of War," *San Francisco Evening Bulletin*, March 16, 1863.

6. "Examination of Prisoners," *Marysville (CA) Daily Appeal*, March 20, 1863.

7. Harpending, *Great Diamond Hoax*, 55.

8. *San Francisco Morning Call*, March 24, 1863. Issues of this newspaper unfortunately are no longer extant for this period, including the date of March 24, 1863, but William A. enclosed the incendiary piece of the article in a communication to Brigadier General Wright and Assistant Adjutant General Drum. Capt. William A. Winder to Asst. Adj. Gen. Richard Drum [and Brig. Gen. George Wright], March 24, 1863, Letters and Their Enclosures Received by the Commission Branch of the Adjutant General's Office, NARA-DC.

9. Asst. Adj. Gen. R. C. Drum to Capt. Wm. A. Winder, March 27, 1863, Letters and Their Enclosures Received by the Commission Branch of the Adjutant General's Office, NARA-DC.

10. Brigadier General Wright to Capt. W. A. Winder, March 28, 1863, Letters and Their Enclosures Received by the Commission Branch of the Adjutant General's Office, NARA-DC.

11. *San Francisco Daily Evening Bulletin*, October 5, 1863, October 19, 1863; Harpending, *Great Diamond Hoax*, 61.

12. "Headquarters Department of the Pacific—Winder Offered Colonelcy," *Sacramento Daily Union*, May 28, 1863.

13. "Rebel Retaliation, Proposed Hanging of Federal Prisoners at Richmond Drawing the Lots," *San Francisco Bulletin*, August 10, 1863.

14. Daughtry, *Gray Cavalier*, 147.

15. W. A. Winder to Montgomery Blair, August 7, 1863, Lincoln Papers, LOC.

16. Montgomery Blair to Abraham Lincoln, August 8, 1863, Lincoln Papers, LOC.

17. W. H. Winder to Edwin Stanton, August 8, 1863, Letters Received by the Office of the Adjutant General, NARA-DC.

7. Invasions, Arrests, and Cannon Fire

1. Kroll, *Friends in Peace and War*, 37–38.

2. Kroll, *Friends in Peace and War*, 51.

3. "British Man of War at the Bay," *Marysville (CA) Daily Appeal*, October 4, 1863.

4. Capt. Thomas O. Selfridge to Gen. George Wright, February 10, 1863, and Capt. Thomas O. Selfridge to Navy Secretary Gideon Welles, February 10, 1863, both in Operations of the Cruisers–Union, from January 1, 1863, to March 31, 1864, *War of the Rebellion*, ser. 1, 2:112–15.

5. Rear Adm. John Kingcome to Gen. George Wright, October 1, 1863, *War of the Rebellion*, ser.1, 50:633.

6. Gen. George Wright to Rear Adm. John Kingcome, October 3, 1863, *War of the Rebellion*, ser. 1, 50:638.

7. Asst. Adj. Gen. R. C. Drum to W. A. Winder, October 5, 1862, *War of the Rebellion*, ser. 1, 50:639.

8. Capt. W. A. Winder to Adjutant General Drum, October 6, 1862, *War of the Rebellion*, ser. 1, 50:640.

9. Rear Adm. John Kingcome to Gen. George Wright, October 15, 1863, *War of the Rebellion*, ser. 1, 50:641.

10. John Martini, author of *Alcatraz at War* and *Fortress Alcatraz*, email to author, November 24, 2010.

11. Brig. Gen. George Wright to Rear Adm. John Kingcome, October 15, 1863, Letters Received by the Office of the Adjutant General, NARA-DC.

12. Lieber, *Instructions for the Government of the United States in the Field*, Article 58, originally issued April 24, 1863. The article reads in full, "The law of nations knows of no distinction of color, and if an enemy of the United States should enslave and sell any captured persons of their army, it would be a case for the severest retaliation, if not redressed upon complaint. The United States cannot retaliate by enslavement; therefore death must be the retaliation for this crime against the law of nations."

13. Blakey, *General John H. Winder, C.S.A.*, 159.

14. "Horrors of the Libby Prison at Richmond–Belle Isle," *San Francisco Bulletin*, December 1, 1863.

15. "Colonel Fish's Detectives," *Baltimore Gazette*, November 23, 1863.

8. The Loyal Man and the Madman

1. Gov. John Goodwin to President Lincoln, February 8, 1864, Letters and Their Enclosures Received by the Commission Branch of the Adjutant General's Office, NARA-DC.

2. Gov. John Goodwin to President Lincoln, February 8, 1864, Letters and Their Enclosures Received by the Commission Branch of the Adjutant General's Office, NARA-DC.

3. Delos Lake, Ogden Hoffman [Judge], Port Surveyor McLean, U.S. Attorney Sharpe, and others to President Lincoln, April 12, 1864, Letters and Their Enclosures Received by the Commission Branch of the Adjutant General's Office, NARA-DC.

4. Ichabod Goodwin to Abraham Lincoln, April 29, 1864, Letters and Their Enclosures Received by the Commission Branch of the Adjutant General's Office, NARA-DC.

5. Martini, "Search and Destroy," 1.

6. [Mark Twain], "Inspection of the Fortifications," *San Francisco Daily Morning Call*, July 14, 1864.

7. Martini, "Search and Destroy," 2.

8. Eliot quoted in Martini, "Search and Destroy," 2.

9. Delafield quoted in Martini, "Search and Destroy," 2.

10. Maj. Gen. Henry Wager Halleck to Maj. Gen. Irvin McDowell, August 1, 1864, *War of the Rebellion*, ser. 1, 50:925.

11. "Fort Alcatraz Taken!," *San Francisco Bulletin*, August 4, 1864.

12. "Fort Alcatraz Taken!," *San Francisco Bulletin*, August 4, 1864.

13. "Civil War at Fort Mason," National Park Service, accessed March 19, 2015, https://www.nps.gov/goga/learn/historyculture/civil-war-at-fort -mason.htm.

14. Testimony of Private Timothy Moran, August 22, 1864, Court Martial Trial of Pvt. Simon Kennedy, Court Martial File NN3499, Record Group 13 7E3/14/12/3, NARA-DC (hereafter cited as Kennedy Court Martial, NARA-DC).

15. [Mark Twain,] "Soldier Murdered by a Monomaniac: Escape and Subsequent Arrest of the Murderer," *San Francisco Morning Call*, August 5, 1864.

16. "The Fitzgerald Inquest," *Sacramento Daily Union*, August 6, 1864.

17. "The Fitzgerald Inquest," *Sacramento Daily Union*, August 6, 1864.

18. Maj. Gen. Irvin McDowell to Adjutant General, U.S. Army, Lorenzo Thomas, August 5, 1864, *War of the Rebellion*, ser. 1, 50:929.

19. "Inducement of General Mason: Statement of Mr. Rulofson," *San Francisco Daily Evening Bulletin*, March 31, 1865.

20. Proceedings of a General Court Martial convened at Point San Jose, August 7, 1864, Kennedy Court Martial, NARA-DC.

21. Second Day's Proceedings, August 20, 1864, Kennedy Court Martial, NARA-DC.

22. Defense counsel William A. Winder's summation, August 29, 1864, Kennedy Court Martial, NARA-DC. Quotations in subsequent paragraphs are from this source until noted otherwise.

23. Judge Advocate George M. Wright for the prosecution, August 29, 1864, Kennedy Court Martial, NARA-DC.

24. Statement of Irvin McDowell, November 22, 1864, Kennedy Court Martial, NARA-DC.

25. Record of Simon Kennedy, vol. 03-04, 1862–70, 358, in Stockton State Hospital Commitment Registers, California State Hospital Records, 1856–1923, accessed at Ancestry.com.

26. Taylor, "Mining Boom in Baja California."

27. McGhee, "E. W. Morse, Pioneer Merchant and Co-Founder of San Diego."

28. W. A. Winder to E. W. Morse, April 7, 1864, Ephraim W. Morse Papers, San Diego History Center, San Diego, California (hereafter cited as SDHC).

29. W. A. Winder to E. W. Morse, September 14, 1864, Morse Papers, SDHC. Quotations in subsequent paragraphs are from this source until noted otherwise.

30. Maj. Gen. Irvin McDowell to Maj. Gen. Henry Halleck, August 1, 1864, *War of the Rebellion*, ser. 1, 50:1083.

31. Davis, *Ghosts and Shadows of Andersonville*, xvii.

9. A Slog to Hell

1. Putnam, *Richmond during the War*, 263.

2. Adj. Gen. J. W. Pegram to Capt. W. S. Winder, November 24, 1863, *War of the Rebellion*, ser. 2, 6:558; Lynn, *800 Paces to Hell*, 2.

3. Marvel, *Andersonville*, 14–15.

4. Davis, *Ghosts and Shadows of Andersonville*, 6.

5. Davis, *Ghosts and Shadows of Andersonville*, 6–7.

6. Blakey, *General John H. Winder, C.S.A.*, 176.

7. Spencer, *Narrative of Andersonville*, 20. Ambrose Spencer, a self-declared Unionist and witness at the trial of Henry Wirz, may not have been present to hear Sidney Winder's order, and it is a matter of debate as to whether his writings are reliable.

8. Hopkins, "Hell and the Survivor," 4.

9. "First Prisoners of War en Route to Andersonville," February 18, 1864, Timeline: Record of Activity-Camp Sumter, http://www.angelfire.com/ga2 /Andersonvilleprison/diary.html.

10. McLean, "Detail of Prison Life at Andersonville," 1. McLean's recollections were written not long after the war ended and should thus be viewed as entirely credible.

11. McLean, "Detail of Prison Life at Andersonville," 2.

12. Sneden, *Eye of the Storm*, 202–3.

13. "General Winder Ordered to Americus, Georgia," *Richmond (VA) Examiner*, June 9, 1864.

14. Goss, *Soldier's Story of His Captivity at Andersonville*, 159.

15. Gooding, *On the Altar of Freedom*, xxxiii.

16. Gooding, *On the Altar of Freedom*, 118–20.

17. John H. Winder quoted in Blakey, *General John H. Winder C.S.A.*, 185.

18. Blakey, *General John H. Winder C.S.A.*, 185.

19. Davis, *Ghosts and Shadows of Andersonville*, 110.

20. Spencer, *Narrative of Andersonville*, 71. Although the actual order to open fire on the prisoners has not been found, it is often recorded in memoirs by Andersonville survivors. The order was deemed a forgery by some researchers, but as many Confederate records were partially destroyed when Richmond fell, it is probable that such an order was found by a clerk salvaging scattered documents and thus did exist.

21. General Sherman to General Grant, August 4, 1864, *War of the Rebellion*, ser. 1, 1:350.

22. General Grant to General Sherman, August 4, 1864, *War of the Rebellion*, ser. 1, 1:350.

23. Marvel, *Andersonville*, 161.

24. D. T. Chandler to R. H. Chilton, August 5, 1864, *War of the Rebellion*, ser. 2, 7:546–49. Quotations in subsequent paragraphs are from this source until noted otherwise.

25. R. H. Chilton to Secretary James A. Seddon, August 18, 1864, *War of the Rebellion*, ser. 2, 7:550.

26. Prof. Robert Scott Davis, author of *Ghost and Shadows of Andersonville*, email to author, August 17, 2010.

27. Blakey, *General John H. Winder, C.S.A.*, 190.

28. Henry Wirz to Gen. J. H. Winder (with recalled quote from Chandler), September 24, 1864, *War of the Rebellion*, ser. 2, 7:758–60.

29. McElroy, *Andersonville*, 561. These alleged last words, whether rumor, gossip, or actually heard by McElroy, were widely read by many thousands of the public.

10. The War Criminal's Son

1. "Eastern Telegraph Still Out of Order," *San Francisco Evening Bulletin*, February 9, 1865.

2. "Sudden Death of General John H. Winder," *Wilmington (NC) Journal*, February 16, 1865.

3. "Gen. John H. Winder—This Monster," *Providence Evening Press*, February 15, 1865.

4. "Sketch of Rebel General Winder," *Beverly (MA) Citizen*, February 18, 1865.

5. "Hog Winder," *Milwaukee Sentinel*, February 21, 1865.

6. "The Death of the Rebel General by Apoplexy Is Reported," *Daily Alta California*, March 19, 1865.

7. "Grand Military Review," *Daily Alta California*, March 19, 1865.

8. "The Notorious Rebel General," *Marysville (CA) Daily Appeal*, March 23, 1865.

9. "Magnanimity," *Sacramento Daily Union*, March 25, 1865.

10. Gov. John Goodwin to Secretary Stanton, March 13, 1865, Letters and Their Enclosures Received by the Commission Branch of the Adjutant General's Office, NARA-DC.

11. Breed and Chase to E. W. Morse, April 1, 1865, Box 1, Ephraim W. Morse Papers, SDHC.

12. Martini, *Fortress Alcatraz*, 52.

13. W. A. Winder to E. W. Morse, April 18, 1865, Morse Papers, SDHC.

14. Breed & Chase to E. W. Morse, April 29, 1865, Morse Papers, SDHC.

15. Whitman, *Specimen Days and Collect*, 70.

16. Robinson, "Ordeal of General Wright," 168.

17. Engstrand, *San Diego*, 78.

18. Pourade, *Glory Years*, 5.

19. Mary C. [Chase Walker] Morse, "Recollections of Early Times in San Diego," 7, Biographical Archives, SDHC.

20. Mary C. [Chase Walker] Morse, "Recollections of Early Times in San Diego," 7, Biographical Archives, SDHC.

21. Morse diary entries, May 10, June 1, June 4, 1866, Register of Ephraim W. Morse Family Papers, University of California, San Diego (hereafter cited as UCSD).

22. Quoted in Cleary, *Quiet, Hard, and Desolated Place*, 16–18.

23. Chipman, *Tragedy of Andersonville*, 28.

24. Lieber, *Instructions for the Government of the United States in the Field*, Article 71, April 24, 1863.

25. Chipman, *Tragedy of Andersonville*, 32–35.

26. Rockwood, *Walking Away from Nuremberg*, 42.

27. Chipman, *Tragedy of Andersonville*, 422.

28. "Trial of Capt. Wirz; Argument at the Closing Scenes," *New York Times*, October 20, 1865.

29. "Another Chapter of Horrors," *Weekly Alta California*, October 28, 1865.

30. Brian P. Luskey, "Men Is Cheap," *New York Times*, February 4, 2015.

31. Capt. W. A. Winder to Gen. Lorenzo Thomas, December 12, 1865, Letters Received by the Office of the Adjutant General, NARA-DC.

32. William H. Winder to E. M. Stanton, December 29, 1865, Letters Received by the Office of the Adjutant General, NARA-DC.

33. U. S. Grant signature on Winder's service record and leave request, along with a note from Asst. Adj. Gen. E. D. Townsend, December 26, 1865, Letters and Their Enclosures Received by the Commission Branch of the Adjutant General's Office, NARA-DC.

34. Wm. A. Winder to Col. T. S. Bowers, December 28, 1865, Letters and Their Enclosures Received by the Commission Branch, NARA-DC.

35. Ichabod Goodwin to Hon. E. M. Stanton, December 29, 1865, Letters and Enclosures Received by the Commission Branch of the Adjutant General's Office, NARA-DC.

11. Of Resignation, Railroads, and Exile

1. Grant's docketed approval noting Capt. W. A. Winder's Application for Leave of Absence, January 4, 1866, Letters and Their Enclosures Received by the Commission Branch of the Adjutant General's Office, NARA-DC.

2. W. M. Stewart to Edwin Stanton, January 9, 1866, Letters Received by the Office of the Adjutant General, NARA-DC.

3. Kelly, *Sarah—Her Story*, 182.

4. Breed and Chase to E. W. Morse, February 2, 1866, Box 1, Ephraim W. Morse Papers, SDHC.

5. "Lower California Matters," *Daily Alta California*, February 18, 1866.

6. Breed and Chase to E. W. Morse, February 17, 1866, Box 1, Morse Papers, SDHC.

7. Breed and Chase to E. W. Morse, March 19, 1866, Box 1, Morse Papers, SDHC.

8. "Mines of the Southern Frontier," *San Francisco Daily Bulletin*, March 24, 1866.

9. Pourade, *Glory Years*, 21.

10. "State Correspondence: Letter from San Diego," *Daily Alta California*, April 22, 1866.

11. "Mines of the Southern Frontier," *San Francisco Daily Bulletin*, April 27, 1866.

12. "San Diego Matters," *Salt Lake (UT) Telegraph*, May 5, 1866; *San Diego Daily Union*, May 11, 1866.

13. William A. Winder to William S. Rosecrans, May 29, 1866, Folder 25, Box 11, William S. Rosecrans Papers, Charles E. Young Research Library, University of California, Los Angeles.

14. Anthony Gilkison to Secretary of War E. M. Stanton, June 13, 1866, Letters Received by the Office of the Adjutant General, NARA-DC.

15. Order of the Secretary of War [Stanton] to W. A. Winder, June 18, 1866, Letters Received by the Office of the Adjutant General, NARA-DC.

16. "Mines of the Southern Frontier," *San Francisco Daily Bulletin*, August 11, 1866.

17. "Mines of the Southern Frontier," *San Francisco Daily Bulletin*, September 3, 1866.

18. W. A. Winder to Edward D. Townsend, September 10, 1866, Letters Received by the Office of the Adjutant General, NARA-DC. Richard H. Linton was a San Francisco real estate broker.

19. Approval docketed by Grant and Stanton, October 13, 16, 1866, Letters Received by the Office of the Adjutant General, NARA-DC.

20. Wm. A. Winder to Gen. E. D. Townsend, dated October 5, 1866, and forwarded to the general on October 19, 1866, Letters Received by the Office of the Adjutant General, NARA-DC.

21. J. C. Kelton to E. D. Townsend, October 23, 1866, Letters and Their Enclosures Received by the Commission Branch of the Adjutant General's Office, NARA-DC.

22. Breed to E. W. Morse, Box 1, Morse Papers, SDHC (underscoring as written in original document).

23. Delos Lake to the Secretary of War, October 27, 1866, Letters and Their Enclosures Received by the Commission Branch of the Adjutant General's Office, NARA-DC. In 1863 Lake defended Harpending, Rubery, and Greathouse during the trial of the *J. M. Chapman* privateers.

24. Breed and Chase to E. W. Morse, November 30, 1866, Box 1, Morse Papers, SDHC (underscoring as written in original document).

25. Wm. A. Winder to President Andrew Johnson, January 15, 1867, Letters and Their Enclosures Received by the Commission Branch of the Adjutant General's Office, NARA-DC. Quotations in subsequent paragraphs are from this source until noted otherwise.

26. Johnson's referral to Stanton and Kelton's report, February 15, 1867, Letters and Their Enclosures Received by the Commission Branch of the Adjutant General's Office, NARA-DC.

27. Breed and Chase to E. W. Morse, February 19, 1867, Box 1, Morse Papers, SDHC.

28. Chase to E. W. Morse, May 7, 1867, Box 1, Morse Papers, SDHC. Breed and Chase refer to Winder as "Captain." They clearly do not know of his army resignation or his immediate request for reinstatement.

29. Nicholas R. Cataldo, "The Serrano's [sic]: The First San Bernardinians," City of San Bernardino, California, 2005, http://www.ci.san-bernardino.ca.us/about/history/the_first_san_bernardinians.asp.

30. "San Bernardino Items," San Francisco Daily Evening Bulletin, May 22, 1867.

31. Tucker and Waring, Mines and Mineral Resources of the Counties of Butte, 19.

32. Harpending, Great Diamond Hoax, 74. Along with Harpending's dramatic account of the J. M. Chapman affair and his devotion to the Confederacy, The Great Diamond Hoax contains Harpending's account of a brazen and costly fraud that began with the supposed find of piles of diamonds and rubies scattered across a vast property in Wyoming. After a proper assay of the land, it was revealed that the area was "salted" with inferior stones. Ruin came to many, but not Harpending, a shareholder in the company that financed the operation.

33. Harpending, Great Diamond Hoax, 100.

34. Mark Muckenfuss, "San Bernardino," Riverside (CA) Press-Enterprise, July 31, 2012.

35. Fogelson, Fragmented Metropolis, 62.

36. Price, "Railroad Stations of San Diego County."

37. W. A. Winder to E. W. Morse, October 20, 1867, Box 6, Morse Papers, SDHC.

38. U. S. Grant to Secretary of State William H. Seward, September 27, 1868, referring to a letter of September 21, 1868, "respecting the return of [William H. Winder's] nephew to this country." Simon, Papers of Ulysses S. Grant, 598.

39. President of the United States of America, "A Proclamation: Granting full pardon and amnesty to all persons engaged in the late rebellion," December 25, 1868, Library of Congress, https://www.loc.gov/resource/rbpe.23602600/.

40. "Land Agency," Daily Alta California, May 14, 1868.

41. Smythe, History of San Diego, 340.

42. Pourade, Glory Years, 11–14.

43. Engstrand, San Diego, 88.

44. "A Little Copper Stain in the Rocks," San Francisco Daily Bulletin, April 14, 1869.

45. W. A. Winder to E. W. Morse, August 30, 1868, Box 6, Morse Papers, SDHC.

46. San Diego Union, October 10, 1868.

47. Smythe, History of San Diego, 479.

48. "Salutatory," San Diego Union, October 10, 1868.

49. "A Railroad Meeting," San Diego Union, October 10, 1868.

50. San Diego Union, October 10, 1868.

12. Heal Thyself

1. "American Hotel," *San Diego Union*, October 10, 1868.

2. E. W. Morse to Mary Walker [the future Mrs. Morse], September 19, 1866, Box 6, Register of Ephraim W. Morse Family Papers, UCSD.

3. Engstrand, *San Diego*, 88.

4. Pourade, *Glory Years*, 48.

5. "Hon. J. H. Ella, M.C.," *Farmer's Cabinet* (Amherst NH), August 19, 1869.

6. Van Dyke, *City and County of San Diego*, 101.

7. "Wm. Winder," census record, United States Federal Census, 1870, San Diego, California, roll M593_78, accessed at Ancestry.com.

8. "Justice of the Peace," *San Diego Union*, January 13, 1870.

9. "San Diego Bay Shore Railroad," *Sacramento Daily Union*, January 14, 1870.

10. Engstrand, *San Diego*, 93.

11. Pourade, *Glory Years*, 74.

12. "Old Town Has Seceded," *San Diego Daily Union*, July 18, 1871.

13. Pourade, *Glory Years*, 75.

14. "San Diego," *Daily Alta California*, December 22, 1870.

15. "Old Town Agent," *San Diego Weekly Bulletin*, January 5, 1871.

16. J. Rowland Hill, "Winder's Reminiscences of Early Days," 1936, Winder Folder, SDHC. This text is based on an article of the same title that was published in *Golden Era* magazine on December 1, 1888.

17. "Impositions in the Healing Arts," *San Francisco Daily Evening Bulletin*, February 14, 1868.

18. Freeman, "Early Western Physicians."

19. Jane Dumas, "Local Edible and Medicinal Plants," Kumeyaay.com, 2017, https://www.kumeyaay.com/local-edible-and-medicinal-plants.html.

20. Smythe, *History of San Diego*, 601.

21. "W. A. Winder Asked to Give an Opinion of Pendleton's Health," *San Diego Union*, January 12, 1871. Pendleton was a member of the county's board of supervisors.

22. Harpending v. Winder, October 17, 1871, PR3.38 District Court, Case Files—Civil and Criminal,
1850–1880, District Court of 17th Judicial District for the County of San Diego, SDHC. Papers contained in typical case files include complaints, subpoenas, affidavits of witnesses, receipts, arrest warrants, testimony, verdicts, and other documents.

23. "Pioneer Society," *San Diego Daily Union*, January 19, 1872.

24. "Old Town Items," *San Diego Daily Union*, January 30, 1872.

25. Medical Care for Estate of C. J. Couts paid to Wm. A. Winder, September 19, 1874, Cave Johnson Couts File, SDHC.

26. "Destructive Fire in Old Town," *San Diego Daily Union*, April 21, 1872.

27. Liberal Republican Party, *Proceedings of the Liberal Republican Convention, Cincinnati, May 1st, 2d and 3d, 1872*, 19.

28. "Democratic Meeting at Old San Diego," *San Diego Daily Union*, June 19, 1872.

29. "Wilmington Breakwater," *Weekly World* (San Diego), August 16, 1872.

30. "Courts," *Weekly World*, August 24, 1872.

31. "A Beautiful Young Lady," *Weekly World*, September 14, 1872.

32. Pourade, *Glory Years*, 83.

33. "Railroad," *San Diego Daily Union*, March 4, 1871.

34. Pourade, *Glory Years*, 102.

35. Pourade, *Glory Years*, 103.

36. "Who Would Have Thought It? A Literary Incognito," *Weekly Alta California*, September 21, 1872.

37. Burton, *Who Would Have Thought It?*, vii.

38. "Who Would Have Thought It? A Literary Incognito," *Weekly Alta California*, September 21, 1872.

39. "Serious Accident," *Daily San Diego Union*, September 10, 1872.

40. "Better," *Daily San Diego Union*, September 11, 1872.

41. "Out of Danger," *Daily San Diego Union*, September 13, 1872.

42. "All Sorts," *Weekly World*, September 14, 1872.

43. "Patient Is Convalescing," *Weekly World*, September 14, 1872.

44. *Weekly World*, October 5, 1872.

45. "Bountiful Supply of Water," *Weekly World*, October 26, 1872.

46. "Picturesque Chapter from Florida," *Weekly World*, November 9, 1872. Quotations in subsequent paragraphs are from this source until noted otherwise.

47. Stanford, "San Diego's Medico-Legal History," 57.

48. "All Sorts," *Weekly World*, December 14, 1872.

49. Quoted in Kelly, *Sarah—Her Story*, 241.

50. Fogelson, *Fragmented Metropolis*, 50.

51. "Physicians and Lawyers," *Daily World*, February 6, 1873.

52. "All Sorts," *Daily World*, March 29, 1873.

53. "Notes," *Weekly World*, April 5, 1873.

54. "New Town," *San Diego Union*, April 22, 1873.

55. "Signs of the Times," *San Diego Union*, April 24, 1873.

56. "Graduates," *Portsmouth Journal of Literature and Politics*, May 31, 1873.

57. Kelly, *Sarah—Her Story*, 243.

58. Estate of C. J. Couts to Wm. A. Winder, Dr., Cave Johnson Couts File, SDHC.

59. Cheryl Anne Stapp, "Pioneer Governors: Newton Booth 1871–1875," *California's Olden Golden Days*, October 28, 2014, http://cherylannestapp.com/pioneer-governors-newton-booth.

60. Pourade, *Glory Years*, 111–12.

61. Pourade, *Glory Years*, 112, 121.

62. "Mr. Wm. Winder, U.S.N., Son of Captain Winder, Who Has Been Visiting His Father," *San Diego Union*, December 17, 1873.

63. "Passengers per *Orizaba*," *San Diego Union*, December 23, 1873.

13. The Lone and Goodly Doctor

1. "Old Town Items," *San Diego Union*, January 25, 1874.

2. *San Diego City Directory*, 1874, 48, in SDHC.

3. "Local Intelligence," *San Diego Weekly Union*, July 23, 1874.

4. Pourade, *Glory Years*, 122–26.

5. "Incorporations," *Sacramento Daily Union*, February 18, 1875.

6. Cited in Pourade, *Glory Years*, 122.

7. Diploma from College of Physicians and Surgeons, Certificate no. 423, for Wm. A. Winder, San Diego, February 17, 1875, "Official Graduates of Keokuk Physicians & Surgeons School of Medicine," Registrar's Office, University of Iowa, Iowa City, Iowa.

8. Stanford, "San Diego's Medico-Legal History."

9. "A Serious Accident Befell Mrs. S. W. Craigue," *San Diego Union*, April 15, 1875.

10. "San Diego Items," *Los Angeles Herald*, May 18, 1875.

11. "The Regatta," *Daily Alta California*, July 6, 1875. As there is no record of William A. ever owning this beautiful vessel, perhaps an admirer had outfitted the craft and christened it in his honor.

12. "War Department Contract: Dr. Winder Does Not Contemplate Removing from San Diego," *San Diego Union*, September 4, 1875.

13. "Ambitious Little Burgh," *San Bernardino Guardian*, September 6, 1876.

14. William A. Winder to Alexander M. Kenaday, May 3, 1876, Letters and Their Enclosures Received by the Commission Branch of the Adjutant General's Office, NARA-DC. Underscores are Winder's own.

15. Adjutant General Townsend to A. M. Kenaday, May 27, 1876, Letters and Their Enclosures Received by the Commission Branch of the Adjutant General's Office, NARA-DC.

16. "Democratic County Convention," *San Diego Weekly Union*, August 9, 1877.

17. "A Serious and Painful Accident," *San Diego Weekly Union*, June 7, 1877.

18. Frederick Low to John W. Satterwhite, March 22, 1878, Letters and Their Enclosures Received by the Commission Branch of the Adjutant General's Office, NARA-DC.

19. John W. Satterwhite and others to Rutherford Hayes, March 23, 1878, Letters and Their Enclosures Received by the Commission Branch of the Adjutant General's Office, NARA-DC.

20. E. W. Morse to W. A. Winder, March 24, 1878, Box 5, Ephraim W. Morse Papers, SDHC. Winder's letter to Morse is not extant.

21. John W. Satterwhite to Peter D. Wigginton, March 25, 1878, Letters and Their Enclosures Received by the Commission Branch of the Adjutant General's Office, NARA-DC.

22. Peter D. Wigginton to Honorable R. B. Hayes, April 2, 1878, Letters and Their Enclosures Received by the Commission Branch of the Adjutant General's Office, NARA-DC.

23. W. A. Winder to P. D. Wigginton, April 9, 1878, Letters and Their Enclosures Received by the Commission Branch of the Adjutant General's Office, NARA-DC.

24. "Local Brevities," *Los Angeles Herald*, July 25, 1878.

25. W. A. Winder to A. Wilcox, February 2, 1879, Box 3, Alfred Wilcox Collection, Local California and Western History Collections, Azusa Pacific University, Azusa, California (hereafter cited as APU). The painting has been lost to history, as have many of the works of William A. that were described and admired in newspapers over the years in which he painted them.

26. W. A. Winder to A. Wilcox, February 2, 1879, Box 3, Wilcox Collection, APU.

27. W. A. Winder to Rutherford B. Hayes, March 19, 1879, Letters and Their Enclosures Received by the Commission Branch of the Adjutant General's Office, NARA-DC (underscoring as written in original document).

28. "How Lincoln Relieved Rosecrans," *Toledo (OH) Journal*, March 7, 1879.

29. "Death of William H. Winder," *Evening Star* (Washington DC), October 20, 1879.

30. Ronald Baumgarten, "Civil War History of the Winder Building," *Tradewinds* (official blog of the United States Trade Representative), April 2011, https://ustr.gov/about-us/policy-offices/press-office/blog/2011/april /civil-war-history-winder-building.

31. W. A. Winder to Henry Worthington, November 23, 1879, Box 3, Wilcox Collection, APU.

32. Morse, "On the Use of the Sub-Nitrate of Bismuth as a Surgical Dressing," 50.

33. Horace Bradt to Winifred Davidson, August 22, 1937, Winifred Davidson Collection, SDHC.

14. Pension or Ruination

1. "Local News," *San Diego Union*, February 29, 1880, referring to an item of January 4, 1880, the date of William A.'s accident.

2. I. McDowell to W. A. Winder, March 19, 1880, Letters and Their Enclosures Received by the Commission Branch of the Adjutant General's Office, NARA-DC.

3. Robert S. Williamson to W. A. Winder, January 27, 1880, Letters and Their Enclosures Received by the Commission Branch of the Adjutant General's Office, NARA-DC.

4. George H. Elliot to Honorable Henry W. Blair, January 16, 1880, Letters and Their Enclosures Received by the Commission Branch of the Adjutant General's Office, NARA-DC.

5. Gen. John Logan in response to Henry William Blair, 46th Cong., 2nd sess., February 24, 1880, General Records of the U.S. Government, Record Group 11, NARA-DC.

6. "What His Brother Officers Think of Him," *Los Angeles Herald*, August 25, 1880.

7. "Winfield Scott Hancock," National Park Service, https://www.nps.gov /people/winfield-scott-hancock.htm.

8. W. A. Winder to A. Wilcox, November 25, 1880, Box 3, Alfred Wilcox Collection, Local California and Western History Collections, APU.

9. Pourade, *Glory Years*, 157.

10. Pourade, *Glory Years*, 159–61.

11. "Died," *Baltimore Sun*, April 12, 1881. See also "Funerals," *Baltimore Sun*, April 13, 1881.

12. "President of Veterans of Mexican War," *San Diego Union*, September 23, 1881.

13. "Dr. William A. Winder Busily Engaged," *San Diego Sun*, September 24, 1881.

14. "Dr. Winder Has Kindly Donated," *San Diego Sun*, October 19, 1881.

15. Smythe, *History of San Diego*, 175–76.

16. Dorris, introduction to *Ramona*, xiv–xv.

17. "New Year Greeting," *San Diego Union*, January 1, 1882.

18. W. A. Winder to A. Wilcox, March 13, 1882, Box 3, Wilcox Collection, APU.

19. "Dr. Winder Who Has Been Indisposed," *San Diego Sun*, March 29, 1882.

20. "We Saw at the Office of Dr. Winder Yesterday Two Very Striking Paintings," *San Diego Union*, May 27, 1882.

21. Kelly, *Sarah—Her Story*, 247.

22. W. A. Winder, late Capt. 3rd Art. Pension Case #6614, Letters and Their Enclosures Received by the Commission Branch of the Adjutant General's Office, NARA-DC.

23. "Local Brevities," *San Diego Union*, December 19, 1882.

24. "Sudden Death of Don Miguel Pedrorena," *San Diego Union*, December 27, 1882.

25. "Reminiscences of an Old Army Officer," *San Diego Union*, January 5, 1883. Quotations in subsequent paragraphs are from this source until noted otherwise.

26. Pourade, *Glory Years*, 160–61.

27. W. A. Winder to A. Wilcox, June 9, 1883, Box 3, Wilcox Collection, APU.

28. "Local Brevities," *San Diego Union*, May 25, 1884.

29. "Local Brevities," *San Diego Union*, July 31, 1885.

30. "Beginning of the War," *San Diego Union*, December 17, 1884.

31. W. A. Winder to W. T. Sherman, November 21, 1884, William T. Sherman Papers, LOC.

32. W. T. Sherman to W. A. Winder, November 30, 1884, Sherman Papers, LOC.

33. W. A. Winder to W. T. Sherman, December 15, 1884, Sherman Papers, LOC. Quotations in subsequent paragraphs are from this source until noted otherwise.

34. "A Chronology of Key Events in the Life of William T. Sherman, 1820–1891," Sherman Papers, LOC.

35. "With All the Coldness and Selfishness in the World," *San Diego Union*, December 25, 1884; Pourade, *Glory Years*, 165.

36. Naomi Baker, "San Diegans Still Fighting toward Early Writer's Goal," *San Diego Union*, August 11, 1949.

37. Naomi Baker, "San Diegans Still Fighting toward Early Writer's Goal," *San Diego Tribune Sun*, August 11, 1949.

38. Sánchez and Pita, introduction to *The Squatter and the Don*, 13.

39. "The Squatter and the Don," *San Francisco Chronicle*, January 11, 1885.

40. "Recent Publications," *San Diego Union*, February 8, 1885.

41. Burton, *The Squatter and the Don*, 314.

42. Winifred Davidson, "When William A. Winder Started for California," *San Diego Union*, August 22, 1937; Naomi Baker, "San Diegans Still Fighting toward Early Writer's Goal," *San Diego Tribune Sun*, August 11, 1949.

43. "Local Brevities," *San Diego Union*, July 1, 1885.

44. *Maxwell's Directory of San Diego City and County, 1887–1888*, San Diego Public Library, San Diego, California.

45. Pourade, *Glory Years*, 166.

46. "Medical Society," *San Diego Union*, August 8, 1886.

47. Pourade, *Glory Years*, 193.

48. "Finest View in San Diego," *San Diego Daily Bee*, June 3, 1887.

49. "His Family Were Disloyal," *Washington Post*, April 12, 1889; Julian Allen Scrapbook, 1860–78, Southern History Collection, Louis Round Wilson Special Collections Library, University of North Carolina, Chapel Hill.

50. "His Family Were Disloyal," *Washington Post*, April 12, 1889.

51. "A Grave Grievance," *Los Angeles Herald*, April 12, 1889.

52. Preston H. Bailhache, Surgeon, U.S. Marine Hospital Service (San Francisco), to John B. Hamilton, Surgeon, U.S. Marine Hospital Service, June 25, 1889, in United States Public Health Service, *Annual Report of the Supervising Surgeon General of the Marine Hospital Service of the U.S for the Fiscal Year 1889*, 117.

53. "Coast Marine Hospital," *San Francisco Bulletin*, June 27, 1889.

54. "Held by the Enemy," *San Diego Union*, December 7, 1889.

55. "Farming Out Sick Seamen," *San Diego Union*, December 19, 1899.

56. H.R. 9057, in United States, *Reports of Committees of the House of Representatives for the First Session of the Fifty-First Congress*, April 7, 1890.

57. Mr. Bowers to the House Committee on Military Affairs, regarding H.R. 704, in United States, *Reports of Committees of the House of Representatives for the First Session of the Fifty-Second Congress, 1891–1892*, January 7, 1892. The subjunctive language, "be it enacted" might be confusing, though it is still used today. In fact, and with the president's silence, nothing happened.

58. Representative Belknap to the House Committee on Military Affairs, regarding H.R. 704, in United States, *Reports of Committees of the House of Representatives for the First Session of the Fifty-Second Congress, 1891–1892*, February 10, 1892.

59. "Personals," *Los Angeles Herald*, September 15, 1892.

60. H.R. 450, in United States, *Reports of Committees of the House of Representatives for the Second Session of the Fifty-Third Congress, 1893–1894*, September 6, 1893.

61. H.R. 450, in United States, *Reports of Committees of the House of Representatives for the Second Session of the Fifty-Third Congress, 1893–1894*, January 23, 1894.

15. Round Valley

1. "Winder Appointed to Be a Special Government Agent," *Washington Post*, January 30, 1894.

2. "An Act to Provide for the Allotment of Lands in Severalty to Indians on the Various Reservations (General Allotment Act or Dawes Act)," 49th Cong., 2nd sess., February 8, 1887, General Records of the U.S. Government, Record Group 11, NARA-DC.

3. Bauer, *We Were All Like Migrant Workers Here*, 12.

4. Jeff Elliott, "The Dark Legacy of Nome Cult," *Albion Monitor*, September 2, 1995, http://albionmonitor.com/9-2-95/history.html.

5. McDonnell, *Dispossession of the American Indian*, 7.

6. Bauer, *We Were All Like Migrant Workers Here*, 117; William Winder to Daniel Browning, May 9, 1894, "Special Cases," 1821–1907, Box 49, Bureau of Indian Affairs, Record Group 75, NARA, San Bruno, California (hereafter cited as NARA-SB).

7. Bauer, *We Were All Like Migrant Workers Here*, 117; William Winder to Daniel Browning, May 20, 1894, "Special Cases," 1821–1907, Box 49, Bureau of Indian Affairs, Record Group 75, NARA-SB.

8. Bauer, *We Were All Like Migrant Workers Here*, 118.

9. Bauer, *We Were All Like Migrant Workers Here*, 118; William Winder to Daniel Browning, May 20, 1894, NARA-SB.

10. Bauer, *We Were All Like Migrant Workers Here*, 118; William Winder to Daniel Browning, May 20, 1894, NARA-SB.

11. Bauer, *We Were All Like Migrant Workers Here*, 118; William Winder to Daniel Browning, May 20, 1894, NARA-SB.

12. Blakey, *General John H. Winder, C.S.A.*, 203.

13. United States, Office of Indian Affairs, *Annual Report of the Commissioner of Indian Affairs* (1895), 21.

16. Rosebud

1. *The Travelers' Official Guide of the Railroad and Steam Navigation Lines of the United States and Canada*, August 1895, 517, in Bruce C. Cooper Collection, Central Pacific Railroad Photographic History Museum, http://CPRR.org.

2. Nostwick, "Nellie Bly's Account of Her 1895 Visit to Drouth-Stricken Nebraska and South Dakota," 41.

3. Roberts, *Encyclopedia of Historic Forts*, 485.

4. "About Us," Rosebud Sioux Tribe, South Dakota, https://www.rosebudsiouxtribe-nsn.gov/.

5. Quoted in Hyde, *Spotted Tail's Folk*, xvi.

6. Hyde, *Sioux Chronicle*, 247.

7. Hamilton and Hamilton, *Sioux of the Rosebud*, 53.

8. Hamilton and Hamilton, *Sioux of the Rosebud*, 53.

9. Hamilton and Hamilton, *Sioux of the Rosebud*, 141.

10. Hamilton and Hamilton, *Sioux of the Rosebud*, 81, 113.

11. Hamilton and Hamilton, *Sioux of the Rosebud*, 141.

12. Hamilton and Hamilton, *Sioux of the Rosebud*, 218.

13. Hamilton and Hamilton, *Sioux of the Rosebud*, 91.

14. Hyde, *Sioux Chronicle*, 7.

15. Russell Eagle Bear, tribal historic preservation officer of the Rosebud Sioux Tribe, telephone interview by author, March 1, 2017.

16. United States, Office of Indian Affairs, *Annual Report of the Commissioner of Indian Affairs* (1895), 21.

17. "Colonel Scott's Appointment," *San Francisco Call*, April 7, 1895.

18. United States, Office of Indian Affairs, *Annual Report of the Commissioner of Indian Affairs* (1895), 39.

19. "Uncle Sam Is Generous," *Valentine (NE) Democrat*, April 16, 1896.

20. Meyn, "Mutual Infatuation," 30, 31.

21. United States, Office of Indian Affairs, *Annual Report of the Commissioner of Indian Affairs* (1896), 298.

22. "This and That," *Valentine Democrat*, February 11, 1897.

23. "This and That," *Valentine Democrat*, August 19, 1897.

24. Hamilton and Hamilton, *Sioux of the Rosebud*, 187-88.

25. United States, Office of Indian Affairs, *Annual Report of the Commissioner of Indian Affairs* (1897), 23.

26. United States, Office of Indian Affairs, *Annual Report of the Commissioner of Indian Affairs* (1898), 42.

27. Hamilton and Hamilton, *Sioux of Rosebud*, 5-6.

28. "For Riverview Park," *Omaha World-Herald*, August 1, 1899.

29. "Brother-in-Law of Dewey," *Sioux City Journal*, August 12, 1899. Quotations in subsequent paragraphs are from this source until noted otherwise.

30. "Hopes to See Admiral Dewey: General Wider [sic] Brother-in-Law of the Admiral Goes East," *Duluth News Tribune*, September 30, 1899.

31. Charles H. Bates to W. A. Winder, November 14, 1899, Letters Received by the Special Allotting Agent from the Office of Indian Affairs, 1893–1901, Volume 2, 2/15/1899-1/5//1901, Records of the Bureau of Indian Affairs (Rosebud Agency), Department of the Interior, Record Group 75, National Archives and Records Administration, Kansas City, Missouri (hereafter cited as NARA-KC).

32. Charles H. Bates to W. A. Winder, November 14, 1899, Letters Received by the Special Allotting Agent from the Office of Indian Affairs, 1893–1901, NARA-KC.

33. "Talk of the Town," *Valentine Democrat*, May 17, 1900.

34. "Personals," *Portsmouth (NH) Herald*, June 20, 1900.

35. "Talk of the Town," *Valentine Democrat*, November 1, 1900.

36. Charles E. McChesney to Dr. Wm. A. Winder, November 14, 1900, Copies of Letters Sent, 1878–1910, Records of the Bureau of Indian Affairs, NARA-KC.

37. "Talk of the Town," *Valentine Democrat*, June 13, 1901.

38. "Personals," *Portsmouth Herald*, December 17, 1901.

39. Charles Reiter to W. A. Winder, January 14, 1902, Folder "1902," Box 9, Letters Received, 1878–1913, Records of the Bureau of Indian Affairs, NARA-KC.

40. "Card of Thanks," *Valentine Democrat*, April 30, 1902.

41. "Major J. C. Minor Dead," *Valentine Democrat*, May 1, 1902.

42. "To Clear a Soldier's Name," *Omaha Daily Bee*, June 29, 1902. Quotations in subsequent paragraphs are from this source until noted otherwise.

43. Charles Reiter to W. A. Winder, May 31, 1902, Box 9, Letters Received, 1878–1913, Records of the Bureau of Indian Affairs, NARA-KC.

44. "Talk of the Town," *Valentine Democrat*, August 14, 1902.

45. "Talk of the Town," *Valentine Democrat*, September 4, 1902.

46. "Talk of the Town," *Valentine Democrat*, October 2, 1902.

47. "Additional Local," *Valentine Democrat*, November 6, 1902.

48. "Says Indians Are Increasing," *Daily Deadwood Pioneer-Times*, January 9, 1908.

49. Abby Winder to Elizabeth Blanchard, February 26, 1903, Box 2, Nathan W. Blanchard Collection, MVC034, Museum of Ventura County, Ventura, California. Quotations in subsequent paragraphs are from this source until noted otherwise.

50. "Captain Winder Is Dead," *Omaha Daily Bee*, March 7, 1903.

51. "One of the Pathfinders Dies at the Millard," *Omaha Morning World-Herald*, March 7, 1903.

52. "Death of Dr. William A. Winder at Omaha," *San Diego Union*, March 7, 1903.

53. Telegram text reprinted in "Death of Dr. William A. Winder at Omaha," *San Diego Union*, March 7, 1903.

54. "Captain William A. Winder Formerly of This City," *Baltimore American*, March 7, 1903.

55. "The Body of Dr. William A. Winder," *Omaha World-Herald*, March 9, 1903.

56. "The Funeral of Capt. William E. [*sic*] Winder Was Held Today," *Portsmouth Herald*, March 12, 1903.

57. "Touching Feature of Captain Winder's Life and Death," *Omaha Sunday World-Herald*, March 15, 1903.

58. A. G. Tonner to Charles E. McChesney, March 28, 1903, Letters Received from the Commissioner of Indian Affairs, 1895–1908, Volume 13, 2/28/1903-7/28/1903, NARA-DC.

17. Of Lives Lost

1. Blakey, *General John H. Winder, C.S.A.*, 207.

2. "Was 71 and Shot Himself," *Baltimore Sun*, February 26, 1905.

3. "Obituary," *Portsmouth (NH) Herald*, May 9, 1906. Quotations in subsequent paragraphs are from this source until noted otherwise.

4. "Capt. Winder a Suicide at Brookline," *Portsmouth Herald*, October 5, 1922.

Bibliography

Archives and Manuscript Materials

Allen, Julian. Scrapbook. Southern History Collection, Louis Round Wilson Special Collections Library, University of North Carolina. Chapel Hill, North Carolina.

Azusa Pacific University (APU). Azusa, California.

    Wilcox, Alfred. Collection.

"Confederate States of America: Jefferson Davis Message to Congress." April 29, 1861. Avalon Project. Lillian Goldman Library, Yale University Law School. New Haven, Connecticut.

Diploma from College of Physicians and Surgeons. Certificate no. 423, Wm. A. Winder, San Diego, February 17, 1875. "Official Graduates of Keokuk Physicians & Surgeons School of Medicine." Registrar's Office, University of Iowa. Iowa City, Iowa.

Library of Congress (LOC), Manuscript Division. Washington DC.

    Lincoln, Abraham. Papers.

    McClellan, George Brinton. Papers.

    Sherman, William T. Papers.

    Taft, Horatio Nelson. "Washington during the Civil War: The Diary of Horatio Nelson Taft, 1861 to 1865."

Maxwell's Directory of San Diego City and County, 1887–1888. SAN DIEGO PUBLIC LIBRARY. San Diego, California.

"Memoirs of Pryce Lewis as told to Major David E. Cronin." Pryce Lewis Collection. St. Lawrence University Archives, Owen D. Young Library, St. Lawrence University. Canton, New York.

National Archives and Records Administration. Washington DC (NARA-DC).

    General Records of the U.S. Government. Record Group 11.

    Letters Received from the Commissioner of Indian Affairs, 1895–1908

    Letters Received by the Office of the Adjutant General. Main Series 1861–70, documenting the period 1850–1917.

Letters and Their Enclosures Received by the Commission Branch of the Adjutant General's Office, 1863–70.

Pacific Division. Letters Received, 1854–58.

Returns from U.S. Military Posts, 1800–1916. Microfilm Publication M617, 1,550 rolls. Records of the Adjutant General's Office, 1780s–1917. Record Group 94. Available at Ancestry.com as U.S. Returns from Military Posts, 1806–1916 (online database).

Trial of Pvt. Simon Kennedy. Court Martial File NN3499. Record Group 13 7E3/14/12/3.

Union Provost Marshal's File of Papers Relating to Individual Civilians, 1861–67. Record Group 109.

U.S. Military Academy Cadet Application Papers, 1840–45. Within Application Papers, 1805–66. M688, Records of the Adjutant General's Office, 1780s–1917. Record Group 94. Available at Ancestry.com as U.S. Military and Naval Academies, Cadet Records and Applications, 1800–1908 (online database).

National Archives and Records Administration (NARA-KC). Kansas City, Missouri.

Records of the Bureau of Indian Affairs (Rosebud Agency), Department of the Interior, Record Group 75.

Copies of Letters Sent, 1878–1910.

Letters Received, 1878–1913.

Letters Received by the Special Allotting Agent from the Office of Indian Affairs, 1893–1901.

National Archives and Records Administration (NARA-SB). San Bruno, California.

"Special Cases," 1821–1907. Box 49, Bureau of Indian Affairs, Record Group 75.

Rosecrans, William S. Papers. Manuscripts and Special Collections, Charles E. Young Research Library, University of California, Los Angeles.

San Diego History Center (SDHC). Document Collection, Special Collections Register of San Diego Historical Research Archives. San Diego, California.

Couts, Cave Johnson. File.

Davidson, Winifred. Collection.

Judicial records. District Court of 17th Judicial District for the County.

Morse, Ephraim W. Papers.

Morse, Mary Chase Walker. Biographical Files.

San Diego City Directory, 1874.

Winder Folder.

University of California, San Diego (UCSD). San Diego, California.

    Morse, Ephraim W. Register of Family Papers. MO689. Special
    Collections.

Winder, Abby, to Elizabeth Blanchard, February 26, 1903. Box 2, Nathan W.
    Blanchard Collection, MVC034, Museum of Ventura County. Ventura,
    California.

Published Works

Asbury, Herbert. *The Barbary Coast: An Informal History of the San Francisco Underworld.* New York: Knopf, 1933.

Bancroft, Hubert H. *The Works of Hubert Howe Bancroft: History of California.* San Francisco: History Company, 1890.

Bauer, William J. *We Were All Like Migrant Workers Here: Work, Community, and Memory on California's Round Valley Reservation, 1850–1941.*
Chapel Hill: University of North Carolina Press, 2009.

Birkheimer, William E. "History of the 3rd U.S. Artillery." In *The Army
of the United States Historical Sketches of Staff,* edited by Theophilus
F. Rodenbough and William L. Haskin, 328–50. New York: Maynard,
Merrill, 1896.

Blakey, Arch F. *General John H. Winder, C.S.A.* Gainesville: University of Florida Press, 1990.

Burton, María Amparo Ruiz de. *The Squatter and the Don.* 1885. 2nd ed. Houston TX: Arte Público Press, 1997.

Casstevens, Frances H. *George W. Alexander and Castle Thunder: A Confederate Prison and Its Commandant.* Jefferson NC: McFarland, 2004.

Chandler, Robert J. "Democratic Turmoil: California during the Civil War
Years." *Dogtown Territorial Quarterly,* no. 31 (Fall 1997): 32–46.

———. "An Uncertain Influence: The Role of the Federal Government in
California, 1846–1880." In *Taming the Elephant: Politics, Government and
Law in Pioneer California,* edited by John F. Burns and Richard J. Orsi,
224–71. Berkeley: University of California Press, 2003.

———. "The Velvet Glove: The Army during the Secessionist Crisis in California, 1860–61." *Journal of the West* 20 (October 20, 1982): 35–42.

Chipman, Gen. N. P. *The Tragedy of Andersonville: Trial of Henry Wirz, the
Prison Keeper.* 2nd ed. N.p.: published by the author, 1911.

Cleary, Guire John, ed. *A Quiet, Hard, and Desolated Place.* San Diego: HITM
Press, 2014.

Cullum, G. W. *Biographical Register of the Officers and Graduates of the U.S.
Military Academy at West Point N.Y.: From Its Establishment in 1802 to
1890; With the Early History of the United States Military Academy.* 3
vols. 3rd ed. Boston: Houghton Mifflin, 1891.

Cutler, Don. "Your Nations Shall Be Exterminated." *Quarterly Journal of Military History* 22, no. 3 (2010): 46–53.

Dana, Richard Henry. *Two Years before the Mast*. 1840. N.p.: Seven Treasures Publications, 2008.

Daughtry, Mary Bandy. *Gray Cavalier: The Life and Wars of General W. H. F. "Rooney" Lee*. Cambridge MA: Da Capo Press, 2002.

Davis, Robert S. *Ghosts and Shadows of Andersonville: Essays on the Secret Social Histories of America's Deadliest Prison*. Macon GA: Mercer University Press, 2006.

Dorris, Michael. Introduction to *Ramona*, by Helen Hunt Jackson. New York: Penguin Group, 2002.

Engstrand, Iris. *San Diego: California's Cornerstone*. San Diego: Sunbelt Publications, 2005.

Fogelson, Robert M. *The Fragmented Metropolis: Los Angeles, 1850–1930*. Berkeley: University of California Press, 1993.

Freeman, Gordon. "The Early Western Physicians." *San Diego County Medical Society Centennial Year*, July 1970, 53–63.

Furguson, Ernest B. *Freedom Rising: Washington in the Civil War*. New York: Knopf, 2004.

Golden, Alan Lawrence. "Castle Thunder: The Confederate Provost Marshal's Prison, 1862–1865." Master's thesis, University of Richmond, 1980.

Gooding, James Henry. *On the Altar of Freedom: A Black Soldier's Civil War Letters from the Front*. Edited by Virginia M. Adams. Amherst: University of Massachusetts Press, 1991.

Goss, Warren Lee. *The Soldier's Story of His Captivity at Andersonville, Belle Isle and Other Rebel Prisons*. Boston: Lee and Shephard, 1867.

Graves, Clifford L. "A Doctor Comes to San Diego." *San Diego County Medical Society Centennial Year*, July 1970, 40–49.

Hamilton, Henry W., and Jean Tyree Hamilton. *The Sioux of the Rosebud: A History in Pictures*. Photographs by John A. Anderson. Norman: University of Oklahoma Press, 1971.

Harpending, Asbury. *The Great Diamond Hoax and Other Stirring Incidents in the Life of Asbury Harpending*. Norman: University of Oklahoma Press, 1958.

Harrison, Donald H. *Louis Rose: San Diego's First Jewish Settler and Entrepreneur*. San Diego: Sunbelt Publications, 2005.

Hayes, Benjamin Ignatius, et al. *Emigrant Notes*. San Diego CA, 1875.

———. *Pioneer Notes from the Diary of Judge Benjamin Hayes, 1849–1875*. Edited by Marjorie Tisdale Woolcott. Los Angeles: Marjorie Tisdale Wolcott, 1929.

Heizer, Robert F., ed. *The Destruction of California Indians*. 1974. Lincoln: University of Nebraska Press, 1993.

Hill, J. Rowland. "Winder's Reminiscences of Early Days." *Golden Era Magazine*, December 1, 1888.

Hopkins, Charles Ferren. "Hell and the Survivor." *American Heritage Magazine* 33, no. 6 (1982). https://www.americanheritage.com/content/hell-and-survivor

Hunt, Aurora. *The Army of the Pacific, 1860–1866*. Mechanicsburg PA: Stackpole Books, 2004.

Hyde, George E. *A Sioux Chronicle*. Norman: University of Oklahoma Press, 1956.

————. *Spotted Tail's Folk: A History of the Brulé Sioux*. Norman: University of Oklahoma Press, 1961.

Jones, J. B. *A Rebel War Clerk's Diary at the Confederate States Capital*. Philadelphia: J. B. Lippincott, 1866.

Kelly, Margaret Whyte. *Sarah—Her Story: The Life Story of Sarah Parker Rice Goodwin, Wife of Ichabod Goodwin, New Hampshire's Civil War Governor*. Portsmouth NH: Back Channel Press, 2006

Kroll, C. Douglas. *Friends in Peace and War: The Russian Navy's Landmark Visit to Civil War San Francisco*. Washington DC: Potomac Books, 2007.

Liberal Republican Party. *Proceedings of the Liberal Republican Convention, in Cincinnati, May 1st, 2d and 3d, 1872: Address of the New York State Committee to their fellow-citizens; Including Horace Greeley's letter of acceptance*. New York: Baker & Godwin, 1872.

Lieber, Francis. *Instructions for the Government of the United States in the Field*. Issued originally as General Orders No. 100. Washington DC: GPO, 1898.

Lynn, John W. *800 Paces to Hell: Andersonville*. Fredericksburg VA: Sergeant Kirkland's Museum and Historical Society, 1999.

Martini, John A. *Alcatraz at War*. San Francisco: Golden Gate National Parks Association, 2002.

————. *Fortress Alcatraz: Guardian of the Golden Gate*. Kailua HI: Pacific Monograph, 1990.

————. "Search and Destroy." *American Heritage* 43, no. 7 (November 1992).

Marvel, William. *Andersonville: The Last Depot*. Chapel Hill: University of North Carolina Press, 1994.

Matthews, Glenna. *The Golden State in the Civil War: Thomas Starr King, the Republican Party, and the Birth of Modern California*. New York: Cambridge University Press, 2012.

McArthur, Benjamin. *The Man Who Was Rip Van Winkle: Joseph Jefferson and Nineteenth-Century American Theatre*. New Haven: Yale University Press, 2007.

McDonnell, Janet A. *The Dispossession of the American Indian, 1887–1934*. Bloomington: Indiana University Press, 1991.

McElroy, John. *Andersonville: A Story of Rebel Military Prisons*. Toledo OH: D. R. Locke, 1879.

McGhee, Earl Samuel. "E. W. Morse, Pioneer Merchant and Co-Founder of San Diego." Master's thesis, San Diego State College, 1950.

McLean, Cpl. Alexander Angus. "A Detail of Prison Life at Andersonville." Appendix to *A history of the One hundred and seventeenth regiment, N.Y. volunteers [Fourth Oneida], from the date of its organization, August, 1862, till that of its muster out, June, 1865,* by J. A. Mowris, M.D., regimental surgeon. Hartford CT: Case, Lockwood, printers, 1866.

Meyn, Susan Labry. "Mutual Infatuation: Rosebud Sioux and the Cincinnatians." *Queen City Heritage* (Cincinnati Historical Society), Spring–Summer 1994, 30–48. http://library.cincymuseum.org/topics/c/files/cintizoo/qch-v52-n1-2-mut-030.pdf

Morse, J. F., M.D. "On the Use of the Sub-Nitrate of Bismuth as a Surgical Dressing." *Western Lancet* 13, no. 2 (February 1884): 49–52.

New York Passenger Lists, 1820–1957. Accessed at Ancestry.com.

Nostwick, T. D. "Nellie Bly's Account of Her 1895 Visit to Drouth-Stricken Nebraska and South Dakota." *Nebraska History* 67, no. 1 (1986): 30–67. http://www.nebraskahistory.org/publish/publicat/history/full-text/NH1986Drouth1895.pdf

Phillips, George Harwood. *Chiefs and Challengers: Indian Resistance in Southern California.* Berkeley: University of California Press, 1975.

Pinkerton, Allan. *The Spy of the Rebellion: Being a True History of the Spy System of the United States Army during the Late Rebellion.* New York: G. W. Carleton, 1883.

Pourade, Richard F. *The Glory Years: The Booms and Busts in the Land of the Sundown Sea.* San Diego: Union Tribune, 1964.

Price, James N. "The Railroad Stations of San Diego County." Journal of San Diego History 34, no. 2 (1988). http://sandiegohistory.org/journal/1988/april/railroad-6/

Putnam, Sallie Brock. *Richmond during the War: Four Years of Personal Observation.* Lincoln: University of Nebraska Press, 1996.

Recko, Corey. *A Spy for the Union: The Life and Execution of Timothy Webster.* Jefferson NC: McFarland, 2013.

Roberts, Robert B. *Encyclopedia of Historic Forts.* New York: Macmillan, 1987.

Robinson, John W. "The Ordeal of General Wright: A Study in Secessionist Sentiment in California, 1861–1864." *The Westerners Brand Book 16,* edited by Raymund F. Wood. Los Angeles: Los Angeles Corral of Westerners, 1982.

Rockwood, Lawrence P. *Walking Away from Nuremberg: Just War and The Doctrine of Command Responsibility.* Amherst: University of Massachusetts Press, 2007.

Sánchez, Rosaura, and Beatrice Pita. Introduction to *The Squatter and the Don,* by María Amparo Ruiz de Burton. 1885. Houston TX: Arte Público Press, 1997.

———. Introduction to *Who Would Have Thought It? A Novel,* by María Amparo Ruiz de Burton. 1872. Houston TX: Arte Público Press, 1995.

Schlicke, Carl P. *General George Wright: Guardian of the Pacific Coast.* Norman: University of Oklahoma Press, 1988.

Scott, Edward R. *San Diego County Soldier-Pioneers, 1846–1866.* National City CA: Crest Printing, 1976.

Sears, Stephen W., ed. *The Civil War Papers of George B. McClellan: Selected Correspondence, 1860–1865.* New York: Da Capo Press, 1992.

Simon, John Y., ed. *The Papers of Ulysses S. Grant:* Volume 19, July 1, 1868–October 31, 1869. Carbondale: Southern Illinois University Press, 1991.

Smythe, William Ellsworth. *History of San Diego, 1542–1907: An Account of the Rise and Progress of the Pioneer Settlement on the Pacific Coast of the United States.* San Diego: History Company, 1908.

Sneden, Robert Knox. *Eye of the Storm: A Civil War Odyssey.* Edited by Charles F. Bryan Jr. and Nelson D. Lankford. New York: Free Press, 2000.

Speer, Lonnie R. *Portals to Hell: Military Prisons of the Civil War.* Lincoln: University of Nebraska Press, 2006.

Spencer, Ambrose. *Narrative of Andersonville, Drawn from the Evidence Elicited on the Trial of Henry Wirz, the Jailer, with the Argument of Col. N. P. Chipman.* New York: Harper & Brothers, 1866.

Stanford, Leland. "San Diego's Medico-Legal History, 1850–1900." *Journal of San Diego History* 16, no. 2 (1970). https://sandiegohistory.org/journal/1970/april/stanford/

Stewart, John. *The Wreck of the "San Francisco": Disaster and Aftermath in the Great Hurricane of December 1853.* Jefferson NC: McFarland, 2018.

Stiles, T. J. *The First Tycoon: The Epic Life of Cornelius Vanderbilt.* New York: Knopf, 2009.

Stockton State Hospital Commitment Registers. California State Hospital Records, 1856–1923. Accessed at Ancestry.com.

Strobridge, William F., ed. "California Letters of Major General James McPherson, 1858–1860." *Ohio History* 81 (Winter 1972): 38–50.

Strong, George Templeton. *The Diary of George Templeton Strong.* Edited by Allan Nevins and Milton Halsey Thomas. 4 vols. New York: Macmillan, 1952.

Taylor, Lawrence D. "The Mining Boom in Baja California from 1850 to 1890 and the Emergence of Tijuana as a Border Community." *Journal of the Southwest* 43, no. 4 (2001): 463–92.

The Travelers' Official Guide of the Railroad and Steam Navigation Lines of the United States and Canada. New York: National Railway Publication Co., August 1895.

Tucker, W. Burling, and Clarence A. Waring. *Mines and Mineral Resources of the Counties of Butte, Lassen, Modoc, Sutter and Tehama.* Sacramento CA: State Printing Office, 1917.

Twain, Mark. *Gold Miners & Guttersnipes: Tales of California.* Selected and with an introduction by Ken Chowder. San Francisco: Chronicle Books, 1991.

United States. *The Reports of Committees of the House of Representatives, First Session of the Fifty-First Congress, 1889–1890.* April 7, 1890, "William A. Winder." Washington: GPO, 1890.

———. *The Reports of Committees of the House of Representatives for the First Session of the Fifty-Second Congress, 1891–1892.* Vol. 1, Report no. 108, "William A. Winder." Washington: GPO, 1892.

———. *The Reports of Committees of the House of Representatives for the Second Session of the Fifty-Third Congress, 1893–1894.* Vol. 1, Report no. 272, "William A. Winder." Washington: GPO, 1893.

———. *The Reports of Committees of the House of Representatives for the Second Session of the Fifty-Third Congress, Second Session of the Fifty-Third Congress, 1893–1894.* Vol. 1, Report no. 272, "William A. Winder." Washington: GPO, 1894.

United States. Adjutant General's Office. *Official Army Register for 1866.* Washington DC: GPO, 1866.

United States. Federal Census, 1870, San Diego, California. Roll M593_78. Accessed at Ancestry.com.

United States. Office of Indian Affairs. *Annual Report of the Commissioner of Indian Affairs.* Washington DC: GPO, various years.

United States. Public Health Service. *Annual Report of the Supervising Surgeon General of the Marine Hospital Service of the U.S. for the fiscal year 1889.* Washington DC: GPO, 1889.

United States. War Department. *General Orders of the War Department, Embracing the Years 1861, 1862 and 1863: Adapted specially for the use of the Army and Navy of the United States.* Compiled by Oliver Diefendorf and Thomas M. O'Brien. 2 vols. New York: Derby & Miller, 1864. https://archive.org/details/generalordersofwunit

U.S. Passport Applications, 1795–1925. Roll 103, December 1861–March 1862. Accessed at Ancestry.com.

Van Dyke, Theodore Strong. *The City and County of San Diego: Illustrated, and Containing Biographical Sketches of Prominent Men and Pioneers.* San Diego CA: Leberthon & Taylor, 1888.

Warner, Michael, ed. *The Portable Walt Whitman.* New York: Penguin Books, 2004.

The War of the Rebellion: A Compilation of the Official Records of the Union and Confederate Armies. 4 series, 129 vols. Washington DC: GPO, 1880–1901.

Whitman, Walt. *Specimen Days and Collect.* 1882. New York: Dover Publications, 1995.

Winder, W. H. *Secrets of the American Bastille.* Philadelphia: John Campbell, 1863.

Index

87; in the Seminole War, 24, 158–59; relationship with Sherman, 28; as surveyor, 145; the *Sutlej* incident, 72–76; in Washington, 15, 18–29; meeting with Webster the spy, 22–27; intercedes for his brother Sid, 69–70

Winder, William H., 6, 11–13, 29, 46, 61, 113, 122, 137, 174–75, 181

Winder, William Sidney, 6, 69, 98–99, 113, 119–20, 122, 137, 181, 231, 234

Winder, Willie, 8, 32, 44–46, 86, 116, 125, 132, 143–44, 161, 164–65, 180, 184, 220–21, 223, 224, 229–30, 232, 235

Winder Building, 175

Winder Street, 236

Wirz, Heinrich Hartmann "Henry", 102, 108–9, 115, 118–19, 122

Witherby, Oliver S., 36, 141, 188

Wood, Benjamin, 5

Wood, Fernando, 5

Wool, John Ellis, 37–38, 241n5

Worthington, Henry, 175–76, 183

Wounded Knee Creek, 213

Wright, George, 4, 51, 53, 55, 57, 59, 60, 66–67, 73–74, 76, 86, 115, 172

Wright, George M., 90, 93

Zoyara, Ella, 15